Making Small Wooden Boxes

James A. Jacobson

Sterling Publishing Co., Inc. New York

Dedicated to
Anita, Karen, Peter, Ann, Chris, Christin
and now, of course, Jessica Helene

Acknowledgments

I wish to acknowledge and thank the following individuals and companies for their assistance:

Mr. L. C. Kind, E.L.P.A. Marketing Industries, New Hyde Park, New York, for providing information and permission to photograph the Thoren's Model 9131 4½″ disc musical movement.

Mr. Jean Reuge and Reuge, S.A. of Switzerland for providing information, technical assistance, and permission to photograph the Reuge musical movements.

Mr. A. Matoesian, master turner, Andreas' Lower State Street Studio for his assistance and consultation.

Ms. Kathy Banghart, Washington University, St. Louis, Missouri, for her assistance in helping me understand the fascinating world of mycology.

In addition, I wish to extend special thanks and recognition to my son, Peter J. Jacobson. Peter, who is a woodworker in his own right, did the photographic work for this book and my previous book, *Woodturning Music Boxes*.

EDITED BY LAUREL ORNITZ

Library of Congress Cataloging-in-Publication Data

Jacobson, James A.
  Making small wooden boxes.

  Includes index.
  1. Woodwork.   2. Boxes, Wooden.   I. Title.
TT200.J33   1986   745.593   85-30330
ISBN 0-8069-6290-9 (pbk.)

  3   5   7   9   10   8   6   4   2

CONTENTS

INTRODUCTION

While crafting certain boxes can challenge the woodworker to use personal ingenuity as well as a range of available tools, other boxes can be crafted with limited woodworking experience and a minimum of tools. This is the joy of crafting boxes: It's within the skill level of the beginning woodworker, yet presents enough of a challenge to test the outer limits of those who are most experienced.

Designing boxes, however, can often be more complex than the crafting process. We tend to think that boxes should be either square or rectangular. Although there are many superb examples of boxes in these traditional shapes, more innovative design possibilities need to be explored. In addition, as you will soon discover, the use of storage trays, hinge systems, and lid and wall embellishments all present the woodworker with an array of design possibilities.

Because I consider planning and design issues critical to successful and enjoyable crafting, one chapter focusses on some of these concerns. While this chapter is not meant to be all-inclusive, it does lay some important groundwork and should stimulate your own problem-solving skills. In this chapter, I encourage you to go beyond the specific projects as they are presented. While the various box designs lend themselves to duplication, I hope you will interject some of your own ideas and methods into their crafting.

The project chapter presents a sampling of boxes that are not only fun to make, but are also excellent vehicles for developing or refining your woodworking skills. Each of the projects was initially created for a particular purpose. However, with minor design modifications, almost all the boxes can be used for a number of different purposes. Most of the jewelry box designs, for example, can be converted into any kind of functional container or even a music box. Boxes that were originally designed to hold cigars or to serve as general storage containers can be modified into jewelry boxes by just adding a tray. The recipe boxes that are presented can also be altered to serve other purposes. While specific instructions are provided for each project, I have sought to eliminate duplication or tedious repetition. When necessary, the crafter is referred to a previous project, where the instructions or methods were initially presented in detail. Methods of modifying various box designs to other kinds of boxes are also included. With few exceptions, most designs lend themselves to this interchangeability. In addition, many components of different box designs are also interchangeable.

As you will discover in the project chapter, there are many ways to enhance a piece. While a box crafted from one of the spalts or a glorious piece of walnut can stand on its own, you may want to enhance a lid with an inlay, a laminated design, or some other decorative configuration. I have found this embellishment process to be one of the most fascinating and difficult aspects of crafting boxes. I hope you find some of the designs and methods I use for embellishing box lids to be interesting and worthy of duplication or modification. The designs tend to range from the tastefully simple to the gaudy.

A number of music box designs, by necessity, are made in traditional configurations, such as squares and rectangles. These designs are presented to introduce the crafter to the various basic design needs and sound requirements of musical movements.

While information on traditional tone woods is presented, a variety of woods that I have enjoyed using for boxes are also discussed. The abundance of woods that are indigenous to most parts of the country provides the box crafter with a renewable source of raw material. Special emphasis is given to the various spalted woods because they are not only real wonderments of nature but also because they are often readily available. The exotic and imported woods are also discussed in brief. In addition to the solid exotics that are available, some attention is given to the diversity of veneers that are on the market.

Various woodworking tools and supplies that I've found useful in crafting boxes are briefly discussed. This area is so unique to each craftsperson that it is difficult to make specific recommendations. The individual projects include suggested tools and supplies that have proven helpful to me. You may very well have tools and supporting devices that can do a job much more quickly and effectively than those that I use. Or you may prefer crafting boxes exclusively with hand tools.

While finishing is a joy to some and a curse to others, no woodworking book would be complete without dealing with this demanding process. As with my crafting, I'm never truly satisfied with my finishes. The last chapter presents some of the products and methods that I use in finishing boxes. As with other aspects of the crafting process, I encourage you to integrate your own finishing methods and products into this task.

If you are making a music box, the time to install the musical movement is after the finishing process is complete. In the Appendix, you'll find detailed instructions on placing the movement in the box as well as directions for cutting the glass insert that can be placed over the movement.

Illus. 1. Sapwood spalt in walnut box lid

5

1
WOODS

As I plan boxes and think about woods to use, I find that I'm often limited by a certain mind-set towards squares and rectangles. Even when buying wood, I examine a board in relation to how many square or rectangular boxes can be made from the piece. Basic shapes seem fixed in my mind, and I tend to perceive design issues only in terms of how the box will be embellished. For example, often my design concerns only relate to the type of wood to be used, whether the lid should have a plug inlay or marquetry, the kinds of joints to be used, and whether to use hinges or not. Even the term "box" has very fixed design implications for most of us. One of the exciting things about wood, however, is its adaptability. I would hope that, as a woodworker, you can move away from the obvious by designing configurations that interest, excite, and challenge you.

Additionally, many of us are inclined to select only those woods that are traditionally used for making boxes. For example, I use a great deal of walnut because jewelry and music boxes are usually crafted from walnut. Or, I use a lot of cherry and oak because they're popular woods. In a world filled with a multitude of different types and qualities of wood, many box crafters limit their work to walnut, cherry, and oak. I do not mean to disparage the traditional, but it does seem that we could be more creative in our choice of woods, especially indigenous ones.

In the part of Illinois where I live, we are fortunate in having a wide variety of hardwoods. I'm certain, however, that you will discover that your locale is also rich with a diversity of wood. While it may be in the form of shipping pallets as opposed to trees, different woods are available. A bit of ingenuity on your part may turn up an ongoing source of wood in your area that you never realized existed. As with many woodworkers, one of my great pleasures is scrounging for wood wherever I can find it. Whether it's kiln dried (KD), air dried (AD), or soaking wet, I will haul it home and work it into shape for crafting.

Pecan is a rather inexpensive wood that I often use for boxes. Similar to hickory, it doesn't seem very attractive. However, if you examine the lower grades of pecan or hickory, you will discover some incredibly beautiful wood for crafting boxes. Both are tough woods to work with and hard on tools, but well worth the effort. Cut to the proper thickness, pecan and hickory also make a good soundboard for music boxes. With a clear lacquer or oil finish, these woods are magnificent for boxes. Incidentally, they are also great for turning. If 8/4's or 12/4's are not available, I will frequently glue and stack 4/4 stock for turning.

Another one of our local woods that lends itself to boxes is Osage orange (commonly called hedge). I also use a great deal of it for my inlay work on box lids. Hedge is extremely hard but finishes beautifully. It is one of the only yellow woods in this country and makes for very attractive boxes or inlays. If you can find old hedge fence posts that have been in the ground, you will have some real treasures for turning. Watch, however, for nails. As with many woods, age and exposure tend to make hedge more

Illus. 2. Collection of spalted pieces

beautiful. It loses its yellow color and turns to a golden brown. This is especially true with the old fence posts. Although various chemicals have been used on hedge so it will retain its yellow color, to my knowledge none has been successful. I prefer to let wood become what it wants to be. While hedge demands the most from both the woodworker and tools, the results are worth the extra time and effort.

Both hard and soft maple, especially the lower grades, are excellent woods for crafting boxes. If you have the shop capacity, either of the maples ripped and planed to ⅛″ or ¼″ make excellent box bottoms or soundboards. Maple that has flaws, mineral staining, a touch of crotch, or some other grain configuration can be an exciting wood for boxes. As with all my boxes, I use a clear lacquer or oil finish on the maple and get outstanding results. The clear

finishes exploit the natural aberrations found in the lower grades of wood.

Other woods that I use regularly in crafting boxes are ash, sycamore, river elm, basswood, and poplar—or anything else that I can find or buy in the lower grades. In point of fact, I have not found a wood that does not lend itself to making boxes. The limiting factor, in most instances, is having the tools, space, and time for working with all the woods that are available.

If woods are not available to you, there are a host of mail-order suppliers that ship all over. Through comparative shopping and by being informed about the various shipping rates, you can easily obtain what you need. Most of the mail-order firms provide toll-free numbers and accept credit cards. I have also found that many companies are willing to discuss the various woods they have in stock and are extremely ac-

7

commodating in meeting their customers' needs.

Many of the exotic or imported woods that I use are from mail-order firms. While I can obtain some imported wood locally, other species must be ordered. As you will note when you begin the projects in Chapter 3, I tend to use a number of the exotics in my lid inlays. In a sculptured-flower lid design, I want the wood colors to approximate the actual flower. This necessitates the use of such woods as padouk, purpleheart, zebrawood, and ebony. I am constantly in search of woods of different colors for both boxes and decorative work. Incidentally, I'm very cautious with the exotics in terms of their potential toxicity or capacity to cause allergic or other reactions. You should find out from the dealer, woodworking magazines, or other woodworkers the potential hazards of a particular wood before you craft with it.

A much maligned wood that is still one of my favorites for making boxes is pine. There is a certain snobbishness afoot among woodworkers and the public alike that is conveyed in the phrase, "It's only pine." However, I learned to work wood from pine and continue to use it on a regular basis. Many of my box designs emerged from a prototype box crafted from pine. While obviously a softwood, it can in many ways compete with the more sophisticated hardwoods. For the beginning or advanced woodworker, pine remains an excellent choice for crafting boxes, and it's relatively inexpensive in comparison to the hardwoods. Pine is an excellent wood to use for the soundboard in music boxes. The lower grades of pine are beautiful and worthy of housing any piece of jewelry or musical movement.

In that I'm inclined to use woods that are victims of a wide range of natural processes, I have a special fondness for spalted woods. The end result of a truly remarkable fungal process, spalting is a phenomenon that occurs naturally in a variety of indigenous woods. For those who are willing to scrounge, the spalts can be an ongoing source of uniquely beautiful, inexpensive wood for crafting. What's more, the use of spalted woods does not deplete our forests; its use allows us to maximize our natural resources without exploiting them.

As with many woodworkers, I've been using spalted woods in my shop for years. I have especially enjoyed turning spalted woods into pieces with unusual designs (Illus. 2). As a matter of fact, I'm so taken with these woods— their strange beauty and unique designs—that I've begun to use them for many of the pieces that I craft as a production woodworker.

I frequently use spalted wood from hackberry, sycamore, box elder, hickory, red oak, black walnut, and the maples. This selection, however, tells more about the areas where I obtain my woods than the trees that are good spalters. Kubler (1980) and others suggest that most domestic trees are, to varying degrees, susceptible to the decaying process that results in spalting. A chart developed by Scheffer and Verrall (1973) identifies the various domestic trees and their ability to resist heartwood de-

Heartwood Decay Resistance of Domestic Woods

Resistant or Very Resistant	Moderately Resistant	Slightly or Nonresistant
Bald cypress (old growth)	Bald cypress (second growth)	Alder
Catalpa	Douglas fir	Ashes
Cedars	Honey locust[a]	Aspens
Cherry, black	Larch, western	Basswood
Chestnut	Oak, swamp chestnut	Beech
Cypress, Arizona	Pine, eastern white	Birches
Junipers	Pine, longleaf	Buckeye[a]
Locust, black[b]	Pine, slash	Butternut
Mesquite	Tamarack	Cottonwood
Mulberry, red[b]		Elms
Oak, bur		Hackberry
Oak, chestnut		Hemlocks
Oak, gambel		Hickories
Oak, Oregon white		Magnolia
Oak, post		Maples
Oak, white		Oak (red and black species)[a]
Osage orange[b]		Pines (most other species)[a]
Redwood		Poplar
Sassafras		Spruces
Walnut, black		Sweet gum[a]
Yew, Pacific[b]		Sycamore
		Willows
		Yellow poplar

Reprinted with permission of T.C. Scheffer and A.F. Verrall.

[a]These species or certain species within the group have higher decay resistance than most woods in this grouping.
[b]Exceptionally high decay resistance.

Illus. 3. Conks on log

cay (see chart). While the chart is but a crude guide and is specific only to heartwood decay, it does target those trees that are most likely to contain spalt. Because much searching for spalted woods is among felled trees that no longer have any foliage, it helps to be able to identify bark of various species. Also it's fun to know the kinds of spalted wood you are using in the shop. Numerous excellent books are on the market that picture and describe the bark of most indigenous trees.

My own searches for spalted woods have been limited to trees that have fallen from either storms or logging. There is no reason to cut down a living tree in search of spalt. For example, I have two huge wild cherry trees in my yard that have numerous large conks on the bark. Conks are the visible fruiting bodies of tree fungus, and their presence indicates possible spalt (Illus. 3.) These conks and the fungi working in the trees have been present for a number of years. The trees look healthy and there is no reason to remove them. Eventually, nature will take its course and they will have to be removed. In the meantime, they are beautiful, shade-giving trees that are priceless. There are enough trees being cut down in the world without what I call "spalt hunters" cutting down more. You will find ample, and usually better, spalted wood in forests or sawmills.

Recognizing conks and other visible signs of decay, as well as the bark of those trees that are likely to have spalt, can be excellent clues in your search for spalted wood. Once you've spotted a potential spalter, chain-saw off a cross-grain slice so you can visually check the sap-

wood and heartwood for black zone lines (Illus. 4). If they are present, immediate excitement will well up inside of you. It's like treasure hunting. The way you plan to use the wood determines your next cuts. Unless you have a tractor or some other means of hauling the log, it will be necessary to cut it into manageable chunks or lengths.

Frequently the bark and immediate outer sapwood of spalted wood is insect infested and full of punk. Punk is decayed wood that is usually white, totally rotten, and falls apart in your hand. It's worthless but an indicator of possible spalt. I usually chain-saw off, with the grain, as much of the bark and outer sapwood as can safely be removed. If I'm lucky, this process exposes more solid wood that is laced with black zone lines, mineral coloring, markings from insects, and who knows what else. Removing the bark and outer sapwood is not so difficult once the log has been cut into manageable sizes. As a rule, I cut the log into lengths that I can carry. With logs of sizeable diameter, I oc-

Illus. 4. Black zone lines in spalted wood

9

casionally rip them through the middle to ease the carrying process. Spalted wood, in good condition, can be quite heavy when you're faced with carrying it any distance.

When a log contains only enough solid spalt for a few small turnings, I cut out blocks from the useable wood. It's much easier to cut and trim the good from the bad while you're still in the forest. For the smaller turnings, I also look at large branches and, if available and exposed, the larger root sections. You may find a superb chunk of crotch or root that the fungi and insects have not invaded yet.

Be sure to always check the hardness of the wood. Sometimes, in the enthusiasm of the moment, you can haul home wood that looks beautiful but the decaying process has gone too far. Wood that you can tear out with your fingernails or poke a knife into is generally too decayed for crafting. Feel the piece, scratch the surface, probe it at various points, kick it, and generally examine it very carefully all over before deciding to haul it back to the shop. Spalted wood is usually soft, but there comes a point when it's almost impossible to use. You will find that your own experience crafting with spalts will help you select wood that is in the proper condition.

Frequently when I haul spalted wood to the shop and cut it to the sizes I want for drying, I will discover that the piece is not as spalted as I originally had thought. When this happens, I throw the wood that needs more spalting in the backyard, on the ground near the firewood pile. Exposed to the weather and the ever-present fungi from the firewood, conks begin to develop and I know the spalting process is continuing. I allow some pieces to lie on the ground for almost a year, periodically checking the end grain to make sure the wood is not decaying too quickly. When it's ready, I cut the wood to working dimensions for drying and eventual use. Incidentally, the backyard woodpile is also a good source of spalted woods. Always examine a piece before burning it. I've found some excellent spalted red oak in my firewood.

The process of drying spalted wood is often simply a matter of bringing it indoors. The size of the piece and the condition of the wood determine the length of drying time. Because spalted wood tends to be porous, most of it air-dries rather quickly. However, some of the pieces—usually heartwood spalt, for example—are extremely hard. Often these finer pieces must be handled more carefully. Generally I paint the end grain with one of the commercial sealants. If a sealant is not available, I use paste wax, candle wax, and, on occasion, even paint. The main thing is to seal the open grain to slow down the drying process and thus reduce splitting. You should check periodically to make sure that the sealant or wax hasn't deteriorated. If it has, you may want to put more on. I often leave these better pieces that are sealed to dry for a year or more. Many of the more porous pieces, on the other hand, will be dry and workable in six months' time or less. The ability to determine when the wood is dry enough to use comes with experience. You can feel a certain coldness and dampness in wood that is not ready for use. Some of my spalted wood has been drying for four or five years. Experimentation and talking to other woodworkers is a good practice when learning to dry spalted woods.

If you're not up to scrounging through forests, another excellent source of spalted woods is the log yards at sawmills. The lower sections of the logs are frequently sawed off prior to hauling the log to the mill. These cut-off sections tend to lie in the yards for months or even years and eventually begin to decay. They have provided the spalted wood for many of my boxes and turned pieces. Usually they are free for the asking. Unfortunately, they are often too heavy to move and must be chain-sawed into chunks that can be handled. These cut-offs can also be found around farms, land that is being

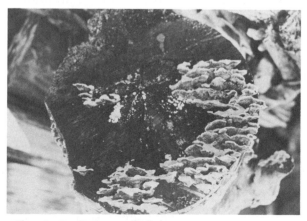

Illus. 5. Conks

Illus. 6. Reuge Model 1.18 movement on hard surface

developed for housing, and areas where new power lines are being strung.

In recent years, I've noticed an increase in spalted woods at lumber suppliers. The growing interest in the spalts among woodworkers has caused the lumber dealers to begin stocking them. When available at a reasonable price, I frequently will buy a variety of spalted woods that are kiln dried and planed from a local dealer. The wood graders often assign a lower grade to spalted woods, making them a bit more affordable. When crafting large functional boxes, I generally use spalted wood from dealers because of the widths they have available.

One of the curious phenomena that emerge when crafting functional and music boxes is the many similarities between them. With a few modifications, as you will see in Chapter 3, a typical functional box can be crafted into a music box. There are, however, a few special considerations to be aware of when selecting wood for music boxes.

The thickness of the walls and lid of music boxes is a significant factor in their crafting.

Except for the sake of appearance, this is not an issue with functional boxes. If you examine commercial music boxes, you will see that the walls and lid are generally about ⅜″ to ½″ thick. This is also true of many of the historic music boxes that are now collectibles. Thin walls and lids tend to resonate and reflect sound; they cooperate with and enhance the work of the soundboard. Thick walls and lids, on the other hand, tend to absorb the sound waves and stifle the work of the soundboard.

It is the soundboard, preferably made from wood, that is the primary resonator of the vibrations from the musical movement (Illus. 6). The soundboard is the major consideration in crafting music boxes (Illus. 7).

Although the thickness of the soundboard is also reasonably fixed (⅛″ to ¼″ at most), the type of wood used for the soundboard is, with a few possible exceptions, wide open for crafter experimentation. On occasion, I will use Sitka or Alaskan spruce for a soundboard. While expensive and somewhat fragile, especially the ⅛″ stock, spruce is an excellent wood for soundboards. Because of its cost, I limit my use of spruce to boxes that will house the larger musical movements. Curiously enough, my purpose in using spruce often has more to do with enhancing the saleability of a music box than with the quality of the sound produced. A Sitka spruce soundboard has a more exotic and, therefore, more marketable ring to it than a plywood soundboard. The average person, however, is not audibly astute enough to be able to tell if there's any sound-quality difference. For many of my music boxes in which the soundboard is not an integral part of the design—in lathed boxes, for example—I frequently use the better grains of plywood.

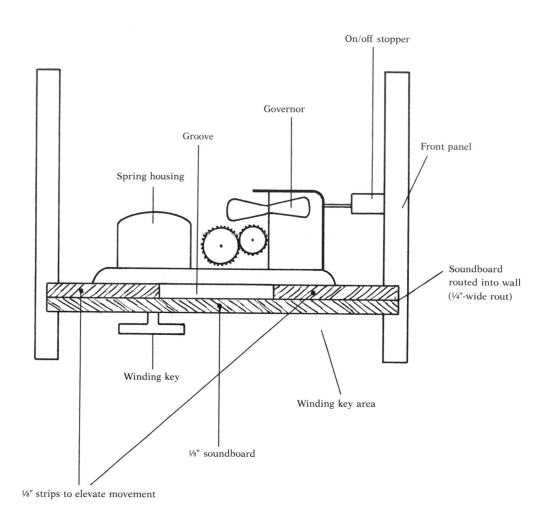

Illus. 7. Elevated soundboard: movement in place

2
PLANNING AND DESIGN

Designing and crafting boxes can be a challenge to anyone interested in working with wood. The curious thing about making boxes is that it confronts you with almost all facets of woodworking. For example, it is imperative that you learn about different woods and their specific characteristics. Box crafting allows you to use traditional or develop innovative joinery techniques. For those inclined to the lathe, it presents opportunities to maximize their turning skills. Music boxes, in particular, mandate planning and design work prior to crafting; they do not allow for careless or shoddy shop behavior. Whatever their eventual shape or use, boxes challenge us to get the most out of our tools.

Tools

In crafting any kind of box, the issue of tools is a major consideration. In an ideal world, the crafter would have a shop filled with every conceivable power and hand tool. While I'm certain there are woodworkers who approach this nirvana, few of us are so fortunate. For that matter, few of us have a shop large enough to accommodate all the tools we would like to possess. Most of us seem to settle for a few basic power tools; a wall full of jigs, clamps, and other clever devices; a great deal of clutter; and a number of fantasies about tools we wish we owned.

In my own crafting of boxes, I try to maximize the tools that I already have in the shop. I crafted the boxes presented in Chapter 3 using a table or radial arm saw, a scroll saw, an electric mitre saw, a band saw, a wood lathe, a table-mounted router, a drill press, and a large belt sander. I used a small pad sander, an electric drill, a Dremel tool, and a flexible shaft tool for preparing the various lid designs. The hand tools I have within reach include a few chisels, some measuring devices, a yankee drill, and the usual collection of screwdrivers, knives, and other minor tools that are in every shop. I've recently added a shaper and a planer that are very helpful but certainly not mandatory in my crafting activities. Many hardwood dealers or local lumberyards will, for a fee, do any mill work that a project may require. Also, mail-order hardwood dealers generally sell their wood in the various thicknesses that a box may require.

The preceding list of tools is not meant to be a shopping list for you. Your own preference may be to use all hand or all power tools, or some combination. The selection of tools is unique to each crafter. However, I have found a number of ways of using particular tools that you may want to emulate. For example, rather than buying the large, expensive multi-spur or Foerstner bits, I use the lathe for making storage or movement holes in many of my boxes. For those without a lathe, the larger bits may be a less expensive alternative. There are numerous ways of maximizing a few select tools, and there are always alternatives to buying an expensive piece of equipment. Alternate ways of using other tools are presented with the projects in Chapter 3.

Rather than providing a detailed list of router bits, saw blades, and other tools and accessories that I use, these specifics also are presented with the projects in the next chapter. Most hobbyist or professional shops already have the various tools and accessories needed for crafting boxes. In general, most woodworkers are inclined to use tools and accessories that have met their needs in the past. For example, I'm inclined to use high-speed steel router bits that I can resharpen; other woodworkers use only carbide bits. Most of what we do in our shops and what we do it with has to do with our own idiosyncrasies and our ability and willingness to spend money.

General Design Issues: Boxes

Before selecting a box to duplicate or before designing your own, it's a good idea to take an inventory of your available tools and crafting skills. Unless you're willing to purchase special tools that can meet your design requirements, it's best to develop or duplicate those box designs that exploit existing shop resources. As you will discover, the projects in Chapter 3 are, for the most part, reasonable in their tool requirements. In regard to matters of crafting skill, the issues are less clear. While some people may not possess the skill for crafting complex designs, I'm convinced the potential is there. The delightful part of woodworking with regard to skill is that almost all problems are solvable. It may take some of us longer but,

Illus. 8. Inlay on pine lids

Illus. 9. Jewelry box with tray

with tenacity, most woodworking projects can be handled. A major problem for many seems to be haste and the driving desire to finish the project. This approach not only dooms us to shoddy workmanship, it also robs us of the pleasure of the process. Crafting is a process and it is in the planning, designing, and doing that the most enjoyment resides. The end product is a visual reminder of a challenging, growth-producing, and satisfying experience. Thus, a seemingly complex design should not necessarily be avoided. It should rather be approached a bit more carefully and without haste.

However, for those who are reluctant to take on a complex project, a good alternative is selecting a less demanding one and crafting it from pine. Given the tool and cost requirements that go along with working with the hardwoods, pine presents an excellent option. Also, pine is a superb wood both in terms of its attractiveness and workability. For example, you can easily place various inlays and sculptured designs in a pine lid (Illus. 8).

When you design a box, you need to consider what it will hold and how much it will hold. While I frequently make jewelry boxes that hold a rather general collection of jewelry, inevitably some pieces do not fit. Some of the project designs in Chapter 3 are quite large, whereas others are diminutive. Prior to making a decision about the size of a box you plan to craft, you may want to address the potential user's needs.

Another aspect of designing boxes that presents the crafter with a quandary is the issue of dividers in trays. Many users of jewelry boxes want trays without dividers separating the various pieces of jewelry. I usually craft a tray with only a few dividers (Illus. 9). Unfortunately, customers often indicate their affection for the box, but want more dividers in the tray. A complaint of too many dividers in the tray is also a common reaction. To avoid such problems, you may want to explore the issue of dividers with the potential user. It may save you some time and grief later.

The thickness of the wood used for the tray and its dividers is also an issue in design. With the larger boxes, I often use stock that is at least ⅜" thick. The joints of the trays are mitred, the bottom fits into routed grooves in the walls, and the dividers are glued and screwed to the base. I tend to craft the tray and dividers so that they will not fall apart with heavy use or abuse. Your preference may be to use much thinner wood, a butt joint, and glue.

The issue of whether or not the tray and bottom of the box should be lined with fabric, leather, or some other soft material is a matter of personal taste. I have found that most users are satisfied with the wood. The wood doesn't scratch nor does it inflict any damage to the pieces contained in the box. I feel that, unless

Illus. 10. Walnut apple jewelry box

the material is cut well, coverings tend to cheapen the appearance of a well-crafted box. As you think about possible designs, you should explore the issue of linings within the box.

Many large boxes that I craft have no trays. I have found that many people prefer just a finely crafted box in which they can arrange things as they see fit. This is true even with jewelry boxes. Apparently, people use the small containers that their jewelry came in and store these containers in a larger jewelry box. The increasing use of large necklaces, bracelets, and earrings also suggests the need for boxes that are not encumbered with trays.

I have noticed that people use many of the large jewelry boxes for items other than jewelry. Everything one can imagine—from junk to cigars to guns—seems to end up in boxes originally designed for jewelry. As you think about crafting boxes, don't limit your designs to jewelry boxes. The possibilities presented by functional boxes are endless.

I have discovered that, in general, boxes I've designed and crafted for a particular use often seem to be used for other purposes. My apple design, for example, was originally crafted to house a musical movement. Now people more frequently use it, split in half, to hold jewelry (Illus. 10). By being aware of the multiple uses of the various designs, more projects are available for your crafting.

There are some special design issues you need to keep in mind when planning and designing music boxes. Your initial planning activities must focus on the space requirements of the musical movement. After deciding which type of musical movement you want to use, it's imperative that you find out the various dimensions of the unit. This is especially true with regard to the winding key and shaft. In dealing with a musical movement, you are working with a mechanism that has fixed dimensions. There is no way to modify the movement's various dimensional demands. Incidentally, musical movements are manufactured using the metric system. This may be the time you begin using this very simple and efficient measurement system in your shop. I have found the metric system to be very effective in all my crafting activities.

The issue of sound is also critical in planning music boxes. As discussed in Chapter 1, you must make some decisions about the type of wood to use for both the box proper and the soundboard. This part of the design process gives you an opportunity to experiment with various woods and thicknesses. I frequently wind a cylinder movement and hold it tightly against a wood's surface to test it for resonance. While the type of wood used for the box is critical in terms of sound reproduction, don't forget the aesthetic needs of your piece. Not only

16

should the box permit good sound, it should also be attractive to you.

Another special consideration has to do with the on/off system. While this is not an issue when working with disc movements, cylinder movements afford a series of stopper options. In part, the type and size of the movement you select determine your on/off options. For example, if you plan on using the small model 1.18 movements, you can get along without an on/off system. The larger movements should definitely employ some kind of stopper system if only to prevent the comb teeth from hanging up on the cylinder pins. The teeth should not, if at all possible, be left under tension when the movement is not in use. There is the possibility of metal fatigue if the teeth remain under tension for extended periods of time. Employing appropriate stopper systems prevents this from happening. It's almost easier to design a box that will readily accommodate the stopper system than to seek alternative designs. This approach, however, often leads to music boxes that are crafted solely along traditional lines. After you craft a few initial boxes this way, I hope your designs will go beyond the tradi-

tional. One of the real challenges in crafting music boxes is solving design problems presented by on/off systems.

Some other design issues specific to music boxes are whether or not to use a glass covering over the musical movement; whether to include a revolving platform; and if the box should have other functions, such as holding jewelry, in addition to playing music. More design considerations are presented with the individual music box projects.

I might add that, using pencil and paper, I make a rough drawing and then a dimensional drawing of each music box I plan to craft. Not only does this approach permit me to better plan the overall project, it also helps me anticipate possible problem areas. The drawing process forces me to deal realistically with possible design limitations that can result from limited tools and the like. It also tends to foster skill development by forcing me to solve those problems anticipated in each step. With the pencil-and-paper approach, I can jot down detailed notes on all aspects of a project. It's a process well worth the time and effort.

General Design Issues: Decorative Lids

One of the most interesting aspects of crafting boxes is creating decorative lids. Even though many of my boxes have no embellishment other than the inherent beauty of the wood, I find decorating box lids endlessly fascinating. By the way, when I'm not using an inlay or some other lid embellishment, I usually select a lower grade piece of hardwood that is laced with natural aberrations to use as a box lid (Illus. 11). With their natural designs, the lower grades of hardwood are ideal for box lids.

When you explore the history of boxes, you discover that the embellishment of the lid, as well as the box proper, is almost a tradition in all cultures. Many boxes belonging to European nobility, now held by museums, are absolute masterpieces of design and craftsmanship. The work of designer-jeweler Carl Fabergé is a magnificent example of the potential that boxes hold for embellishment. Although Fabergé worked primarily in precious metals, his work

affords the designer-craftsman an exposure to some historic treasures. The intricate inlays found on Oriental boxes, as well as the marque-

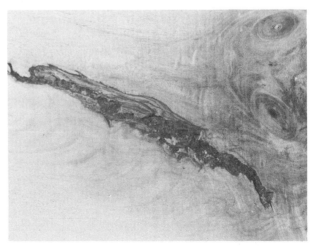

Illus. 11. Walnut board with character

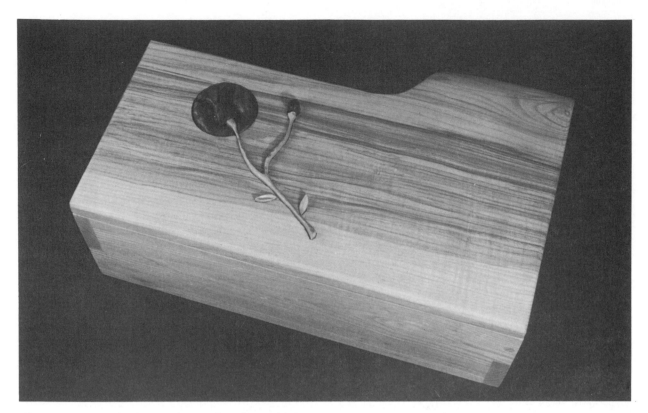

Illus. 12. Ash jewelry box with raised sculptured lid

try and intarsia of Italian boxes, are evidence of our historic fascination with the enhancement of boxes.

In recent years, I've experimented with different designs and techniques that can be used for decorating box lids. It's very easy to over-decorate lids because the process is so much fun. In looking over some of my lids that I considered tastefully designed and well crafted, one of my daughters said simply: "Too gaudy." From an artistic point of view her assessment may be accurate, but the buying public seems to like my gaudy boxes. The purpose of a box will, in part, determine the extent of embellishment. As you design box lids, try to take a balanced and tasteful approach.

In addition to determining how much embellishment to use, you need to decide what kinds of designs or decorations to use. While both these issues relate to personal taste, the possible designs are somewhat easier to address. In recent years, many of my box lids have reflected my interest in flowers. Flowers are relatively easy to design and craft on box lids, and the

different-colored hardwoods—such as padouk, purpleheart, hedge, and poplar—lend themselves to use in flowers. I have found that there are so many common everyday things that can be designed and crafted for lid decoration that the issue becomes one of time. In addition to representational decorations, there are endless abstract designs that can also be used on lids.

As you think about designs for lids, consider other skills you have in addition to woodworking. Lids provide an excellent opportunity for decorative work with a woodburning unit. Woodworkers who are also painters have a great combination of skills for decorative lid work. As you plan your decorating, reflect on other skills you currently possess or would like to develop. Box lids provide an excellent opportunity for both.

You may want to develop or use your skills at marquetry on your box lids. The wide range of veneers that are available makes possible a diversity of designs. For those so inclined, there are prepared veneer designs and edgings that can be readily adapted to box lids. I frequently inlay an attractive piece of veneer in the lid of a box. This process is done with the lathe.

I use an inlay process called intarsia even more often. Intarsia is an ancient technique for doing inlay work. My intarsia techniques are much simpler, though, and the results less intricate. Essentially, intarsia is the inlaying of metal, stones, ivory, or anything else into a solid wood surface. In contrast to marquetry, where you form a pattern by inserting veneer pieces into a base, intarsia involves cutting a recess in the wood surface to receive the inlay (Illus. 12). In addition to making raised sculptured designs, with intarsia you can also make designs that are flush with the surface (Illus. 13). I use small micro-bits, Dremel tools, and other small tools for making the designs and inserting them into the lids. There is considerable detail on this technique in the next chapter.

General Design Issues: Wood Joints

In general, the use of wood joints for boxes is more a matter of aesthetics than of function. As boxes are not usually subject to significant amounts of user or wood stress, they do not require strong joints. However, if you feel the stronger joints would enhance a box, by all means use them.

Joinery is probably the area of crafting that most challenges and frustrates the woodworker. By definition, it simply means the process of joining wood together. While simple in concept, joinery in practice can be rather intimidating to the beginning and even experienced woodworker. Much of it seems related to geometry and algebra and other subjects that many of us found difficult in school. There also seems to be a certain mystique that accompanies a well-executed joint. It has become, for many, a yardstick by which woodworking skill is measured. People always seem to look at the joints of a box

Illus. 13. Surface inlay on lids

Illus. 14. Decorative joints

first unless, of course, you have a gaudy lid design.

While joinery is a critical part of crafting boxes, the use of some joints can be more demoralizing than they're worth. As you plan your box designs, select joints that you can handle and that will give you a sense of accomplishment. You may even want to plan for a sequence of joints that escalate in complexity.

I use mitre, butt, lap, and a few other rather standard joints on my boxes. While I'm interested in joints, I'm more interested in how I can make them decorative (Illus. 14). There are numerous techniques you can use to accentuate the corners of a box in addition to the joint itself. The use of splines on mitres, for example, tends to sharpen up an otherwise rather drab joint. Incidentally, I've devised a fairly simple jig that I use with a table-mounted router that you may find useful in cutting splines.

Another aspect of joinery you need to consider has to do with securing the bottom section of functional boxes and the soundboard of music boxes. This is not an issue, of course, with turned boxes. You need to plan ways of securing the bottom of functional boxes that are both attractive and strong. Usually, I rout a groove in the walls of the box that will hold the box bottom securely in place. Also, I seldom use stock less than ¼″ thick for the bottom of functional boxes. To prevent the bottom of a large functional box from sagging in the middle, I often use an additional support piece. With music boxes, the issue of support is less of a problem, but you still need to plan how the soundboard will be placed and secured in the box. If the soundboard is not firmly attached, you will have an ongoing rattling noise whenever the musical movement plays. The movement must be a tight-fitting, integral component of the music box design. To hold the soundboard firmly in place, I generally rout a groove similar to that used in functional boxes. You may, however, prefer a small support frame secured at the corners of the box for holding the soundboard in place.

Issues related to specific types of joints and techniques for crafting them are covered in the next chapter. In working with joints, step-by-step procedures are often the most helpful.

General Design Issues: Hinges

Making boxes provides the crafter with opportunities to use a wide range of hardware. In addition to lid supports and hinges, key-lock systems, lid catches, and other clever devices are available for use on boxes. You may want to become familiar with the wide range of box hardware that is on the market. Within this wide range, there is a great diversity in quality. You also need to plan for hardware that is compatible with the dimensions of the wood you will be using.

Despite all that's available, I usually limit my hardware to hinges. As a number of projects demonstrate, I often use an extension on the lid that serves as a restraint (Illus. 15). This extension prevents the lid from opening too far and eliminates the need for chains or other lid stoppers. It also adds an interesting appearance to the lid. In your planning and design activities, you may want to consider using this type of lid restraint or developing an alternative design.

My usual choices for hinging boxes are small butt hinges and piano-type hinges that are manufactured for boxes (Illus. 16). However, as you will discover in numerous mail-order catalogues, there are many other styles that lend themselves to use on boxes. You may want to consider some of the hidden hinges or special-function hinges that are currently available. You also may want to think about crafting your own hinges from wood. In Chapter 3, I discuss ways of making wood hinges, as well as ways of routing and attaching hinges to the box and lid.

I use ¼″ or ⅜″ dowels as the hinge system on many of my small boxes (Illus. 17). For a sliding lid, a dowel system is an excellent alternative. I have found birch dowels to be preferable to the many beech dowels that suppliers seem to be marketing. Also, there are numerous nylon and other kinds of synthetic dowels available that make for very smooth and long-lasting hinge systems. In your planning activities, you should familiarize yourself with the range of materials that are available for crafting this type of hinge system. Various dowel systems are discussed in detail in the next chapter.

Although a variety of hardware for raising the lid is available, I use a sanded finger-grip

Illus. 15. Box lid stopper

recess in the lid for most of my boxes. A subtle but very effective way of opening a lid, the recess is usually placed on both sides of the bottom of the lid. You may want to use this type of design or a number of others that are presented. Clearly some method of opening the lid should be examined in your planning.

There are a number of designs in Chapter 3 that employ a lift-off lid. These lids can be either crafted or turned, depending on your preference. These designs, of course, eliminate the need for hardware. Closely related to these designs are fulcrum lid designs and designs with lids that slide in grooves. Band-saw boxes offer you another range of designs that do not require hardware.

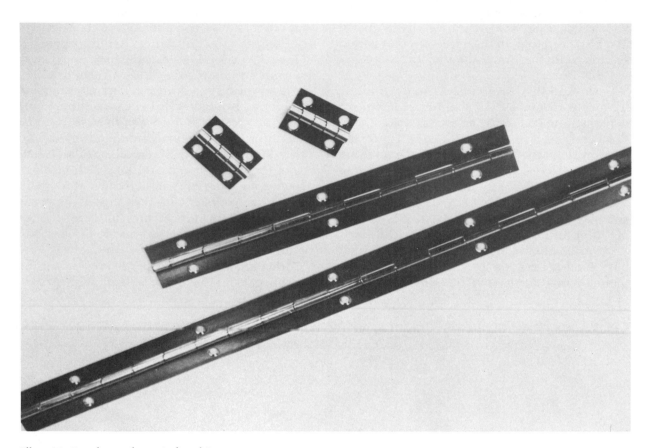

Illus. 16. Jewelry and music box hinges

General Design Issues: Turning

In designing boxes, it's important to consider how the wood lathe can be used to supplement other tools. All too frequently we think of the lathe as a primary tool used for crafting a total project—for example, a bowl. In point of fact, the lathe has all kinds of possibilities for use as a secondary tool. For example, with my apple design, I did the initial shaping and created the storage or movement area using the lathe. I did the final shaping of the apple, stem, and leaf with other tools. When its potential is explored, the lathe can provide you with numerous options for crafting boxes. These options are secondary but critical to the overall design. As you plan your crafting, do not overlook the possibilities that the lathe offers as a support tool.

Illus. 17. Sliding-lid hinge system

Summary

The foregoing discussion was presented to assist you in your design and planning activities. It is critical that you explore some of these issues and options before beginning the crafting process. When you initiate some prior planning, you are not so tied to specific project directions. Often, when projects are started without prior thought, the woodworker is hidebound to the instructions. This usually results in an overriding fear of making a mistake and thus takes much of the pleasure out of crafting boxes.

3

PROJECTS

While much of the fun in woodworking is designing your own projects, most of us need a few ideas to get started. In addition, examining projects designed by others can be both interesting and helpful because it allows you to see how someone else does a particular task. The following projects are presented as ideas that you may want to duplicate or modify.

The more boxes I make, the more I'm amazed at their potential uses. For example, a friend of mine uses my boxes for what she calls "grimple." According to this friend, grimple describes any small object that needs to be picked up and put someplace. Buttons, pins, paper clips, broken cup handles, and pennies are all grimple.

As you begin making small boxes, you will not only be continually surprised by their diversity of uses, but also by their design possibilities. Boxes can be designed to duplicate all kinds of objects—birds, animals, people, or anything else you may encounter in the world. If you're not interested in duplicating the real, there is always the abstraction or the surreal. Anything, even ideas and emotions, can be transformed into a box.

Many components of different projects are interchangeable, further expanding your design possibilities. For example, as you examine a particular box design, you may decide to use an alternate joint rather than the one presented with the project. Box lids and their embellishments also lend themselves to this interchange process. Hinges confront you with a range of options. The various components of each design

reflect my tastes, but are not mandatory to a given project. This is also true of the woods suggested for both boxes and decorative lids.

The various woods that are used in the projects are those that are indigenous to the area where I live. I encourage you to maximize the woods that are indigenous to your own locale. As mentioned earlier, do not rule out the use of pine for pilot or final boxes. Pine is generally available in all areas.

For each project, I have tried to provide sufficient detail for the completion of the box. I have, however, deliberately sought to eliminate the kind of detail that keeps you chained to the page. The instructions assume both a willingness and an ability on your part to solve some aspects of each project yourself.

Before beginning a project, it's a good idea to get a sense of its procedures and overall design. Try to figure out specific procedures that you feel could or should be done differently. Do some pencil-and-paper design modifications or simply make some notes of your own. It's best to rely on your own ideas, abilities, and resources as much as you can.

While I suggest various techniques and tools that work best for me, your own may be preferable for accomplishing a given task. I tend to do as much of my crafting as possible with power tools. Thus, I often do not address ways of accomplishing a particular task with hand tools. For those inclined to use hand tools exclusively, some translation of tasks may be necessary.

I have deliberately omitted any discussion of the finishing process from the individual projects. I have similarly omitted instructions for installing the musical movement. Instead, I discuss the finishing process in the next chapter and the procedures involved in installing the musical movement in a separate appendix. Because these final tasks can be done with any number of projects, it seems most useful to present them separately.

I present the various projects in three sections based on the tools and techniques that are used. The first selection of boxes can be made using the band saw and the lathe. This does not, however, rule out the use of other tools; it simply presents a series of projects in which these two tools are especially useful. The second series of boxes can be made with the lathe. While the band saw is critical in preparing the turning blocks, the lathe and various turning meth-

ods are essential to making these boxes. The final selection of projects employs various joinery techniques and the tools they require.

To identify each box design, I use a letter and number system, along with a descriptive name. Following the descriptive name, I indicate the number of the illustration that shows the finished box. A quick review of the many projects should give you an idea of how they are labelled.

To minimize detail and redundancy, specific procedures are stated once even though they may be required by another project. When necessary, a reference is provided to assist you in locating the appropriate information. Working wood can be addictive. Relax; enjoy the process.

A: Band-Sawed and Turned Boxes

The following projects represent just a sampling of the many boxes you can make when you use a band saw and the lathe as a secondary tool. While you may prefer to use large wood bits or a plunge router for accomplishing tasks I've assigned to the lathe, at least consider using this versatile tool. If you don't own a lathe, when you can afford it, buy one. They're the greatest.

When you use the lathe as a secondary tool, you will have to use scrapers as opposed to gouges. The use of the scraping method, however, will be a good change of pace for those wed to the cutting method. The use of the lathe in preparing the storage area in boxes also reduces the need for expensive bits or a separate tool. Don't rule out the lathe until you've used it in making a few boxes.

Illus. 18. Mushroom and apple music boxes

Most of the box designs include dimensional requirements. It is important to realize that each project can be reduced or increased in size. Some of the designs are a bit wasteful of wood. You may prefer a dimensional change that will use your materials more efficiently. As previously mentioned, the dimensional requirements for music boxes are more fixed than those for other types of boxes.

The lid designs also present various options. For those not inclined towards decorative lids, simply omit the embellishment procedures. Once you have a sense of some of my techniques for crafting lid designs, you can easily modify them to suit your own taste and designs.

As part of my own design process, I usually prepare a pattern for each project. I make my initial pattern on construction paper that I can easily cut with a pair of scissors. The paper-and-scissors approach permits quick and easy changes in any design. It also allows me to discard the design with nothing lost other than a little time and paper.

Paper patterns are durable enough for tracing a number of projects. I strongly recommend their use. When I finally develop a design and pattern that satisfies me, I transfer the pattern to metal. There are numerous lightweight metals available that make for excellent permanent patterns. I often obtain used metal sheets from print shops that are flexible and easily cut with a pair of scissors.

While the use of patterns may seem unspontaneous and terribly uncreative, patterns are critical to the production woodworker. They assure uniformity of design and dimensional accuracy. Also, patterns are an excellent way of saving designs that you've worked very hard to develop. You may want to make the same design at some point in the future. I suggest you make patterns for some of the projects that follow when you do your initial design work.

To assist you in your planning and pattern-making, I've included a profile of some designs. These profiles do not provide or suggest dimensions, but rather give you an idea of the configuration of a particular box design. They should be especially helpful with some of the rather unusual shapes that are presented.

Design A 1-1: Heart Box (Illus. 19)

1. The box presented in Illus. 19 requires 2" (8/4's)-thick stock for the base and 1" (4/4's) material for the lid. References to wood thickness are nominal dimensions as used by the hardwood industry. This design is approximately 5" wide and 5" long. You may prefer crafting it from thinner stock, however, to cut down the cost. Another alternative is gluing two 1" (4/4's) boards together to obtain the desired thickness. For an interesting effect, you can use two different woods for the laminated base. When laminating two similar 1" (4/4's) boards for the box base, I occasionally place a contrasting veneer between the pieces. This gives the base an interesting appearance, especially when I'm using wood that otherwise may not be very attractive. For example, a strip of padouk veneer can greatly enhance two pieces of white ash. The heart-box design lends itself to a range of thicknesses. Your selection should be based on available stock and how you anticipate the box will be used.

2. To assure uniformity of design, I recommend the use of a pattern (Illus. 20). A good pattern procedure to follow with a heart design starts with folding a piece of construction paper

Illus. 19. Heart box

evenly in half. Mark the length of the heart on the fold; mark half of the width out from the fold. Draw half of a heart within these dimensions. Cut and then open to the full-sized pattern.

3. Trace the heart pattern, with the grain, on the base block (8/4's stock). I do not use the pattern, however, for the lid. Instead, I trace the lid from the cut base. The way I band-saw the patterned base is not always perfect. By using the base as the pattern for the lid, you can obtain a much neater match of the edges.

4. Cut the heart base along the pattern line. For this procedure, I use a band saw with a ¼″ five-and-one-half-teeth-per-inch skip blade. While there are better blades to use for this procedure, this blade gives a reasonably smooth finish and can be used for other band-saw work.

5. Mount a 3″ faceplate, centered on the base. Select the best face of the block for the top surface of the box.

6. Secure the faceplate with the attached heart base to the lathe. Align the tool rest in front of the base in order to tool out the storage area (Illus. 21).

7. When turning out the storage area in boxes, I generally run my lathe at 2220 rpm. You may want to reduce your lathe speed if you are working on an initial box. After some experience, you will feel more comfortable working

Illus. 20. Heart box profile

on the blocks at the higher speeds. For purposes of safety, you may want to bring your lathe tailstock with a revolving center forward against the block. This will hold the block secured in place while turning out the storage area. As the last step in the turning process, tool out the wooden support pillar that develops.

8. For turning out the storage area, I use a ½″ square-nose scraper. This tool allows for quick

Illus. 21. Heart box on faceplate

Illus. 22. Dowel hinge in bottom of lid

as large as possible. You will want to leave some reasonably thick walls, however. Make your decision in relation to the anticipated use of the box.

9. After removing the faceplate from the turned base, trace the top edge of the heart on the 1″ (4/4's) lid stock. Cut the lid from the stock. Mark the bottom surface of the lid to assure proper alignment when you assemble the two parts.

10. For the hinge system on this design, I use a ⅜″ dowel (Illus. 22). With a ⅜″ wood bit in the drill, align the box and lid, upside down, under the bit (Illus. 23). On this design, I drill the dowel-hinge hole through one of the upper portions of the heart. Be certain not to drill too close to the edge or the dowel will split out. If possible, set your drill so that the bit penetrates the base no more than two thirds of the way into the lid. If the bit is too deep, it will penetrate the top surface of the lid. By the way, should you inadvertently drill through the lid, don't throw the lid away. Simply place a ⅜″ decorative plug in the hole and use it as the first plug in a three-or-more-plug inlay. After the plug glue is dry, the hinge dowel can be inserted and glued in place. Holding the box and lid tightly together, aligned under the bit, drill the dowel hole. You may want to use clamps to

removal of wood as well as a straight wall. When turning the storage area, be careful not to go too deep or you will hit the faceplate screws. Depending on the thickness of your faceplate, you may want to secure the block with screws that are no more than ⅝″ long. I tend to make the diameter of the storage area

Illus. 23. Drilling dowel-hinge hole

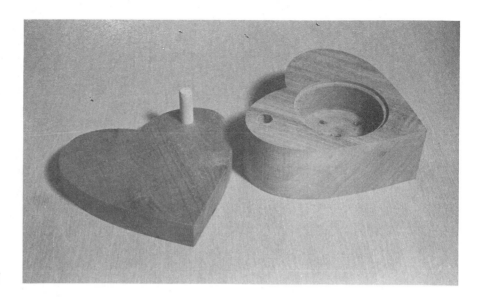

Illus. 24. Dowel hinge in lid

be sure the assembly doesn't move as it's being drilled. The hole and the alignment need to be near-perfect for a properly fitting lid and base. Incidentally, you should use birch or maple dowels, if available. The beech dowels tend to tear and wear down very quickly when used as a hinge. In place of wooden dowels, you may want to use the new synthetic dowels or rods that are on the market. These synthetics always have uniform diameters and they wear much better than wood. Unlike wooden dowels, these products are not affected by temperature or moisture.

11. After the hole has been drilled through the base and into the lid, cut a 1½″-long piece of ⅜″-diameter dowel. Also, cut a ¼″ piece of the same dowel to be used as a plug in the bottom of the base where the bit entered. To facilitate placement of the dowel into the lid hole and to avoid splitting, I slightly round the edge of the dowel end. It's also worth rounding the other end of the dowel that will enter the base portion.

12. After lightly spreading glue on the wall of the lid hole and also on the dowel, tap the dowel in place (Illus. 24). Be sure the dowel is straight in the hole or the lid will be elevated from the surface of the box when in place. Allow the glue to dry properly before placement in the base hole. If the glue is not dry, the dowel will twist out of the lid when placed in the base.

13. When the glue is dry, test the fit of the dowel in the base hole. If it is too tight, lightly sand the entire length of the dowel, all the way around it. You want a snug fit, but not one that's too tight. If the fit is too tight, the lid will not slide properly or you will twist the dowel out of the lid. Using the ¼″ piece of dowel and a touch of glue, fill the drill hole at the bottom of the base.

14. If the lid and base are not flush when assembled, either the hole was not drilled straight or the dowel was glued into the lid at an angle. There are a number of procedures that will remedy this problem. If the gap between the lid and base is slight, sometimes sanding over the hole in the top surface of the base will solve the problem. However, be sure you don't remove too much wood from the surface. Another solution is cutting the dowel off near the undersurface of the lid. Sand the remaining dowel flush with the undersurface of the lid. Carefully centering the ⅜″ wood bit over the dowel surface, drill it out while being careful not to penetrate the lid. After spreading glue and placing the new dowel in the lid hole, lightly tap the dowel towards the area where the lid was elevated from the base. This procedure usually results in a flush fit.

15. If you want to embellish the lid with a plug inlay, there are a number of options (Illus. 25). I generally use ⅜″-diameter plugs that I cut with a plug cutter from a type of wood that will look good with the box. Often the wood of choice for the heart box is padouk. After drilling the plugs with a cutter in a board, I saw them out using the band saw and its fence. It's a quick, easy way of cutting plugs from a board and it also ensures uniform length. An alternative to using a plug cutter is using dowels or commercially prepared plugs. Many suppliers stock walnut, cherry, and oak dowels in a range of diameters, including ⅜″. You can also use plugs cut from the dowel left over from making the hinge. As a rule, whether using a plug cutter or dowels, I cut the plugs to a length of at least ⅜″. Plugs of this length are more than adequate for decorative purposes and fairly easy to glue in place.

16. To inlay the plugs in the lid surface, first decide where you want the design to be placed. For our purposes, I assume you are following the three-plug-overlay design, shown in Illus. 25. Using a ⅜″ wood bit, drill a hole in the surface of the lid to a depth of a little less than ⅜″. After placing wood glue on the wall of the hole, tap the plug in place. You must allow the glue to dry before you drill the next hole. If the plug is not firmly glued in place, it will tear out when the next overlapping hole is drilled. When dry, sand the plug flush with the lid surface. Drill the second plug hole overlapping the first plug's surface by at least ¼″. Glue and tap the plug in place. Again, allow sufficient time for the glue to dry and then sand the plug flush with the lid surface. The third hole should be drilled so it overlaps at least ¼″ of the surface of the other two plugs. When the glue is dry, sand the inlay flush with the lid surface.

Illus. 25. Heart lid with three-plug inlay

17. With the lid in place, sand the side surfaces of the base and lid. Also, sand the bottom of the base in preparation for finishing. If desired, rout the lid edge and bottom base edge with a rounding-over bit. Do not rout the bottom edge of the lid or the top edge of the base. This would be a distraction from the overall appearance of the design. Be sure to remove any band-saw marks from the sides of both the lid and base.

18. Finish the box as desired or refer to the next chapter for a few ideas and products that I find helpful.

Design A 1-2: Heart Music Box (Illus. 19)

1. Although this design is essentially the same as the previous heart box, it has a turned-out area for holding a Model 1.18 musical movement. Refer to Design A 1-1 for specifics on the dimensions, pattern, and preparation of the base and lid.

2. Mount the base on a 3″ faceplate and secure it on the lathe. Align the tool rest in front of the block in order to tool out the musical movement area. It is also necessary to cut a shoulder in the movement area where a glass insert can be placed and secured.

3. For turning out the movement area, I use a ½″ square-nose scraper. This is also a good tool for making the glass-insert shoulder. Illus. 26 depicts the movement area and glass-insert shoulder, along with their dimensions. It also shows the soundboard, with the appropriate thickness, and the winding key area. You should check the length of the movement's winding key because sufficient depth must be allowed for it in the base of the block. When turning the various areas in your music box, you will want a ruler handy for monitoring dimensions. Remember, a musical movement is an object with fixed dimensions.

4. Turn out the musical movement area and the glass-insert shoulder. Carefully monitor their dimensions. With the corner of the scraper, make a small dimple in the middle of the bottom of the movement area after it has been turned. This point is where you will eventually drill a hole through the base for mounting a chuck to turn out the key area. As Illus. 26 indicates, I generally turn the movement area to a depth of at least ⅞″. The movement hole, including the insert shoulder, is approximately 3″ in diameter. The shoulder for the glass insert is usually about ¼″ wide and ¼″ or less deep. I use standard-thickness window glass for the inserts so a ¼″ depth is ample. The extra depth for the insert shoulder allows for any finish-sanding you may want to do on the top surface of the base.

5. After turning out the movement area and the glass-insert shoulder and placing the dimple in the middle of the bottom, remove the faceplate from the base.

6. Place the Model 1.18 musical movement in the turned hole and center it. When properly centered, press down on the spring housing. This pressure forces the key shaft to make a slight indentation in the surface of the bottom.

7. Using a ⅜″-diameter or slightly larger bit, drill a hole through the entire base at the key-shaft indentation. This hole is where the key shaft will eventually penetrate the soundboard.

8. For turning out the key area, I use a self-made chuck with a ¼″-diameter lag screw extending from the middle (Illus. 27). You may want to make your own chuck or purchase one of the numerous commercial ones available. Because accuracy is not all that critical in turning the key area, a self-made chuck is adequate. I usually make my chucks from 2″ (8/4's) ash,

oak, or hackberry. If you want to make your own chuck, turn a piece of 2″ (8/4's) stock, using a 3″ faceplate, to a throat diameter of about 2½″. This diameter allows for easy mounting of a base that has a 3″-diameter musical movement area. Cut a dimple in the middle of the front surface of the throat. Drill an undersized hole at the dimple and through the entire chuck. The hole is undersized because it must tightly accommodate the ¼″-diameter lag screw. If you have to remove the faceplate for this procedure, be sure to put alignment marks on the edges of both the chuck and the faceplate. After the lag screw has been screwed through the chuck, you may want to remove some of its length. The screw tends to extend too far from the face of the chuck if some of it is not cut off. You may want to square the end of the screw and deepen its gullets for better holding power. A file works well for deepening the screw's gullets.

9. After the chuck is made, mount it on the lathe and turn the machine on. Watch the lag screw as the chuck rotates. If it is running off-center, tap the screw until it runs perfectly straight.

10. Using the same bit that was employed in drilling the lag-screw hole through the chuck, drill a hole through the box base. The hole should be drilled at the dimple you made earlier in the middle of the bottom of the movement area. Mount the base on the chuck while it is secured to the lathe.

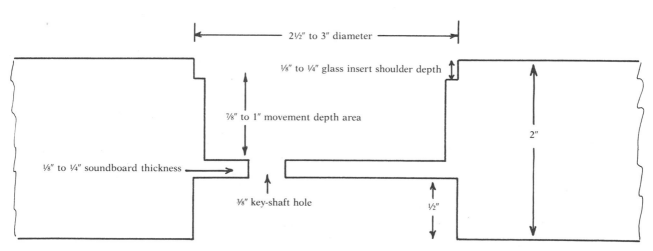

Illus. 26. Music box dimensions

Illus. 27. Self-made chuck

11. For removing wood from the winding key area, I again use a ½" square-nose scraper. If you lack confidence in your chuck or want to be certain of safety, bring your lathe tailstock forward against the base. You will want to have a revolving center in the tailstock for this procedure. If the lag screw protrudes through the box base, use a piece of dowel to thread on it. Secure the tailstock and revolving center against the end of the dowel (Illus. 28). Incidentally, the use of a dowel also gives you more room for your tool when turning. As you turn out the key area, leave a pillar of wood around the lag screw. You need this wood in place for support

while turning. Remember to check the depth of the area. A guide for checking the depth of the area and the thickness of the soundboard is the ⅜"-diameter key-shaft hole that you drilled in the base.

12. After removing the base from the chuck, chisel out the wooden pillar that formed in the middle of the key area. Remove it carefully so you don't split the soundboard.

13. Place the musical movement in the base with the key shaft penetrating through the ⅜"-diameter hole in the soundboard. You need to center the key shaft in the hole and the movement in the box. This centering procedure is necessary because you will be marking the exact places where the holding screws penetrate the soundboard. It's an awkward but manageable task, often requiring both hands. You want the key shaft centered in the hole so that when the key is in place and unwinding, it does not rub against the wall of the hole.

14. When the movement and key shaft are perfectly aligned, using a sharp pencil or scribe, mark through the three holes in the movement baseplate and onto the surface of the soundboard. You may want to darken these marks so they will be more visible when you drill holes through them. Using a ⅛" or slightly larger bit, drill through the soundboard at the three points you have marked. These holes will accommodate the screws that secure the musical

Illus. 28. Winding key area being turned

Illus. 1. Spalted black walnut box

Illus. 2. Triangle box with sculptured inlay

A

Illus. 3. Turned boxes with sculptured inlays

Illus. 4. Band-sawed/turned box with sculptured inlay

Illus. 5. Spalted sycamore and black walnut musical apples: turned and shaped

Illus. 6. Turned off-center box with lid

Illus. 7. White ash box with sculptured floral inlay

Illus. 8. Spalted hackberry mushroom music box: turned

B

Illus. 9. Box with sculptured goose inlay

Illus. 10. Wooden hinges: white ash and padouk

C

Illus. 11. Pencil box with sliding lid

Illus. 12. Emeri box with sculptured floral inlay

Illus. 13. Emeri box with picture inlay

D

movement to the surface of the soundboard.

15. Just for the fun of it, secure the movement in the box with the appropriate screws, wind the movement, and listen. After enjoying the sounds of clockwork music in your box, remove the movement in order to complete the project. Avoid getting sawdust in the movement.

16. This box uses the same dowel-hinge system described in Design A 1-1. For specific procedures and suggestions related to the dowel-hinge system, refer back to that design.

17. Design A 1-1 also presents step-by-step procedures for making a three-plug-inlay design in the lid of the box. If you want to use this type of lid embellishment, you may want to follow these procedures.

18. Rout the top edge of the lid and bottom edge of the base with a round-over router bit. If you do not have a router, roll the edges carefully using abrasive papers.

19. Finish the box as desired. You may want to refer to the next chapter for finishing procedures and the Appendix for specifics on installing the musical movement and cutting the glass insert.

Design A 2-1: Square Box with Floral Inlay (Illus. 29)

1. This design calls for 2″ (8/4's) stock for the base and standard 1″ (4/4's) material for the lid. If the stock is too costly or not available, laminate a number of boards together to achieve the desired thickness. You also may want to laminate a piece of veneer between the laminated boards. Instead of veneer, you may want to use stock that is ⅛″ or ¼″ thick. Select wood that contrasts well with the other material used. Whatever way you laminate the base, be sure to spread glue on all surfaces and clamp until dry. The design is approximately 3½″ wide and 3½″ long. You may, of course, choose to increase or reduce the size of this design. In part, your decision should be based on the anticipated use of the box. This size is appropriate for a ring or an earring box; it's also appropriate for a standard grimple box. Think about possible uses before finalizing your dimensional plans.

2. The best way to cut this design, both base and lid, is with a band saw. Because it's a square design, setting the rip fence 3½″ from the blade solves the dimensional cutting problems. You may want to cut the base and lid a tad oversize to allow for the sanding of the various surfaces.

3. Before turning or drilling out the storage area in the base, I generally begin the lid-inlay process. While the stem is drying in the lid, you can work on the storage area in the base. Veneer or a thin slice of wood that contrasts with the lid wood is a good choice for the stem. The veneer or slice of wood should be about the same thickness as your band-saw blade. Using your band saw, make a curved cut resembling a flower stem, with the grain, into the lid. The cut

should extend from the edge to approximately the middle of the lid. If you want two flowers for your design, cut another slot in close proximity to the first but separated at the top of the

Illus. 29. Square box with floral inlay

cut. You need to leave enough space between the stems to allow for placement of the plugs for the flowers. To be able to visualize the finished inlay, you may want to refer to Illus. 30.

4. Using a scissors or other cutting device, cut a strip of veneer, with the grain, a little longer than the stem cut. The veneer should also be cut a little wider than the thickness of the lid.

With this oversize cut, it is easier to slide the piece of veneer into the lid. Spread glue on both surfaces of the veneer; then slide the veneer into the cut. Clamp; then wipe off any excess glue. By the time you've prepared the storage area in the box base, the glue should be dry.

5. There are a number of ways of making the storage area in the base. One alternative to using the lathe is using a large multi-spur bit. Another comparable bit is the Foerstner. While expensive, these bits are available in diameters up to 3″. The larger bits, of course, must be used in a drill press. You can also use bits with smaller diameters for making a series of storage areas to be used in this box and in other boxes as well. This approach is especially useful if you are making a box that has a number of storage areas as opposed to one large one. For those with a standard or plunge router, with appropriate bits, storage areas can be easily routed. On some of the box designs, using an edge guide, the storage area can be routed to conform with the box design. You may want to explore with a router and various bits if you have access to them. If you prefer the lathe for making the storage area, refer to Design A 1-1 for specifics on turning procedures. If you use a multi-spur bit for drilling the storage area, you may want to prepare a felt or leather insert for covering the bottom of the area. These bits tend to cut a rather unsightly groove in the bottom of the box. After the box is totally finished, the insert can be glued to the bottom of the storage area. It makes for a more finished appearance.

6. Before you begin the floral inlay in the lid, cut off and sand the excess veneer. You will want the stem to be flush with the lid surface before you begin drilling holes for the inlay plugs.

7. Natural-colored hardwoods are the best woods to use for the floral plug inlay. I use padouk for red petals and purpleheart for purple. I usually use hedge (yellow) or ebony (black) plugs for the central seed pod. If you want yellow petals in the design, use the hedge. Flower-plug inlays challenge the woodworker to find and experiment with different-colored woods. Although I never stain any of the hardwoods that I use in making boxes, you may want to consider using some of the excellent colored stains that are now on the market. They can be used for staining the entire box or to add color variety to the inlay. Incidentally, the floral inlay design can be easily modified into a design of colored balloons on strings. When I do the balloon design, I generally make four or five cuts in the lid for holding strips of veneer.

8. To make the plugs for either inlay design, you need a plug cutter and a wood bit of the same diameter. As indicated, I generally use a 3/8″ wood bit and a 3/8″ plug cutter for much of my inlay work. You may, of course, prefer a 1/4″- or 1/2″-plug diameter, or some combination of diameters. Often I will make a seed pod from a 1/4″ plug when the petals are 3/8″ in diameter. Plan the overall size and shape of the flower and cut a sufficient quantity of plugs to do the job. As mentioned, I cut the plugs to a length of approximately 3/8″. For quick removal of the cut plugs in a board, using the saw fence, saw them out on the band saw.

9. Drill a series of holes in the lid, placed around the outer edge of the flower design. Be certain the holes don't overlap at this point. That part of the inlay process comes after the plugs have been glued in place. When drilling the holes, set your drill so that the depth does not exceed the length of the plugs. I generally plan to let at least 1/16″ of the plug extend out of its hole. Spread a touch of glue in the drilled holes and tap the plugs in place. Allow the glue to dry thoroughly before drilling any overlapping holes. If the glue is not dry, the plugs will move out of place when you drill into them for the overlapping hole.

10. Continue the process of drilling holes and inserting plugs, each overlapping the others. It's best to work from the outer edge of the flower towards the middle. The last plug to be inserted should be the seed pod. To make the drilling process easier and more accurate, sand the plugs flush to the lid after each is dry. When the entire inlay is complete, again sand it flush with the surface of the lid.

11. While small brass hinges can be used on this design, you may prefer the sliding lid, dowel-hinge system. For specifics on the dowel hinge, refer to Design A 1-1.

12. Rout the top edge of the lid along with the bottom edge of the base. Using abrasive papers, prepare all surfaces for finishing. Finish the box.

Design A 2-2: Square Music Box with Floral Inlay (Illus. 30)

1. This design is essentially the same as Design A 2-1. To alter the box so that it will house a Model 1.18 musical movement, you need to use 2″ (8/4's) stock for the base. Illus. 26 shows the dimensional requirements of a box that will house a Model 1.18 musical movement. You can, of course, laminate 1″ (4/4's) boards to achieve the necessary base thickness.

2. The area that will house the musical movement should be turned on the lathe. A shoulder for holding the glass insert also needs to be made while you turn the movement area. For specifics on these procedures, refer to Design A 1-2. You should also refer to this design for information on the self-made chuck and turning the movement key area in the bottom of the box. Other procedures that have to do with preparing the base for housing the musical movement should also be reviewed.

Illus. 30. Floral inlay

Design A 3-1: Bird Box 1 (Illus. 31)

1. This is a rather tough box to cut with a ¼″ band-saw blade, but it's well worth the effort. Illus. 32 shows a profile of the design that should assist you in making a pattern. You will want to be certain that your pattern does not have a curved neck area that is too sharp for the radius of the band-saw blade. An obvious solution is using a ⅛″ band-saw blade if you have one. I generally make the base of this design from 2″ (8/4's) stock and the lid from 1″ (4/4's) stock. With the smaller boxes, you need thick stock in order to have a reasonable storage area. When you shop for 2″ (8/4's) lumber, be sure to examine the lower grades of hardwood. As mentioned earlier, I usually buy the lower grades because they're not only less expensive, but also more attractive. For functional boxes, you can also use 2″ × 4″ or 2″ × 6″ pine for the base. Don't rule out pine for both the base and the lid. When the 1″ lid stock is embellished and a clear finish is applied, pine makes for a very attractive box.

2. The lid of the box should be traced from the cut base rather than the pattern. This allows for those variances that inevitably result when cutting a piece on the band saw. It also eliminates a lot of sanding that is often necessary if the lid and base walls are not flush. Some sanding of the base and lid edges will be required, but it's best to minimize it as much as possible.

3. If you want a few tail feathers on the lid, you may want to begin this process prior to making the storage area in the base. Refer to Illus. 31 to orient yourself to the approximate placement of the feathers. Depending upon the wood used for the lid, select a veneer or cut stock that contrasts well with the color of the lid. As Illus. 31 indicates, I cut three straight lines, about 1″ long, into the lid. Where the tail feathers should be placed is arbitrary. The thickness of the veneer and the band-saw blade should be compatible because it's very difficult to clamp a round lid. I usually make the cuts with a blade that is a bit thinner than the veneer. You will want the veneer to fit as tightly as possible into the cuts.

4. Cut oversized veneer strips, apply glue to both surfaces, and slide the strips into the lid

Illus. 31. Bird box 1

cuts. As you will discover, making the veneer strips oversized allows them to slide into the cuts much more easily. Wipe away the excess glue and allow it to dry.

5. For the adventurous, a wing slot can also be cut into the lid. Approximate the location of the wing on the lid; then, with a pencil, draw a curved line about ¾″ long. Using a Moto-Tool electric hand grinder with a router base and a micro-burr, the wood can be removed to accept an inlay. This routing procedure is discussed in detail in a number of later projects. An alternative procedure involves using an X-acto knife or any knife that's similar and carefully cutting the area out. The micro-burr leaves rounded ends in the groove, whereas the knife can make them square. You may want to use both tools. Depending upon the width you've selected for the wing groove, glue in veneer or other stock cut to the correct length, width, and thickness. Wood filler, properly packed into the cut, can also be used in the inlay process.

A final task in preparing the lid is drilling a ⅜″-diameter hole and inserting a plug for the eye. You need to approximate its location and decide on a possible wood to use. I often cut the plug from hedge, giving the bird a yellow eye.

6. While I'm inclined to use my lathe for making the storage area in this design, you may prefer drilling or routing the area. Refer to De-

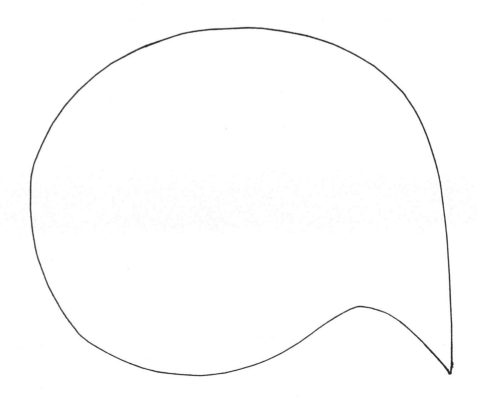

Illus. 32. Bird box 1 profile

sign A 2-1 for some of these alternate ways of preparing the storage area. Those who prefer to use the lathe should refer to Design A 1-1 for specifics.

7. The final procedure for the lid, when the glue is dry, involves breaking off the excess veneer and sanding the entire inlay flush with all surfaces.

8. This design lends itself to using a sliding lid, dowel-hinge system. There is not enough space for using traditional hinges. Check with Design A 1-1 for specific procedures involving preparation and placement of the dowel hinge.

9. Sanding the outside edges of this design can be a problem. This is especially true if you have extensive band-saw marks in the neck area. This curved area is almost impossible to get at with a power hand sander. If you have a Moto-Tool with sleeve-sanding capacity, the task will be much easier. If not, the hand method of sanding is recommended.

10. You will want to rout the top lid edge and the bottom of the base. Boxes look better if the edges are rolled a bit. Be careful when routing over the veneer tail feathers. Keep the edge of the lid tight against the router bit or you may get some tear-out. This tearing out also happens with a dull bit.

11. Finish the box using your own procedures or refer to mine in the next chapter.

Alternate Use: This design can also be made to house a Model 1.18 musical movement. Refer to Design A 1-2 for the specifics on making a music box.

Design A 4-1: Bird Box 2 (Illus. 33)

1. Birds can provide a range of design ideas for the box maker. This design presents another one that you may want to consider. While consuming a bit more wood than the previous bird design, this design has more storage area and a plain or carved lid. To assist you in your design work, Illus. 34 presents a profile of this design. You may want to play with a few ideas of your own in designing a bird box. Designs are based on our own perceptions and you may prefer to use yours rather than mine. These designs are, at best, approximations of an object. Why not make your own unique design? You can use this design as a guide for preparing the various components of the box.

2. I use 2″ (8/4's) stock for the base and 1″ (4/4's) stock for the lid. The length of the box is approximately 5½″ and its width is at least 3½″. These dimensions allow you to make one large storage area or a series of smaller drilled storage areas. The design also lends itself to using a router for making a large storage area that con-

Illus. 33. Bird box 2

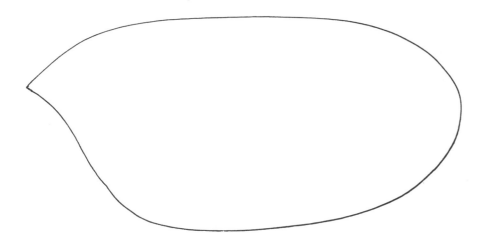

forms to the shape of the box. You may want to consider possible uses for the box as you explore alternative storage areas. You may prefer to laminate the base from 1″ (4/4's) stock. To provide a storage area of greater depth, you can enlarge the box to a thickness of 3″. Strips of veneer or solid woods can be placed between the laminated boards for an interesting effect.

3. Prepare a pattern, then trace and cut the base of the box (Illus. 34). To assure a good-fitting lid, trace the base onto the 1″ (4/4's) lid stock. As mentioned, this process usually results in edges that are more flush and minimizes the need for sanding.

4. The storage area can be readily turned on the lathe using a 3″ faceplate centered on the bottom of the base. A ½″ square-nose scraper or similar turning tool works well for removing wood from the storage area. When turning, be sure to monitor the depth of the storage hole so you don't hit the ends of the faceplate screws. A single large storage area can also be made with a multi-spur bit or a large Foerstner bit. A number of mail-order clock suppliers stock a 3″-diameter bit that works well for drilling storage areas in boxes. While costly, these larger bits are effective and simple to use. The router and appropriate straight bits are another alternative for preparing the storage space. Those who want a series of small holes for a range of storage areas should use small Foerstner or multi-spur bits. I generally use 1″- or 1¼″-diameter multi-spur bits to drill holes for accommodating rings or other small jewelry. You can, of course, vary the depth of the holes depending upon the anticipated use of the box.

5. While the lid on this design can be hinged with small brass hinges, you may want to use the ⅜″ dowel hinge described in Design A 1-1. I hinge the lid at the head portion of the bird. If you refer back to Illus. 33, you will see that a plug has been inserted for an eye. You may want to add tail feathers and a wing line using veneer strips. For those with carving tools or a woodburning unit, detail can be easily added to the lid. It's a good idea to draw your design on the lid surface prior to carving or burning. Use your imagination. There's sufficient surface on this lid for considerable detail.

6. Using appropriate abrasives, prepare all surfaces for finishing. The chapter on finishing also includes procedures for preparing the surfaces. Finish the box.

Alternate Use: As with most of these projects, this design can also be made to house a small Model 1.18 musical movement. In fact, it has sufficient space for a musical movement as well as a storage area. For specific procedures for modifying the design into a music box refer to Design A 1-2.

Design A 5-1: Kidney Box (Illus. 35)

1. While the name of this box is not especially artistic, it is descriptive. Illus. 36 provides a profile of the design that will help you make a pattern. The design allows for two storage areas. It has opposite opening lids that have ample surface for a range of interesting inlay

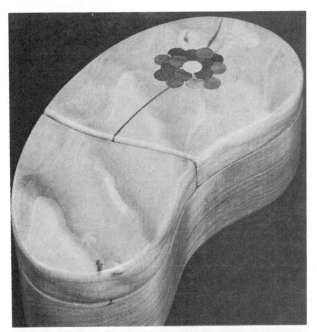

Illus. 35. Kidney box

work. This is one of those designs in which the inlay can easily become gaudy, but it's an ideal box to embellish. Because the box requires some rather high-risk turning, if you use a lathe, you may want to drill or rout the storage areas. It's a bit disconcerting the first time you turn a large block off-center on the lathe. An alternative is to turn out a large storage area in the wide end of the box and drill a hole in the smaller end of the base with a multi-spur bit. More about this shortly.

2. For this project, 2″ (8/4's) stock is necessary for the base and 1″ (4/4's) material for the lids.

It's best to pattern the lids from the base and cut them as one piece. A later procedure explains how the lid is cut into two sections. The box is approximately 7¾″ long and 3½″ wide. Because this design uses a sizeable piece of wood, you may want to reduce its overall dimensions. You may want to consider laminating the base from 1″ (4/4's) boards, as opposed to using the more costly 2″ (8/4's) stock.

3. Pattern and cut the base section of the box. Using the cut base as a pattern, trace and cut the lid. As previously mentioned, do not cut the lid piece into two sections at this point. You will eventually cut the lids when you know exactly where the two storage holes are located in the base. While you can begin planning and designing your lid embellishment, the actual work should not begin until the lids have been cut.

4. If you want to turn one of the storage areas, mount a 3″ faceplate in the middle of the widest end of the base. As you know, the faceplate should be secured directly below where the hole is to be turned. This placement of the faceplate should be clearly off-center in relation to the total base (Illus. 37). The tailstock with a revolving center should be used to support the block when turning. It will give you a measure of safety when turning off-center.

Reduce your lathe speed to the slowest possible rpm before turning on the lathe. I usually turn off-center at 990 rpm. You may, however, want to set your lathe at a slower speed if this is your first attempt at turning off-center. As you will quickly discover, this type of turning can move your lathe around on the floor unless it's

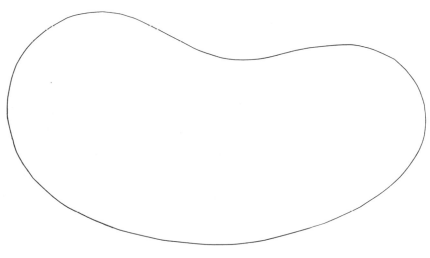

Illus. 36. Kidney box profile

Illus. 37. Kidney box block off-center on lathe

secured or weighted down. It also could be hard on the headstock bearings. By way of reassurance, I've turned many off-center blocks on my Rockwell Model 46-111 lathe and the bearings are fine. This lathe, by the way, is a rather inexpensive model made some years back for the hobbyist wood turner. Despite the possible drawbacks of turning off-center, it's a great way to turn some fascinating and different effects in blocks. If you have access to large bits, you may want to drill both storage areas. Most of the time, I only turn the larger storage hole with the lathe; I drill the smaller one using a 2" multi-spur bit. For the confirmed turner, both holes can be turned off-center on the lathe.

5. After both holes have been made in the base, place the lid piece on its top surface in such a way as to show the edges of both storage holes. Draw a line on the lid surface where it should be cut into sections. The lid that will cover the larger hole is generally the larger of the two lids. I make a curved cut when separating the two pieces. A curved cut is much more attractive than a straight cut. You may want to refer back to Illus. 35 to see how the two lids are cut and aligned when finished.

6. If you plan to do a plug-inlay floral design, now is the point in the process for these procedures. This floral design is the same as the one presented in Design A 2-1. I often limit the inlay to the larger lid. Frequently, because of its size,

I inlay two flowers in the larger lid. You may want to do some design work before beginning the inlay process. Some alternative designs are presented with the next project.

7. The dowel-hinge system is mandatory with the kidney-box design. The procedures for making the hinge system are the same as those presented with Design A 1-1. However, with the kidney box, remember that the two lids should

Illus. 38. Kidney box: dowels in lids, holes in base

slide open in opposite directions. Thus, one lid is hinged on one side, and the other lid is hinged on the opposite side. The dowel holes must be planned and drilled with this in mind. Also, it's a good idea to use clamps when drilling holes through the base and into the lids. Working with two lids can be rather difficult, especially when you're trying to drill a hole. Take your time on this procedure and reflect on each step prior to initiating it. Illus. 38 shows the kidney box with the two holes drilled for the dowels.

8. Using a round-over bit, rout the top edges of the lids and the bottom edge of the base. A table-mounted router works best for these procedures. The dowels can be in place and the lid can still be routed.

9. Finish the box, after all surfaces have been sanded.

Alternate Use: This design can also be made into a music box. In addition to turning the musical movement area off-center, you will need to turn the winding key area off-center and mount it on a chuck. The design has a musical movement in the larger area and a drilled hole for storage in the small end of the base. It makes for an excellent small box that both performs music and provides some storage space. For specific procedures, refer to Design A 1-2 and to the previous discussion of off-center turning.

Design A 5-2: Kidney Box with Sculptured Inlay (Illus. 39)

1. This box is presented as a separate design because it involves a rather elaborate lid embellishment. The inlay process I use with this design is a type of intarsia that's both fun and a challenge.

2. Prior to beginning the inlay process, the base and lids of the box should be prepared according to the procedures presented in Design A 5-1. For those who prefer making this design into a music box, refer to the procedures presented in Design A 1-2. You may also want to examine the brief discussion on off-center turning presented with Design A 5-1.

3. After the base and lids are prepared, be certain the surfaces, especially the lids, are ready for final finishing. Once the inlay is glued in place on the lids, the use of abrasives is very limited. Thus, it's important that the surfaces be adequately prepared. While you may prefer another lid design for this box, for our purposes the discussion will focus on duplicating the floral inlay presented in Illus. 39. Once you have

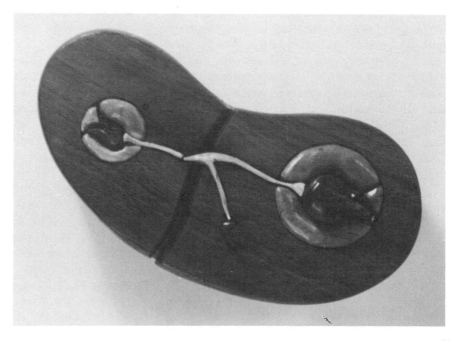

Illus. 39. Kidney box with sculptured lid

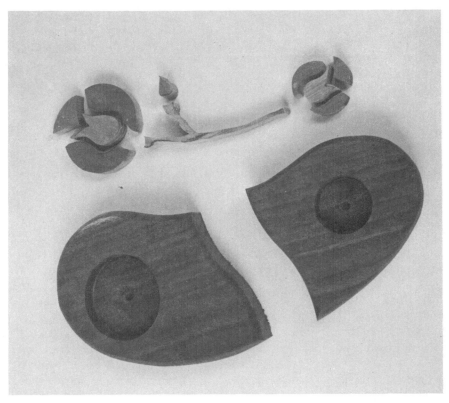

Illus. 40. Kidney box: insert holes and inlay components

an idea of the various methods and tools that are employed, you can easily develop your own alternative designs.

4. The inlay design consists of two different-sized flowers, a bud, a leaf, and a stem. Additionally, there are two round lid inserts that serve as margins to offset the flowers. Two different-sized holes are drilled or turned in the lids to a depth of approximately ¼″ to ⅜″. The larger hole should have a diameter of 2″ and the smaller one a diameter of 1¼″. Multi-spur bits work well for making these lid-insert holes. The larger hole should be drilled or turned in the larger lid piece. Illus. 40 shows the holes in the lids, along with the other inlay components.

5. The best way to drill the holes in the lids is by using multi-spur or Foerstner bits. If these bits are not available, you can turn the insert holes on the lathe using a self-made screw chuck. Drill a hole through the lid in the middle of the planned insert hole. The hole should be undersized in relation to the screw chuck. Mount each lid on the chuck and turn out the insert areas to the dimensions previously stated. A ½″ square-nose scraper works well for making the insert holes. You can fill the screw

holes in the bottom of the lids with wood filler. The holes on the top surface will, of course, be covered by the inlay.

6. Cut two round inserts that will fit perfectly into the prepared holes in the lids. These two pieces will serve as the background for the flowers. You should cut them from a wood that contrasts well with the wood used for the flowers. It also must look good with the stock from which the lids are made. For example, in a walnut lid when the flowers are from padouk (red), I often use wild cherry or white ash for the background inserts. The thickness of the inserts should be at least ⅛″ greater than the depth of the two holes. You want the inserts to extend above the lid surface for a more impressive-looking inlay. I use a plastic template with marked diameters for patterning the inserts. A school compass also works.

7. The flowers in Illus. 39 are supposed to resemble roses. You may want to make a pattern for your flowers. On the pattern, you may want some details regarding how the flowers should be shaped. Although the size of the flowers is arbitrary, the flowers should not exceed the outer edge of the inserts. Also, you need to al-

low some space at the base of both flowers for the stem to butt against. The flowers should have a thickness of ½″ to ⅝″. This thickness should permit the flowers to extend out of the lid inserts by at least ¼″. The thickness also provides enough wood for sculpting the flowers. Prepare and cut the two flowers from a wood of your choice. I do my cutting of inlay parts using either a large scroll saw or a band saw with a ⅛″ blade. If necessary, the parts can be cut using a sabre saw with a fine-tooth blade.

8. A bud also needs to be cut from the same wood as the flowers. It needs to be only about ¼″ to ⅜″ thick because it requires no background insert. The bud is routed directly into the lid. Use your imagination when designing and cutting the bud. You may want to duplicate the rather simple bud design in Illus. 39. This picture may also give you some ideas about the shapes of flowers. Refer to Illus. 40 for some ideas on how the flowers and bud appear when rough-cut and prior to shaping.

9. Place the inserts in their respective holes in the lid and lay the rough-cut flowers on them. I usually place the bud on the lid near the larger flower insert. These procedures are necessary so you can visualize and prepare the stem. The stem needs to connect both flowers and the bud. It should penetrate the inserts and butt against the bases of both flowers. You may want

to examine Illus. 39 and Illus. 40 to see the end result of these stem procedures. You should also note how the stem widens as it makes contact with the flowers and the bud. This makes the design appear more realistic.

I usually draw the stem, freehand, on the wood to be used. This is done after making a few rough measurements to determine the overall length of the stem. Normally I cut the stem from ¼″-thick poplar or hedge that has been ripped on the band saw. I use the green section that is often found in poplar. The yellow hedge also makes for an attractive stem. The stem is separated where the two lids make contact. This is one of the final procedures in the inlay process. This procedure permits the lids to open, but presents a total picture when the lids are closed. With a scrap of poplar or hedge, cut a small leaf that will be placed along the stem.

10. After the stem has been cut, trace the two flowers on their respective inserts. The traced area is cut out so that the flowers will fit neatly into the inserts. Trace the flowers with the insert grain; it looks much neater. After the flowers are traced, place the stem ends on the inserts, touching the flower lines, and trace. Remember, the stems need to touch the bottoms of the flowers so an area must also be cut for them. Cut along the traced lines on the insert. You should also mark the top of each piece of

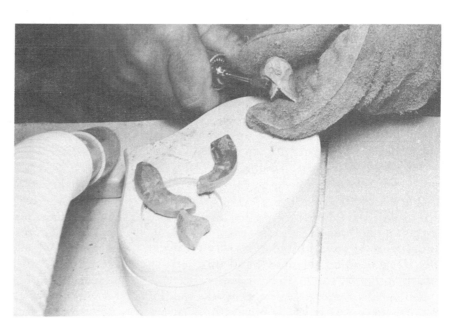

Illus. 41. Shaping inlay parts with burr and flex-shaft tool

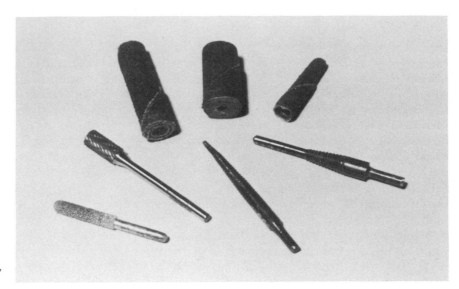

Illus. 42. Abrasives, mandrels, and burrs for shaping inlays

the insert as it is cut. The flower should also be marked. When the insert cutting is complete, you should have three pieces left (Illus. 40). To test the fit, place the flowers in the insert holes and put the pieces of the cut inserts around them. You can place the stem against the flowers but, at this point, it will not fit into the inserts. An area must be routed out of the surface of the lid for the stem. If the fit between the flowers and the insert pieces is too tight, you can grind off any oversized parts when you begin shaping the various pieces of the inlay. While these procedures may seem rather tedious and confusing, once you understand the basic methods of this design, similar designs can be done the same way. If you're having some problems, study the illustrations again.

11. Before beginning the shaping process, assemble the various parts in the lid-insert holes. Be sure you have marked the top of all the pieces. This will serve to remind you, when you begin shaping the various pieces, which surface is up. Only the top and side surfaces are shaped. When you're dealing with a lot of small parts, it's very easy to shape the wrong surface.

12. I shape the various pieces using a carbide burr in a flexible shaft tool (Illus. 41). The burr I use is a standard cut, somewhere between coarse and fine. The diameter of the cutter head is ¼″ and the diameter of the shank is ⅛″ (Illus. 42). The cutting area of the burr is ½″ long. This type of burr removes wood very quickly and is an efficient way to do initial shaping. Burrs of this type can also very quickly cut a finger. Thus, as the picture indicates, I generally wear a leather glove to hold the piece being worked on. Be careful that the burr doesn't grab any portion of the glove. The type of burrs and small end mills that I use for routing are available from various mail-order tool and die supply houses. There are some excellent carbide cutters used by wood carvers that are also very effective for shaping the inlay parts. The carbide burrs are rather expensive but, properly cared for, they will last for years. Moto-Tools also work just as effectively as the flexible shaft tool. They are larger than the flexible shaft tool, but can do any shaping just as well. The Moto-Tools are considerably less expensive. Most local hardware dealers carry a wide range of burrs and other accessories for these small Moto-Tool electric hand grinders.

Another effective way to rough-shape the inlays is by using a mandrel and abrasive sleeves. These are also readily available for the Moto-Tools. It's best to use the coarser grit (80-grit) abrasive sleeves. You will find that on the softer hardwoods, the coarse abrasives are extremely effective. Hedge, however, requires a bit more time to shape with abrasives than with carbide burrs. The way each piece should be shaped is a matter of personal preference. I tend to roll the edges of the lid-insert pieces and randomly grind some dips and rolls in them. There is no fixed way of shaping the insert pieces. The main thing is not to grind the bottom or bottom edges of the pieces. To do so would reduce their size and thus cause a problem with their fit in the insert hole. If one of the pieces was too tight when you rough-assembled the design, you may want to remove a little wood from the side for a better fit.

The flowers, of course, are even more fun to sculpt. You can give them as much or as little detail as you want. I tend to roll the edges and the petals to give them a look of realism. Again, don't remove wood from the bottom edge because it will affect the fit when the flower is placed into the insert. As you shape the flowers, you will probably begin to see possibilities for other inlay designs. It's great fun to plan a design and then make it take shape on a box lid.

13. You also need to shape the stem and the leaf. However, avoid removing any wood from the bottom or bottom edge of the stem and leaf when shaping them. You will need sharp edges for tracing the stem and the leaf onto the lids' surfaces for eventual routing of a groove to hold them. Because the stem is very fragile, I tend to minimize its shaping. It's best to use only a me dium- or fine-grit abrasive on the stem. Shape it to resemble a stem, but exercise caution so it doesn't break. I usually taper the leaf and grind an indentation down the middle of it. The lower end of the taper is then placed next to the stem. You may want to give it even more detail.

14. When the various pieces are shaped and the surfaces are prepared for finishing, place the flower and insert pieces into their respective holes in the lid. Do not glue them in place. Next, align the stem so that it touches the bottom of each of the flowers. If the stem is a bit long, carefully sand off some of it from one end. For the next procedure, you need a sharp pencil or scribe. I find it's much easier with a pencil, and the traced line that's produced is easier to see. For very detailed work, I use a scribe and then spread blue chalk dust in the marks. The blue chalk makes the lines highly visible. While holding the stem firmly in place on the surface of the lid, carefully trace it. Be certain the ends of the stem are in contact with the bottoms of the flowers. The outline of the stem that is traced on the lid surface will be cut out so that the stem, bud, and leaf will fit snugly into the grooves. After tracing the stem, you need to trace the bud, at the end of its stem, and the leaf, placed somewhere along the larger stem. After the tracing is completed, remove all parts from the lid including the flowers and insert pieces.

15. There are a number of ways of cutting the grooves in the lid. If you have carving tools of the appropriate style and size, they can be effective. The small X-acto-type knives also work well. These methods require considerable patience, but are efficient and cost-effective. When cutting the grooves, do not exceed a depth of ⅛". You will want the stem, leaf, and bud to extend above the lid surface.

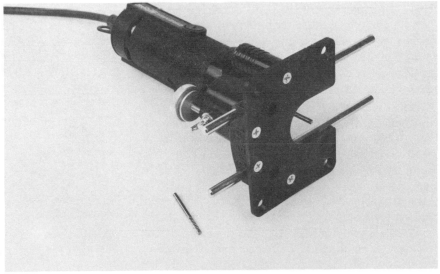

Illus. 43. Moto-Tool with router attachment

An easier way to cut the inlay grooves is by using a Moto-Tool and very small end mills or router bits. I usually make my stems wide enough so that I can use a carbide-end mill with a ⅛"-diameter cutter. For the points of the leaf and bud and the sharp corners of the stem, I use either a 1/16"-diameter end mill or router bit. You can also cut these areas out with a sharp knife. I have a router attachment on my Moto-Tool so the grooving procedure is relatively simple (Illus. 43). Do not, however, exceed the ⅛" depth of cut if you decide to rout the grooves. If you have not used these electric tools with a router attachment, I suggest you practise for a while before cutting the groove in the lid. Unless the tool is held tightly and guided with a firm hand, it can easily cut into areas beyond the traced line. You need good lighting when routing the traced outline. By all means, take your time with the procedure. If you do cut beyond the traced lines, you can make a filler paste from sawdust and white glue. A careful filling job hides most cuts that are made beyond the traced outline.

For those not inclined to cutting or routing a groove for the stem, leaf, and bud, there is no reason these parts of the inlay cannot be glued directly to the lid surface. Should you decide on this approach, be certain to clamp the parts while the glue dries. To clamp, use a small piece of wood that will cover the length of the stem and wrap large rubber bands around the entire box. Then glue and clamp the leaf and bud. Be certain you wipe off the excess glue so that it doesn't stain the lid surface.

16. To secure the inlay in place, spread glue in the two insert holes and the grooves that will hold the stem, leaf, and bud. Place the various inlay pieces in their respective locations and clean off any excess glue. Before placing the stem, cut it into two pieces where the two lids come together. You may want to clamp the stem in place while the glue dries. A block of wood and large rubber bands work well for clamping the stem pieces.

17. Finish the box and inlays using your preferred materials and finishing techniques. You may want to turn to the next chapter for some specifics on how I finish boxes and lid inlays.

Design A 6-1: Box with Lid (Illus. 44)

1. This box does not lend itself to a descriptive name. It is, however, another multifunction design that can be used for jewelry, a musical movement, grimple, or anything else you may want to place in it. The lid presents sufficient surface for a range of decorative work or, if preferred, the use of a highly figured piece of wood.

2. The box is made from 2" (8/4's)-thick stock. As with many of the designs, it can be laminated to the preferred thickness. If you're not going to install a musical movement, you can make the design from thinner stock. I find, however, that when you reduce the thickness too much, you eliminate considerable storage area. The lid for the design is from 1" (4/4's)-thick stock. The approximate length of the box is 6½"; the approximate width is 4½". Illus. 45 presents a profile of this design.

3. Pattern and cut the base and the lid to the desired dimensions. It will help to know that this box can employ either a dowel hinge or standard brass butt hinges. Should you decide to use a single jewelry box hinge or two small butt hinges, be certain the back wall on the

Illus. 44. Box with lid

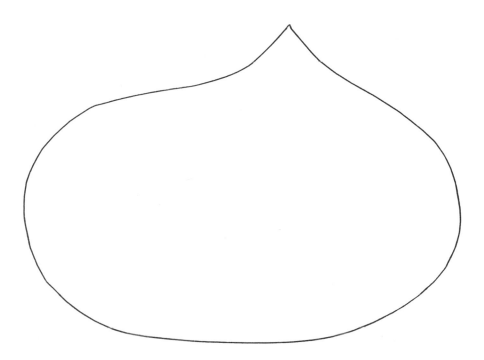

Illus. 45. Box profile

base and lid are straight over most of their lengths. As you will see in Illus. 45, the design begins to round towards the two ends of the box. Plan your pattern and cutting work so that the back surfaces will accommodate a metal hinge system if desired.

4. The storage area in this design can be easily turned on the lathe. Be certain you center your faceplate so you don't find yourself turning off-center. If you want to make the design into a music box, refer to Design A 1-2. The base of this box is large enough for a number of storage holes rather than just a single large one. I recommend you use multi-spur or Foerstner bits for making these holes. Again, the issue is the anticipated use of the box. Design and prepare your storage areas according to how the box will be used.

5. When the storage area(s) or musical movement hole has been prepared, you must deal with the issue of the hinge system. As mentioned, you can use the dowel system that is presented in Design A 1-1. If you want to use a dowel hinge, place it in one of the ends of the base and lid. When the entire lid slides open, you have better access to the items stored in the box. Metal hinges can also be used as an alternative.

6. The use and placement of hinges on boxes can be problematical for the woodworker. For those who want a quick and easy hinge system, simply place the hinges on the back of the box and lid and secure them with screws. This is not the most attractive or functional way of placing hinges, but it does work. Some of the larger boxes presented in later projects sport wooden hinges. These hand-crafted hinges are also placed on the back surface of the base and lid. You may want to consider making a set of small wooden hinges for this design. Not only are they great fun to design and craft, they're attractive and functional. There is nothing wrong with placing hinges on the back surface of a box. If you follow this procedure, I suggest you place a piece of construction paper between the lid and the base. Secure the lid, paper, and base together with a large rubber band. Then apply and secure the hinges. The piece of paper elevates the lid and prevents the hinges from binding and thus raising the front part of the lid off the base edge. There tends to be a perpetual crack between the front part of the lid and the base if the two aren't separated when the hinges are mounted.

In selecting brass or other metal hinges to use on your box, the size of the hinge is a major consideration. While this is less of a problem when the hinges are attached to the back sur-

Illus. 46. Large jewelry box with hinge in place

face, you need to be aware of the dimensional options presented by the array of available hinges. While the base and lid dimensions place restrictions on hinge size, you also need to consider whether the hinges are in proportion to the box. While many hinges may fit, they may be out of proportion to the size of the base and lid. Although the issue of proportion is rather subjective, it must be considered when planning hinges.

While hinges are decorative, they are more importantly functional. You should carefully examine the thickness and quality of each leaf when shopping for durable hinges. You should also examine the knuckle to which each leaf is attached for ease of movement and durability. You will find that there are many hinges for boxes on the market that effectively balance aesthetics and durability. They're often rather costly but, on your prize box, it may be worth spending a little extra for quality. If you must choose between decoration and durability, go with durability.

Hinges should be placed on the top edge of the base wall and the rear underside of the lid. This placement necessitates hinges that are dimensionally compatible with the wall thickness. As you can see in Illus. 46, the hinge leaf is recessed into the wood surface. Also, you should note the small wall at the front edge and

sides of the hinge leaf. While the wall at the front edge is not mandatory, it certainly enhances the inside appearance of the box. I generally use hinges that dimensionally allow for a recess that leaves a front wall of wood. You will usually have recessed walls at the sides of the hinge leaf. Prior to cutting the recess for the hinge leaf on the base of the box, do some tentative placement and measurement. I place one hinge leaf on the edge of the base to determine the best location in terms of function and appearance. You need to consider the weight and size of the lid, in addition to appearance, when planning where to place the hinge(s). The one-piece jewelry box hinge, in part, eliminates placement problems. This hinge simply needs to be long enough to carry the weight of the lid and needs to be centered on the base edge.

The small butt hinges or those without removable pins are best for small boxes. The other option is the long piano-type hinge that is designed for use on jewelry or music boxes. These longer hinges are available in 6″ and 12″ lengths and are usually ¾″ wide when open. Numerous mail-order suppliers of wood products and tools generally stock these types of hinges. The metal on jewelry box hinges is rather thin. This does, however, facilitate cutting them when a certain size hinge is required. Small butt hinges are available in a wide range of sizes. As a rule, the thicker the hinge metal, the more costly the hinge. Hinges that you buy to recess in the box surface should have countersunk screw holes in the leaves.

After you've determined the proper placement of the leaf on the base edge, make a line around the three edges with a sharp pencil or scriber. When the leaf is placed on the edge, the hinge knuckle should extend out from the base wall. Make your line tight against the edge of the leaf so you will have a good fit when the recess is cut. The depth of the recess should be enough to allow the top surface of the leaf to be flush with the edge surface. This, of course, assumes that the screw heads can be countersunk in the leaf. When leaf thickness is used as the guide for the depth of the recess, a similar recess is required in the lid. If both leaves of the hinge are not recessed, the hinged back of the base and lid will be elevated. You will have a nice slope running from the back to the front of the lid.

A method that I use involves making the initial recess in the base wall deep enough for accommodating the thickness of both leaves. While probably not a proper way to place a hinge, it works quite well for me. This method works only with the thinner, less expensive butt and jewelry box hinges. Cutting a deeper recess that will accommodate both parts of the hinge when the lid is closed eliminates the need of cutting a recess in the lid. This method is a lot simpler, especially when a lid stopper extends from the lid. Lid stoppers are simply an extension on the back of the lid that prevents the lid from falling backwards when it is open. Lid stoppers are discussed in greater detail with a later project.

7. For reasons of speed and accuracy, I use an electric Moto-Tool with a base and router attachment to make a hinge recess (Illus. 47). I use small carbide-end mills with a cutter diameter of ⅛". There are numerous small router bits available for these small tools. Most are made from high-speed steel and are adequate for the average user. The carbide-end mills are rather expensive, but they do outlast the other bits.

8. Using the lines marked or scribed on the base edge as a guide, set the router attachment for the width of cut. As with any router, the guide, when properly set, limits the cut. Also, set the depth of the cut in relation to the thickness of the leaf or leaves and proceed to rout out the recess. Be sure to have a firm grip on the

Illus. 47. Routing a hinge recess

tool because it can get away from you very quickly. Also, you need to balance the tool with the router base riding on the ball in front of the recess. You may want to have a little experience with the tool and bit prior to making the hinge recess. Place a pine board in a vise, edge up, and practise routing a recess. It's a great way to develop some skill with the tool and its attachment. After the recess has been made in the box, clean up the recessed area with abrasive paper. Remove any remaining pencil marks as well. For those without a Moto-Tool or attachment, a good sharp chisel and a mallet accomplish the same job.

9. Brass flathead screws that come with hinges can be a real nuisance. They're usually very small, difficult to start in the wood, and easily twisted into two pieces. Frequently the head slot is stripped with the screwdriver. To eliminate some of these problems, a few suggestions seem appropriate. After proper placement of the hinge leaf in the recess, drill a small pilot hole for each screw. Be sure the bit you use is much smaller than the screw diameter or the screw will not hold in the hole. Center the pilot hole in the countersunk screw area in the leaf. If the hole is not centered, the screws will not center properly. The screws can be cut in two pieces from the sharp edge of the hinge-leaf screw hole. To eliminate stripping the slot in the small screwheads, grind your screwdriver tips so they fit perfectly in the slot. Small screwdrivers are rather inexpensive so you can have a series of them ground to fit the various screw-slot sizes. I grind the ends of the screwdrivers on a 1″ belt grinder or else on a grinding wheel using a light touch. You can also accomplish the same job using your belt sander or file. When working with the smaller screws, this process can save you a lot of grief. It also pays to have a supply of extra-small screws of all sizes

available. Often those that I don't ruin, I lose.

10. Secure the hinge leaf in the recessed area on the base edge first. Whether the other leaf will be recessed or not, you can easily mark where it should be placed. To accomplish this, place and center the lid on the base. Make a pencil mark on the back edge of the lid at both ends of the hinge knuckle. Using a small square, transfer these lines to the underside of the lid surface. Another similar hinge can also be used as a template. The other option is to measure the exact dimensions of the hinge leaf and transfer them onto the lid surface. Drill pilot holes and secure the leaf with screws. To facilitate this last step, it helps to place the lid flat on a surface. Put a piece of stock the same thickness as the lid under the back of the box and slide the lid under the hinge leaf. This will give you easy access to the leaf to be attached as well as a solid surface for working.

If the fit is not good between the base and the lid after the hinge is attached, light pressure in the right direction can sometimes solve the problem. Apply pressure sparingly or you will damage the hinge knuckle or pull the screws loose. A better option is using abrasive paper or a power sander to make the edges of the lid and base flush. If the fit cannot be remedied with these procedures, you will need to reset the lid-hinge leaf. Usually only the lid leaf of the hinge requires resetting.

11. The lid on this design can be left unembellished or, if desired, a sculptured design can be prepared. If you decide on an inlay, refer to the discussions in the next few projects. A plug-inlay design can also be effectively used on this box lid, even with the hinges in place.

12. Finish the box as desired. Avoid getting any finishing products on the hinges. You may want to refer to the next chapter for a few ideas.

Design A 6-2: Box with Sculptured Lid: Apple Inlay (Illus. 48)

1. Except for the sculptured apple on the lid, this design is a duplicate of the previous one. Refer to Design A 6-1 for all procedures necessary for making the base and the lid.

2. The sculptured apple is not only a fun design to make, it also demonstrates one of the many possibilities for embellishing box lids. To approximate the apple, I use either padouk (red) or hedge (yellow). For green apples, I cut out the section of poplar that often has green in it. The stem for the apple is made from ebony or walnut and the leaf is made from poplar. One of the interesting aspects of designing inlays is that you can experiment with small pieces of

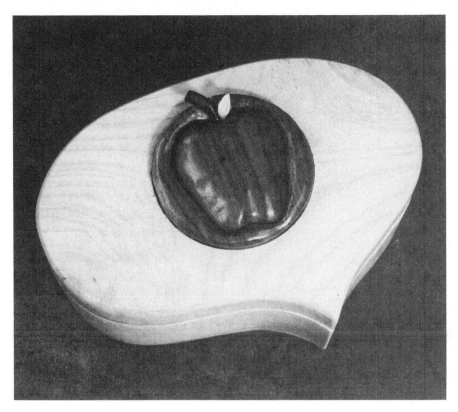

Illus. 48. Box with apple inlay

various hardwoods. You can purchase small amounts of some of the more exotic woods to use in your inlay work. If you use indigenous wood for the base and lid of the box, small amounts of the exotic woods can be affordable. Many hardwood suppliers sell small pieces or scraps of their exotics.

3. For the apple inlay, I use a 2½″ multi-spur bit or turn the lid-insert hole on the lathe. It's best to use a screw chuck if you plan to turn the insert hole on the lathe. Drill an undersized hole through the lid in the exact center of the planned insert if you're using a screw chuck. Keep the diameter of the turned recess at about 2½″. This will simplify the preparation of the insert that is placed in the hole. As a rule, for the apple inlay, I place the hole in the middle of the lid. The hole should be drilled or turned to a depth of at least ¼″.

4. Using a 2½″-diameter circle template, trace and cut an insert for the lid hole. This insert should be at least ⅜″ thick. You want the insert to extend out of the lid hole. It tends to make the entire inlay more attractive. I often cut the insert from wild cherry, ash, walnut, or some other wood that will look good with a padouk apple. The insert should fit snugly in the turned or drilled lid recess.

5. Pattern and cut an apple that is at least 1¾″ long, 1½″ wide, and approximately ½″ thick. This thickness permits you to roll the edges, giving the apple a more realistic appearance. You may want to purchase an apple and carefully examine it before sculpting the detail in this inlay.

6. After the apple inlay has been cut, center it on the lid insert, trace, and cut. You will need a scroll saw, a band saw with a ⅛″ blade or, if necessary, a sabre saw with a fine-tooth blade. In cutting the traced apple from the insert, I begin the cut at the top portion of the traced apple. The stem and leaf can then be placed in such a way as to cover this entry cut.

7. Cut a stem and leaf to sizes that are in proportion to the apple. As previously mentioned, I often cut the stem from ebony or walnut and the leaf from poplar. You may want to experiment with other woods for these parts.

8. Assemble all the pieces in the lid recess and check the fit. To shape the inlay parts, use the various techniques and tools described in Design A 5-2. I generally flatten the insert at the top area where the entry cut was made. This becomes the area where the stem and leaf are placed. It provides sufficient glue surface for both of these pieces. This removal of wood at the top of the insert also enhances the overall appearance of the design. It makes the leaf and stem appear to be in the middle of the apple.

9. When all the parts are shaped, spread glue in the insert hole and place the apple and insert in place. After spreading a touch of glue on the stem and leaf, place them at the top of the insert. As a rule, you don't need to clamp inlays while the glue is drying.

10. Finish the box and the inlay as desired. Be careful that the padouk doesn't bleed onto the insert pieces when applying your finishing product. You may want to refer to the next chapter for a few ideas on the finishing process.

Design A 6-3: Box with Sculptured Lid: Bird Inlay (Illus. 49)

1. Another interesting inlay that can be used on the lid of Design A 6-1 is a cardinal or some other bird. All of the procedures for preparing and making the base and lid are the same as those described in Design A 6-1. For specifics on the various inlay procedures and tools, refer to Design A 6-2.

2. I use padouk for the cardinal inlay. You may, however, prefer to design a different bird profile and employ another wood. This inlay design is used to demonstrate another possibility for embellishing a box lid.

3. You should refer to Design A 6-2 for all the procedures that have to do with preparing the lid and the insert components. Design A 6-2 also presents the various dimensions necessary for this type of inlay work. One significant difference between previous inlays and this one is that the tail of the cardinal extends onto the lid. Allowing the inlay to extend beyond the background insert and onto the lid proper adds an interesting touch to the inlay.

4. It's a good idea to draw the cardinal freehand on construction paper that will serve as a pat-

Illus. 49. Box with bird inlay

tern. As the procedures in Design A 6-2 indicate, the insert that will accommodate the cardinal is usually 2½" in diameter. Thus, the bird must be designed in relation to this dimension. With the cardinal, however, you will be extending a portion of the tail onto the lid. As you design and make your pattern, keep this in mind.

5. After you trace and cut the cardinal from the insert (remember: a portion of the tail will extend beyond the insert), place the cardinal and insert pieces into the lid recess. Using a sharp pencil or a scribe, trace onto the lid surface that portion of the tail that extends onto it.

6. Using a Moto-Tool and bit, rout the traced area to the same depth as the lid-recess hole. Refer to the discussion in Design A 5-2 for routing procedures. Check for fit after the area has been routed.

7. Use the procedures for shaping and securing the inlay that are presented in Design A 6-2.

8. Finish the box and inlay using the products and methods you prefer.

Design A 6-4: Box with Sculptured Lid: Flower Inlay with Petals (Illus. 50)

1. For those who would like to use an inlay of a flower with detailed petals, here's your opportunity. Portions of the insert can be seen between each of the petals. Also, the inlay has a seed pod that extends up from the middle of the flower. All of the procedures for preparing and making the base and lid are the same as those described in Design A 6-1. For specifics on the various inlay procedures and tools, refer to Design A 6-2.

2. I make the pattern of the flower design with a series of pointed petals. I usually use either padouk or hedge for the flower. When you make your design, don't make too many petals because, when cut and shaped, they may become too thin and break off. The flower should not exceed 2" in diameter so that it will fit well within the 2½"-diameter insert. The insert, as you may recall, is the background for the flower inlay and fits into a 2½"-diameter recess in the lid.

3. Trace and carefully cut the flower from the wood you decide to use. The flower should be made from a thickness that will extend above the insert. Trace the flower on the lid-insert piece and carefully cut. I use a scroll saw or band saw with a ⅛" blade for the cutting procedure. Because you will have numerous parts from cutting the insert, it's a good practice to number the flower petals and the insert pieces that fit next to them. This is critical for assembling the inlay. After the traced flower has been cut from the insert, assemble the pieces and the flower into the lid recess and check the fit. You will no doubt have to reduce a few of the insert pieces. This can be done in the sculpting process.

4. Prior to shaping the flower and insert pieces, drill a small hole in the middle of the flower for holding the seed pod. Cut and shape a small

Illus. 50. Box with flower inlay

shaft of wood that will serve as the seed pod. As mentioned, I often use ebony for the seed pod. The seed pod should be long enough to extend at least ¼" above the flower's surface. You can shorten it, if desired, during the final shaping process.

5. For details on shaping procedures, refer to Design A 5-2. When shaping this design, I begin with the flower. Each petal is grooved out to suggest depth. I try to approximate the actual petals of a flower. The edges of the petals are usually quite thin when the shaping procedures have been completed. You will want to approximate some degree of realism as you sculpt the petals and the rest of the flower. When the flower is adequately shaped, you will need to shape each of the insert pieces to fit neatly between the petals. Remember not to cut wood from the bottom edges or it will affect the fit when placed back into the lid recess. After all the insert pieces are shaped, assemble the entire inlay in the lid recess. Do some final shaping on the seed pod.

6. Remove the flower and the insert pieces from the recess. Spread glue in the recess and place the flower and insert pieces back into the recess. Put a touch of glue in the seed-pod hole and put the pod in place. Allow the glue to dry.

7. Finish the box with your usual methods and products. You may want to refer to the next chapter for a few suggestions and products that I've found helpful.

Design A 6-5: Box with Sculptured Lid: Flower Inlay (Illus. 51)

1. This design presents another floral inlay that can be prepared and inserted into the lid of the box presented in Design A 6-1. The design is a modified version of the rather elaborate one presented in Design A 5-2. I use this inlay design on many of my boxes. As shown in Illus. 51, the stem of the inlay extends from the base of the flower onto the lid. The procedures for making this extension are the same as those presented with Design A 6-3. You simply rout a traced outline of the stem into the lid surface to the same depth as the insert hole. All of the procedures for preparing the base and lid are the same as those described in Design A 6-1. For specifics on the various inlay procedures and tools, refer to Design A 6-2.

2. Because the flower is the same as the one presented in Design A 5-2, refer to Design A 5-2 for specifics on the preparation of the background insert and the flower. The procedures for shaping the flower are also the same. The stem for this design should be approximately 1" long and made from poplar or hedge. Refer to Illus. 51 to get an idea of how the stem is cut and shaped. Again notice how the stem extends onto the lid.

3. Secure the inlay in the insert recess with glue. You should also place glue in the groove that has been cut into the lid for holding the stem. Finish the box as desired.

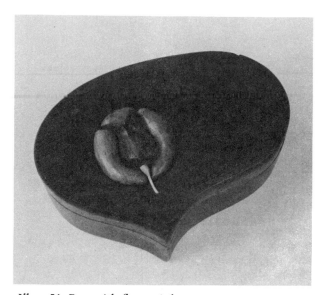

Illus. 51. Box with flower inlay

Design A 6-6: Box with Sculptured Lid: Pear Inlay (Illus. 52)

1. The use of a pear further demonstrates the possibilities for inlay designs. Incidentally, I'm currently looking for some orange wood for a carrot inlay. One of my boxes has a lid embellished with bunches of grapes made from purpleheart. While the objects I select for some of my inlays may seem a bit odd, they make for interesting and unique boxes. You can even design an inlay to correspond to the items stored in the box or to the room where the box will be used. The procedures for making the base and lid of this box are described in Design A 6-1. For specifics on the various inlay procedures and the required tools and accessories, refer to Design A 6-2.

2. The pear for the inlay is made from hedge. While hedge tends to turn a rather golden brown in time, its initial yellow color makes for a good approximation of the color of a pear. I might add that pears also tend to turn rather brown in time. The stem on the pear is made from ebony. You may, of course, prefer to use walnut or some other dark wood for the stem. You should make a pattern that approximates the shape of a pear and then trace and cut it from hedge.

3. The insert or background piece for the pear inlay should be 2½″ in diameter. Refer to Design A 6-2 for procedures regarding the lid recess and the insert. After the pear is traced on the insert piece, make one cut from what will be the top portion of the pear. As with the apple inlay, the stem of the pear can be placed to cover the initial cut into the insert. Shape the pear with the various abrasives and burrs to give it a rounded appearance. You may want to examine a real pear before you begin the shaping process. The insert or background piece that surrounds the pear in the lid recess should also be shaped. Make the top portion of the insert somewhat flat so that the stem can be easily glued to it. As suggested, you can place

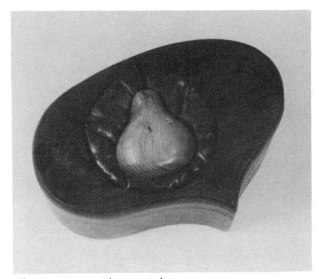

Illus. 52. Box with pear inlay

the stem over the saw cut to hide it. I do not use a leaf with the pear inlay, but I do round the stem a bit with abrasives.

4. Glue the insert and pear into the lid recess. Place a touch of glue on the stem and place it so that it touches the top of the pear and covers the insert cut. Refer to the next chapter for some finishing ideas, methods, and products that you may find helpful.

Design A 7-1: Pointed Oblong Box (Illus. 53)

1. I often make this box from lower grade ash because its size tends to showcase the attractive nature of this wood. The box is approximately 8″ long and 4″ wide. Illus. 54 presents a profile of the design. I generally use 2″ (8/4's) stock for the base and 1″ (4/4's) for the lid. If you want to make this design into a music box, you will definitely need wood this thick. Refer back to Design A 1-2 for specifics on preparing a music box. This design can be increased or decreased in its overall dimensions. A smaller design can be made that is very attractive and functional. You may also decide to laminate 1″ (4/4's) stock to build up the base to 2″ (8/4's). Don't rule out placing a piece of veneer between the boards being laminated. Because of the size of this design, you have some options in preparing the base.

2. Pattern and cut the base. Using the base as a pattern, trace and cut the lid. A lid from a different wood is especially attractive on this design. You may want to use a walnut lid if the base has been made from ash or some other lighter wood. Remember to mark the bottom of the lid after it has been cut. This will be helpful when you begin making the hinge system for the box. You should also mark the surface of the base that was used to pattern the lid. The lid and base need to be assembled in the same way they were cut or they probably will be out of alignment. Our patterning and cutting work is not always precise. Marking the various surfaces will solve any possible problems.

3. If you want a large storage area in the base, you may want to turn the base on the lathe. There is a lot of wood in this design so you can

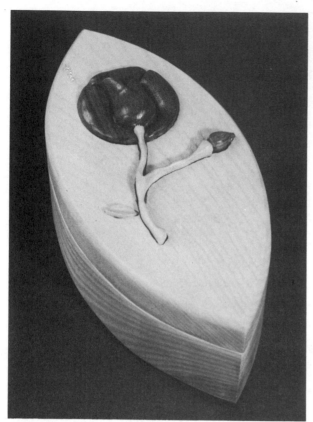

Illus. 53. Pointed oblong box with floral inlay

depths, depending upon their anticipated use. Because the base is large, there are a number of ways you can make the storage areas. When the design is not used for a music box, I often turn a storage area in the middle of the base and then drill two smaller holes, one near each end. You may want to consider this type of storage layout.

4. The curved lines of this design prohibit the use of brass hinges. You will want to use the dowel hinge or one of your own designs. If you use a dowel hinge, it should be placed near one end of the box. You will want the entire lid to slide open so you can have easy access to the storage areas. Refer to Design A 1-1 for specifics on procedures for preparing the hinge system.

5. Because of its size, this box looks very nice with a plain lid. You may want to use one of your choice pieces of wood that's loaded with character. On the other hand, if you prefer an inlay, you should prepare the lid surfaces for finishing. You should also rout the top edge of the lid and the bottom edge of the base with a rounding-over bit. This same procedure can also be done using abrasive paper. Illus. 53 shows an inlay that I frequently use on this design. It's a kind of modification of the inlay shown in Illus. 39. The procedures involved in preparing the inlay are the same as those presented in Design A 5-2. With this design, however, you will have only one flower and a bud, thus only one lid insert. Given the size of the lid on this design, you may want to pursue an alternate inlay. Do some design work. Explore some ideas of your own. The procedures will still be the same.

prepare a rather sizeable storage area. Refer to Design A 1-1 for procedures on turning the storage area. Multi-spur or Foerstner bits can also be used for preparing the storage area. You may prefer to drill a series of storage holes in this box. The holes can be of differing diameters and

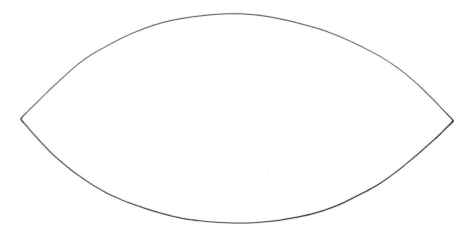

Illus. 54. Pointed oblong box profile

6. Finish the box as desired or refer to the next chapter for some products and methods that I use. If you made the box to house a musical movement, refer to the Appendix for the procedures that have to do with placing the movement in the box and cutting the glass insert.

Design A 7-2: Pointed Oblong Box: Apple Inlay (Illus. 55)

1. While the box is the same as the one presented in Design A 7-1, the inlay that's used is quite different. This design is presented to demonstrate another option for embellishing box lids. As Illus. 55 indicates, the apple is placed in the middle of the lid. The apple can be made from either padouk or hedge.

2. For specific procedures on preparing the lid and the inlay, refer to Design A 6-2.

Illus. 55. Pointed oblong box with apple inlay

Design A 7-3: Pointed Oblong Box: Fish Inlay (Illus. 56)

1. This design offers you another way to embellish a lid. As you might guess, the box is essentially the same as the one presented in Design A 7-1. The nature of this lid inlay almost necessitates using the overall box dimensions suggested in the procedures for Design A 7-1. The inlay in this design is white ash veneer. As the illustration indicates, the lid is made of walnut. The ash and walnut contrast well together for this type of inlay work. The eye in the fish is a ⅜"-diameter padouk plug.

2. To prepare the inlay, make lines of varying lengths for the various fins and tail. I simply pencil on marks for the location of the eventual cuts and their lengths. I also make a pencil line for the mouth. You can, of course, increase the number of inlaid pieces to add more detail to either the tail or the fins. Using the band saw with a blade that is close to the thickness of the veneer you will be using, cut into the lid along each pencil mark. As you would guess, the lid-dowel hinge cannot be in place for this procedure. The lid is hinged later. Cut oversized pieces of veneer for each cut made into the lid. Spread glue on both surfaces of the veneer and slide the veneer into the lid cuts. Allow the glue to dry.

3. After the glue is dry, trim the veneer off the edges of the lid with a band saw. Be careful not to cut into the lid as you do the trimming. Carefully break the excess veneer that may be extending from the top or bottom of the lid. Using

Illus. 56. Pointed oblong box with fish inlay

a belt sander, sand the top, bottom, and edge of the lid. You will want to remove any excess glue and pieces of veneer. Pencil a mark where you want the eye to be located. I usually cut a ⅜″ plug for placement in a ⅜″ hole. Glue the plug in place and, when dry, sand it flush with the lid surface.

4. A rather interesting scale effect can be made on the lid surface. Using either a large nail set or a metal punch, you can make indentations in the lid that resemble scales. I make the indentations in rows, tapping the punch or nail set with a small hammer. It's a good idea to practise the procedure on some scrap material before starting on the finished lid.

5. Finish the box as desired.

Design A 8-1: Musical Note Music Box (Illus. 57)

1. Although obvious, the musical note is still a great design for a music box. You may, of course, prefer to make this box into a general storage container for someone who is very interested in music. Either way, it's a fun design. I usually make the box from walnut and leave the lid plain. While you can easily embellish the lid, I prefer this design with a plain lid. The design presents some potential hazards when the musical movement area and the key area are being turned on the lathe. The upper portion of the note has some rather sharp edges that are rotating at a considerable speed so you need, to exercise caution when turning it. The design is crafted from 2″ (8/4's) stock with a lid from 1″ (4/4's) material. The length of the note is 7¼″; its width is 4¼″. You may want to reduce the size to save wood. If you plan to make the design into a music box, don't reduce the dimensions too much.

2. Before making a pattern, refer to Illus. 58 for a profile of the design. You also may want to look at a musical score to get an idea of the shape of a note. There are certain nuances in the neck and tail of the note that you may want to check and integrate into your pattern. Because this design uses a dowel-hinge system, you need to allow sufficient width in the lower neck area for the dowel to penetrate. Keep this in mind as you pattern your design.

3. Trace the note pattern, with the grain, on the base stock. Your lid will be more precise if it is traced from the cut base. However, if you are unusually skilled with the band saw, use the pattern for both.

4. Using a band saw with a ¼″ blade, cut out the patterned base of the note. Trace and cut the lid. You will want to use a fine-tooth blade on your band saw to minimize saw marks on the edges of the base and lid. The neck and tail

Illus. 57. Musical note music box

Illus. 58. Musical note profile

areas of the design can be difficult to sand so try to prevent as much saw marking of the surface as possible.

5. For turning the movement and key area, follow the procedures in Design A 1-2. The note should be turned at a slow speed, especially if you are using a chuck to turn the winding key area. *I always wear a glove when turning this design. The glove would probably do little to prevent hand injury if struck by the rotating note, but it does serve as a constant reminder of the potential danger.* Use your tailstock and revolving center to support the block when turning this design.

6. As I mentioned, I use a dowel-hinge system for this design. The dowel should be placed in a wide area in the lower neck section of the note. Placing the dowel in this location permits the entire musical movement area to be seen when

the lid is moved to the side. Refer to Design A 1-1 for procedures on the dowel hinge.

7. Rout the top edge of the lid and the bottom edge of the base. Finish the box as desired or refer to the next chapter. If you made a music box, refer to the Appendix for information on cutting the glass insert and installing the movement in the box.

Design A 9-1: Hinged Box with Sculptured Lid (Illus. 59)

1. This small box has a hinged lid and employs an extension to stop the lid at an appropriate position. The lid on this design is attractive either plain or with an inlay. The dimensions of this box allow you to make it into either a music box or a functional container. It's an excellent box for small jewelry because of its size

and the lid stopper. The box requires 2" (8/4's) stock for the base and 1" (4/4's) stock for the lid. The design is approximately 4½" long and 3⅗" wide. The length is distorted because it includes the extension on the lid that serves as the lid stopper.

2. For assistance in making your pattern, see

Illus. 60 for a profile of both the base and the lid. With this design, I generally make two patterns and cut them out carefully using a band saw. You should note in the profiles that the base is square along the back while the lid curves to a point on one side. This pointed area is the lid stopper and will prevent the lid from falling over the back of the box when opened.

3. Whether you're planning on using the design as a storage box or music box, you may want to turn out the base. It's a rather easy design to mount and turn on the lathe. Depending on the way you plan to use the box, refer to either Design A 1-1 or Design A 1-2 for assistance in turning.

4. This design permits an inlay that is at least 2″ in diameter. To make the lid recess for the inlay, you can either turn out the area or use a multi-spur or Foerstner bit. Refer to Design A 5-2 for the procedures involved in preparing this type

of flower inlay. The top edge of the lid and the bottom edge of the base should be routed be-

Illus. 59. Hinged box with floral inlay

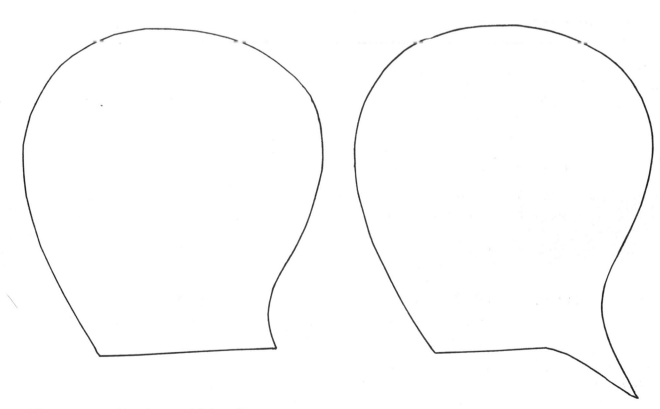

Illus. 60. Hinged box base and lid profiles

fore the inlay process begins. You may want to place the hinge right away also.

5. The lid is hinged on this design with a single brass butt hinge. Refer to the discussion of hinges in Design A 6-1. Take your time in plac-ing the hinge on this box because the lid stop-per can present problems.

6. Finish the box as desired or refer to the pro-cedures in the next chapter.

Design A 10-1: Cat Box 1 (Illus. 61)

1. For those who have a fondness for cats, this and the following box design may be of special interest. This design can be made as a general

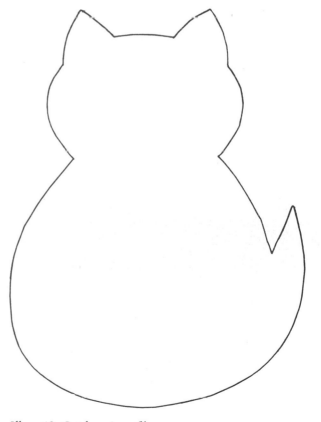

Illus. 61. Cat box 1

storage, special use, or music box. You may want to consider possible uses of the box before beginning any planning activities. It's es-pecially important to consider its use before you plan the dimensions. The length of the box is 6½"; its width is 4½". The width is somewhat deceiving because it includes the tail portion of the cat on both the base and the lid. There is, however, considerable area in the lower portion of the design for storage. I have not inlaid this box. You may, however, want to add eyes made from hedge or some other wood that suggests

cat eyes. For those with a bent towards detail, you could consider a nose and some whiskers. The lid is of sufficient size for any type of detail or inlay you may want to place on it.

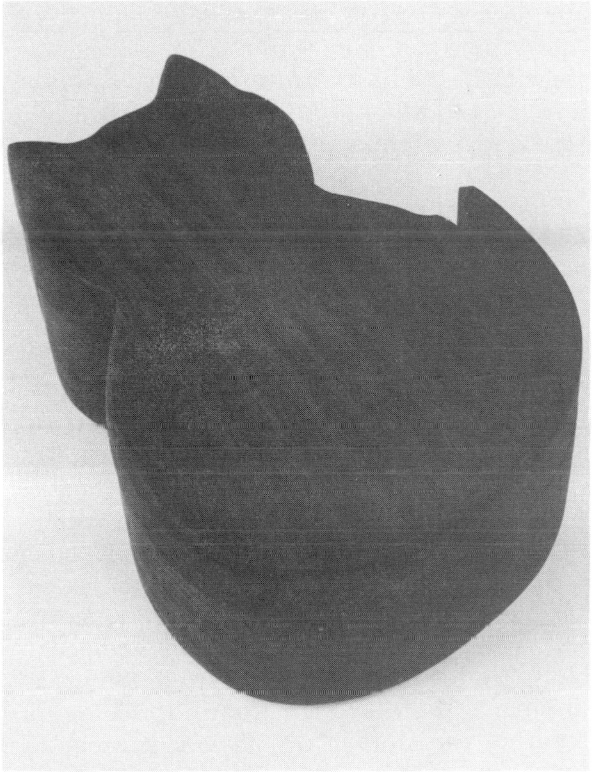

2. You will want to prepare a pattern for cut-ting this design. Illus. 62 presents a profile of the design that may assist you in designing your pattern. This is one of those patterns that can be tough to draw. Don't get discouraged. The de-sign is only an approximation of a cat. We're making boxes, not cats. When you've finalized your pattern, trace it on the base stock.

3. I use a band saw with a ¼" blade for cutting out the design. The only area on the pattern that's difficult to cut is around the ears and the

Illus. 62. Cat box 1 profile

top of the head. Simply take your time. When the base has been cut, trace the lid using the base as the pattern. Trace and cut carefully to minimize the need for sanding the edges. You will want the edges of the lid and base to be flush all over. If the lid is traced and cut over-sized, it can be time-consuming to sand it flush with the base.

4. Depending on the use of the box, prepare the storage or musical movement area in the base. I would recommend using the lathe unless you have very large multi-spur bits. The base can easily accommodate a storage area with a diameter of at least 3½″. You can readily turn out this diameter on the lathe. When turning this block, you will be dealing with an off-center piece. You may want to refer to the discussion in Design A 5-1 regarding off-center turning. Design A 1-1 provides information on turning a storage area; Design A 1-2 has similar information for the musical movement area. Refer to these designs if you use the lathe.

5. You will want to use a dowel for a hinge on this box. While a small butt hinge could be used, the lid is a bit too large and heavy for one hinge. A hinge could be placed between the ears. Refer to Design A 1-1 for procedures on preparing and placing a dowel-hinge system. The dowel should be placed in the upper portion of the head in the middle. This placement allows the lid to slide open in such a way so that the user will have complete access to the storage or musical movement area.

6. If you plan to put eyes in the lid or do some other embellishment, begin preparing your design and materials. Before proceeding, you should rout the top edge of the lid and the bottom edge of the base. You should also sand the entire box to finishing readiness. Incidentally, oversized ½″-diameter eyes look interesting on this design.

7. Finish the box using either an oil or a surface finish. You may want to refer to the next chapter for some ideas on the finishing process.

Design A 11-1: Cat Box 2 (Illus. 63)

1. As you can see in Illus. 63, the cat design on this box is carved into the lid. A small portion of one ear extends out from the edge of the box. Also, the tip of the tail is exaggerated by a cut into the wall of the box and lid. The design is supposed to approximate a curled-up cat. The shape of the box is a bit oblong. Its length is 5½″; its width is 5″. In your design and pattern work, you may prefer to make the box round with a 5½″ diameter. The ear and tail extensions can then be added to the circle. As the dimensions suggest, the box provides considerable space for storage or, if desired, a musical movement. You may want to use the lathe for preparing the storage or movement area. Although you can use large bits, the lathe allows you to make the storage area of a greater diameter. This is also true with the previous cat design.

2. Illus. 64 presents a profile of the design, along with some detail that should assist you in preparing a pattern. The head and tail need to be carved or cut into the lid. The profile should provide you with some ideas on how and where to sketch these details on the lid. Prepare a pattern and trace it on the base stock. Using a band saw, cut the base, carefully following the pattern lines. Trace the lid using the cut base as the pattern. Again, take your time both in tracing and cutting. You will want edges that are flush with one another. If you cut the lid too

Illus. 63. Cat box 2

Illus. 64. Cat box 2 profile

open and expose the entire storage or musical movement area. Refer to Design A 1-1 for procedures on preparing this type of hinge system.

5. With the lid hinged to the base, the details of the cat can be cut into the lid. It's best to draw the ears, head, and tail of the cat freehand on the lid. I simply pencil them in, erase, and try again until I'm satisfied with the drawing. You may want to refer to Illus. 64 for some assistance. When you're satisfied with your drawing, cut or carve it into the lid. If you have carving tools, you may want to use them for this procedure. I use either a flexible shaft or Moto-Tool with a burr for the initial cutting of the design. With the burr, I make a trench about ¼" deep all along the traced lines. Generally, I use a burr with a ⅛" cutting diameter. You can also use one of the small carbide carving burrs that are available.

After the trench has been cut, using 80-grit abrasive sleeves on a mandrel, I begin rolling the edges of the trench on both sides. These mandrels and sleeves, referred to in Design A 5-2, mount easily on the flexible shaft or Moto-Tool. Keep rounding the edges of the trench until the details appear to have depth. Be careful with the abrasives when rounding on the ears. It's very easy to reduce their size. I usually taper the trench more on the lid side than on the cat side. You will want the cat profile to stand out and this tapering procedure helps to achieve this. The top edge of the lid should be routed with a round-over bit so you don't have to do any shaping on it. Continue using the abrasive sleeves until you're satisfied with your cat profile. Again, the procedure should result in an approximation of a cat profile. It does not have to be all that precise and detailed.

6. Finish sanding the entire base and lid. You may want to refer to the next chapter for some methods and products for finishing the box. Also, you may want to refer to the Appendix for some methods for cutting glass inserts.

large, it can be reduced using a belt sander. The best time for this procedure is after the base and lid have been hinged. If available, a 1"-wide belt sander or grinder also works well, especially in sanding around the ear and tail extensions. You will want the edges to be perfectly flush.

3. You need to prepare the base for storage or a musical movement. I suggest you use the lathe so you can maximize the potential space in the base. Refer to Design A 1-1 for procedures on turning the storage area; refer to Design A 1-2 for specifics on turning the base so it can hold a musical movement.

4. Before beginning any detail work on the lid, you should hinge the box. You will want to use a dowel hinge on this design. I place the dowel in the head area of the base and lid, near the edge. With this placement, you can slide the lid

Design A 12-1: Four-Hole Box (Illus. 65)

1. This box not only looks interesting with its four lids, it is also rather fun to make. The lids are arranged and cut in such a way that they must be opened in sequence or they will not open at all. With this design, you can insert a musical movement in one of the larger holes.

This design does not lend itself to turning. It can, in part, be turned but at such a high risk that the end result is hardly justified. I usually drill all four holes using various-sized multi-spur bits. You can embellish the lids with shaped or inlaid designs. You can also cut the entire lid into sections and laminate them with strips of veneer. As will be discussed, the lid piece must be cut oversized to allow for the dimensional loss that results from the various cuts that need to be made. The cutting of the four individual lids is one of the last procedures to be done. The box shown in Illus. 65 has lids laminated with padouk veneer.

For storing jewelry and other items, the box has holes that vary both in diameter and depth. You can increase or reduce the overall dimensions of the design to suit your planned usage. The design is approximately 5½″ square. For this design, you should use 2″ (8/4's) stock for the base and 1″ (4/4's) material for the lid. To increase the depth of the storage holes, you may want to laminate the base to a thickness of 3″. It looks great if you use various woods for a laminated base. If desired, include a piece of veneer between the laminated boards. You may also prefer to use a contrasting wood for the lid section. There is no reason the base and lid have to be made from the same wood. As with all the box designs, do some planning and design work prior to beginning your crafting procedures.

2. Cut the base of the box to a 5½″ square or to whatever other dimensions you plan to use. It's probably easier to use a band saw and fence for cutting the base if you're using 2″ (8/4's) stock. When I make boxes, I tend to use the band saw more often than the table or radial arm saw for cutting the bases and lids. You may want to cut the box base a bit oversized to allow for a possible reduction in dimensions that can result from sanding the sides. You should also cut the lid section. You should increase its size by at least ⅜″. This added dimension allows for wood loss that will result when the lid section is cut into four pieces. It also allows for dimensional loss if you decide to laminate the entire lid section before cutting it into the four small lids.

3. With the base and lid cut, you will need to plan how and where to drill the four storage holes. As mentioned, I use various sizes of multi-spur bits for drilling the storage areas in this design. You may want to use large spade bits to keep the expenses down. While the spade bits are not as efficient or accurate as the multi-spur bits, they are considerably less expensive.

Illus. 65. Four-hole box

Illus. 66. Four-hole box with lids open

While you can be more sophisticated with this design in terms of the placement of the holes and their lids, your initial box should probably be made the easiest way. I drill the holes in the base near its four corners. This design uses a hinge-dowel system, usually with ¼"-diameter dowels, so you need to allow for them when you drill the storage holes. The dowel hinges are placed in the four corners of the base. The first drilled hole usually has a diameter of 1¼". I often place a ¼" dowel piece in the center of this hole that designates it for ring usage. The dowel gives support to the rings and allows them to be stacked in the hole. The next two holes are usually 2" in diameter. The last corner area is usually drilled with a 2½"-diameter bit. This area, if desired, can accommodate a musical movement. If you plan to include a musical movement in your design, you also need to drill a winding key area in the bottom of the base. Refer to Design A 1-2 for the approximate dimensional needs of the movement. While a 2½"-diameter hole is a bit small for a musical movement, the unit will fit. With this design, you will have to give up some sound

quality in favor of box design. I do not put a glass insert over the movement in this design. You may want to vary the depth of the various storage holes, depending on the way you plan to use them. It is often much easier to retrieve a piece of jewelry or some other object from a shallower storage hole.

4. If you plan to embellish the various lids, include this planning in your pencil-and-paper design work. As suggested, you may want to laminate strips of veneer throughout the entire lid. These strips give an interesting appearance to the box after the lid section has been cut into the four smaller parts. The various pieces with the veneer glued in place must be clamped until dry. Radical curves or small pieces can be tough to clamp. When making your design, remember that all the pieces must be clamped back together. When cutting the veneer to be inlaid between the lid pieces, you should cut both the length and width oversized. This makes the veneer easier to work with and clamp. It also assures that the veneer strips will show through on both sides and edges of the lid.

Another inlay design involves cutting and inlaying stems into the lid and then placing flowers from plugs on an adjoining lid. This inlay design is similar to the one used in Design A 2-1. Before starting the design, you must cut the lid section into four pieces. The pieces also need to be cut before you attach the dowels for the hinge system. Surface inlays, such as the flower and stem, can overlap onto all four lids. For example, you can have a flower on one lid, a bud on one lid, a leaf on another lid, and a connecting stem system beginning on the fourth lid. You can also make sculptured inlays on the various lids and then connect them with a surface inlay. Do some inlay design work with this project. It offers a range of possibilities for lid embellishment.

You can also place various objects, such as stones and glass, into the lids. For most of this type of intarsia, you should micro-rout a total or partial recess into the lids for holding the objects in place.

An entire box made from pine presents other options for enhancing the lids. These options include tole painting, woodburning, and carving, to name a few. Don't rule out making this box from pine.

5. As mentioned, I use a dowel-hinge system with this design. Refer to Design A 1-1 for the dowel-hinge procedures. With this design, you will want to use ¼″-diameter dowels for the hinges. To simplify the drilling of the dowel-hinge holes through the base and into the lid, it's best to have the lid section in one piece. While your veneer laminating or flush-surface-inlay work may be done, this should not present a problem when drilling the hinge holes. Obviously, any inlay work that extends beyond the surface of the lid must wait until the hinge holes have been drilled. Illus. 66 shows how the box appears when the hinge dowels are in place and the four lids are open. As the picture indicates, I have drilled the four hinge holes near the corners of the base. With a ¼″-diameter bit in place, the lid and the base should be set upside down on the drill press. Set the drill bit so that it penetrates only about two thirds of the way into the lid. Very carefully drill the four dowel-hinge holes.

6. Before placing the hinge dowels into the lid section, you need to cut the lid into the four separate pieces. This procedure tends to be pretty much of an eyeball task. While looking at

the surface of the base and the four holes, draw the four lids on the surface of the lid section. Using a ruler, check to make sure that each lid you've drawn will adequately cover its respective hole. Also, remember that each lid must be placed with and over its dowel-hinge hole. If you interchange the drilled pieces, the lids will not fit when the hinge dowels are in place. Keep this in mind when you draw the cutting lines for the four lids.

Plan to leave the outer edges of the four lids square to the base walls. It tends to look much neater. You may want to refer to Illus. 65 to get an idea of how the lids and base will look when assembled. In order to slide past one another in sequence, the lids need to have rounded corners. The corner where the lid is hinged should not be rounded. Also, to make them open in sequence, make each lid a little larger than the previous one. Thus, the lid over the smallest hole would be the smallest and it also would be the first lid to open in the sequence.

After cutting the four lids from the lid section, place them over their respective storage holes to get an idea of fit. If it's visually apparent that they will not slide by one another in sequence, remove some wood from the appropriate edge or edges. Be sure you don't reduce the lid size too much or the lid will not cover the storage hole. The type of lid inlay you use determines when you should put dowel-hinge pieces in place. You will want to rout the top edges of the lids and the bottom edges of the base.

Before gluing the dowel hinges into the lids, be certain the bottoms of the lids have been prepared for finishing. Do any sanding that may be necessary. After gluing the dowels into the lid holes, allow ample time for the glue to dry or the dowels will pull out when placed in the base. You should also glue pieces of dowel in the entry holes in the bottom of the base.

7. With the dowels glued in place and dry, place the lids on the base to check for fit. You may have to reduce the diameter of the dowels if they fit too tightly in their respective base holes. Abrasive paper, lightly applied around the entire surface of the dowel, usually does the job. Be certain you are placing the correct lid into its base-hinge hole. To make the lids open in sequence, you may have to remove more wood from their edges. It's best to start with the smallest lid and work on up through the various sizes. With this design, as indicated, the smallest lid should be opened first in order to allow the others to be opened. To get the lids to slide in sequence is simply a matter of removing wood from the appropriate edge or edges, trying the fit, and repeating the process until the system works. There is no easy way of accomplishing this task. Take your time and remove only small amounts of wood at a time. Eventually the lids will open and close, very easily, in sequence. They will not, however, open out of sequence.

8. When the lids have been fitted in place and routed on the top edges, begin the process of making your shaped inlay if you've decided to use one. You should have the lid surfaces ready for finishing before beginning the raised inlay procedures.

9. Prepare the base for finishing and do any touch-up surface work on the lids and the inlay. Using abrasive paper, be sure to remove any excess glue. Finish the box. You may want to refer to the next chapter for some suggestions on this process.

Design A 13-1: Small Heart Box (Illus. 67)

1. The heart design is always a good one for tiny boxes. This box makes an extremely useful storage container for rings, earrings, or other small items. To make sure that the heart box will have use scraps if they are available. While the dimensions may vary depending on the thickness of the wood, the quarter shown with the boxes in Illus. 67 gives you some idea of possible size.

Illus. 67. Small heart box

a balanced design, you should make a pattern. You may want to refer back to the heart profile in Illus. 20 for some assistance. While the heart design can be done freehand, when it's done this way, it tends to have a freehand appearance. Designing and cutting a small pattern are well worth your time and effort.

2. The heart box can be made from 2″ pine stock or 2″ (8/4's) hardwood. You may want to

You can, of course, make the dimensions considerably smaller if desired. The very tiny boxes are great fun to design and make. As you can see in Illus. 67, the lid has two overlapping plugs. You may want to consider embellishing the lid with some type of inlay design.

3. After tracing the pattern onto the stock, cut out the heart with a band or scroll saw. When I use a band saw, I usually use a ⅛″- or ¼″-wide

blade. The corners of the design are too sharp for a wider blade. The lid for this design is eventually cut off the base piece. More about this procedure shortly.

4. After the box has been cut, sand off the saw marks on the surfaces using a finishing sander or a 1″ belt sander or grinder. No matter how small and fine the teeth are, the band saw tends to mark the surface of the wall. You will want to clean up the edges of the box before cutting the lid.

5. This design uses a dowel hinge similar to the one described in Design A 1-1. Although the procedures are the same, you will need to use a ¼″-diameter or smaller dowel for this hinge. The dowel hole should be drilled into the box before the lid is cut off. Drill the hole to within ¼″ from what will be the top surface of the lid. After you drill the dowel-hinge hole, the lid can be cut from the block. You can readily accomplish this procedure using the band saw and its fence. Set the fence for cutting a ⅜″- to ½″-thick slice off the top of the block. Remember to cut the lid piece from the correct surface. The base surface should have a hole drilled into it for the dowel hinge.

6. Before placing the piece of dowel into the lid hole, sand the bottom surface of the lid and the top surface of the base. Be careful not to sand too much. If you do, you won't have a flush fit. Carefully remove the saw marks that were made on the surfaces when the lid piece was separated from the base section. The hinge dowel should be cut so it extends from the lid to at least halfway into the base. You should also cut a piece of the same dowel for plugging the drill hole in the bottom of the box. Glue the hinge dowel into the lid hole and allow the glue to dry. Be certain the dowel is placed straight up and down in the lid so it fits flush to the surface of the base.

7. Drill a storage area in the middle of the base. The size of the storage area depends on the size of the base. I often drill to ⅛″ from the bottom of the box. If you want to add some class to the box, cut a piece of felt or leather and place it at the bottom of the storage hole. It should not be glued in place until the box has been finished.

8. Assemble the lid onto the base. I rout the edges of both the lid and the base with a small round-over bit. Abrasive paper can also accomplish this procedure. You can put a plug-inlay design on the lid.

9. Sand the entire box to finishing readiness and finish as desired.

Design A 14-1: Scrap Boxes (Illus. 68)

1. Not only do these boxes look like scrap pieces of wood, they are actually made from pieces of 2″ (8/4's) scrap. While dimensions are of little significance when it comes to making scrap boxes, the quarter in Illus. 68 provides some perspective on size. These boxes lend themselves to some simple lid embellishments. I often inlay the lid with a single ⅜″-diameter plug. You may want to come up with your own design.

2. Whenever a piece of wood is cut from a large project, I always save it for either inlay work or scrap boxes. Seldom do you ever have two pieces of scrap that are shaped exactly the same. Thus, you have an unending supply of free-style designs for small boxes. You may, on occasion, want to trim a sharp edge off the block prior to making a box from it. Usually, however, the blocks can be used exactly as they come out of the scrap pile.

3. The scrap boxes require the use of a dowel-hinge system, as described in both Design A 1-1 and Design A 13-1. Refer to these designs for some ideas and procedures on making the hinges for a sliding lid.

4. The lid on the scrap boxes is cut from the block. For this procedure, refer to Design A 13-1. Before cutting the lid from the block, you should sand the edges of the box. Also, you may want to rout the top and bottom edges of the piece. It's much easier to rout the edges before the lid is cut from the block. When I use an inlay on the lid, I do these procedures before cutting off the lid piece.

5. For a truly unique box, the block can be ripped and a strip of veneer can be laminated between the pieces. You can cut the block at various angles and glue them back together with veneer strips between the pieces. When you make these cuts, remember that the pieces must be clamped until the glue is dry. Some angled cuts make it almost imposible to clamp

Illus. 68. Scrap boxes

the parts. These laminating procedures should be done prior to drilling the dowel-hinge hole. If you want the laminate in the lid, do the procedures before the lid is cut from the box. This kind of design is an excellent way of honing your laminating skills while obtaining some design experience. Some very exciting effects can be achieved rather quickly and with a minimum of effort. Also, you're working with scrap pieces of wood so your costs are minimal.

6. Follow the procedures for preparing the storage area and finishing the box that are presented in Design A 13-1.

B: Turned Boxes

As you look over the various projects in this section, you'll discover that the range of sizes and designs is limited only by your imagination and turning skills. It's worth noting, however, that your imagination can be easily tapped and, with persistence, your turning skills can be systematically improved.

Many turned boxes can be made from scrap material. In fact, I have turned several boxes in this section from pieces of scrap material salvaged from other projects. Usually any piece of scrap material can be used for a tiny box. Wood that is 2″ to 3″ long and 1″ in diameter can provide sufficient material for turning a box with a lid. These very small boxes can be used for holding any number of items from needles to pills. Many people collect small boxes. I've found that the smaller the box, the more it is prized by collectors. As you begin the process of designing and turning small boxes, you will be amazed to see how tiny you can make a box.

In addition to the very small boxes, you can

design and turn a range of larger boxes. Many of the larger turned boxes can be used to store jewelry or anything else that requires a fine storage container. The larger turned boxes can also be turned to house a Model 1.18 musical movement.

While boxes can be turned between spindles, many designs require the use of a faceplate. I generally turn my boxes using either a faceplate or a self-made chuck. The chuck is ideal for turning the lids, especially on some of the larger box designs. In addition to using glue blocks, I often use double-face tape for faceplate-turning boxes. Once you develop some confidence in the tape, it can be excellent for turning small boxes.

In turning boxes, you will find that either the cutting or scraping method can be used. I tend to use scrapers, especially when turning the base and lid from separate blocks. You will definitely want to use scrapers when turning the inside storage areas of the boxes. Due to their size or design, some boxes may require special turning tools, but most can be turned with the standard array of available tools. When a specialized tool is required for a box, I usually make it from a file. There are numerous books available that will assist you with both turning methods and tools.

The lids of turned boxes offer the turner a range of design options. While some designs lend themselves to a turned knob, others can be prepared for holding an inlay. You will find that the turned lid provides you with some unusual and very interesting possibilities for inlay work.

Both the bases and lids can be laminated from various woods. Not only does laminating produce an unusual-looking box or lid, it is also cost-effective. You can laminate either solid wood or veneer to enhance the overall appearance of a box. On the larger boxes that require 2″ (8/4′s)-thick stock, you may want to consider laminating two 1″ (4/4′s) boards together. A strip of veneer between the boards adds a nice touch to the base.

Although this section presents designs made on the lathe, you can also enhance a turned piece by using other tools and procedures. For example, a number of the projects present designs that are turned on the lathe but shaped further on a belt sander. The reshaping of a turned piece will add a different dimension to your turning.

While I encourage you to duplicate at least one of the box designs in this section, I hope you go beyond this and turn some designs of your own. The delightful thing about the lathe and turning tools is that you can make any shape or design you want. Maximize this marvellous potential. Turn your boxes and lids in a way that you find interesting. More importantly, turn them in a way that gives you the most pleasure and satisfaction.

Design B 15-1: Small Turned Box with Lid (Illus. 69)

1. While not what the collectors would call a tiny box, this design is sufficiently small to give you an introduction to turning small boxes with lids. It can, of course, be reduced or increased in size. The box in Illus. 69 is 2½″ high and 1¾″ in diameter. It was turned from a scrap piece of wild cherry. The collection of small boxes in Illus. 70 was turned from scrap pieces of various hardwoods. You can salvage many scraps from the projects you've made in the previous section.

2. I turn this box design between centers using a small drive center in the headstock and a revolving center in the tailstock. If you lack the small drive center, the block can be centered and glued to a scrap block attached to a 3″ faceplate. With these smaller designs, I glue the

block to be turned directly to the scrap block. I use a piece of pine that is 3″ in diameter and ¾″

Illus. 69. Small turned box with lid

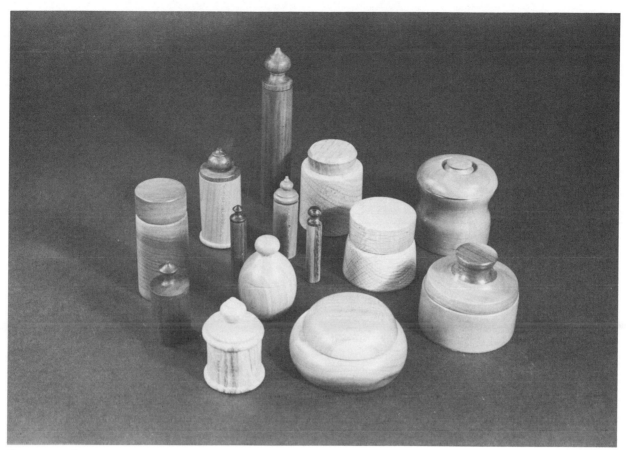

Illus. 70. Collection of small turned boxes with lids

thick for the glue block. The assembly should be clamped until the glue is dry. After the base and lid have been turned, I cut the turned piece off the glue block with the band saw. This procedure allows you to use the pine glue block again. Sand its surface clean and flush on a belt sander. If you want, you can put a piece of paper between the turning block and the glue block with glue spread on both surfaces. This assembly should also be clamped until the glue is dry. You can chisel off the turned piece when completed. In either of the glue-block procedures, the turning block should be glued to the center. With these small turning blocks, you can't afford to waste wood by turning the piece to roundness.

3. This box design is turned with the grain. You should prepare a block that is at least 3″ long and 2″ in diameter. Using either the drive-center or glue-block method, mount the assembly on the lathe. Illus. 71 shows the assembly between centers. It also identifies the various parts of the assembly and the different turned sections of the base and lid.

As you can see in Illus. 71, an extra-small knob is turned on the lid piece. This knob holds the point of the revolving center and is later removed. If this procedure were not used, the final lid knob would have a hole in its top from supporting the point of the revolving center. Turn the design to shape, including the lid and its two knobs. Decide where the lid and base should be separated. The lid tenon is cut at this point. The tenon should fit snugly into the base of the box. I drill the storage area in the base of this design using a 1¼″ multi-spur or Foerstner bit. Thus, the lid tenon must be turned to a diameter that is slightly less than 1¼″. You don't want the lid tenon to fit too tightly into the piece. On the other hand, you don't want it too loose. I usually make the lid tenon about ¼″ long. It's best to cut into the turned piece and to make the lid tenon using a parting tool. Using a vernier caliper, monitor the diameter of the

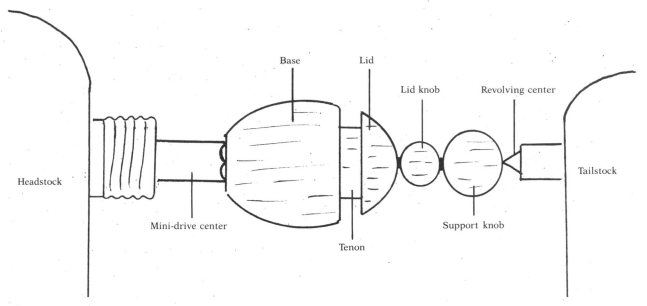

Base   Lid   Lid knob   Revolving center

Headstock   Tailstock

Mini-drive center   Support knob

Tenon

Illus. 71. Small box and lid on lathe

tenon until it is slightly less than the 1¼" required. Do not separate the lid and the base at this time. When the tenon has been turned, if necessary, use abrasive paper to bring the box to finishing readiness. Be careful not to round over the top edge of the base or the bottom edge of the lid. You want to leave sharp edges for a nice clean fit. The point where the base and lid come together should hardly be visible when the box is completed.

4. Remove the turned piece from the lathe. Using a band saw, cut off the extra knob that held the revolving center. Next, cut the base and lid apart where the tenon joins the base section. It's best to leave a little excess tenon on the base and then sand it off. This will prevent you from cutting into the top of the base wall. You should sand both the base of the box and the base of the lid tenon. If you used a drive center, locate the exact center at the top surface of the base and mark. This will be the entry point for the 1¼" bit when drilling the storage area. The storage hole can be drilled within ¼" of the bottom of the base. You will, of course, have to do the drilling using your drill press. When drilling, hold the base firmly so that the drill bit doesn't pull it from your hand.

If you used a glue block, after the tenon and lid have been separated from the base, remount the assembly on the lathe. Place a Jacobs chuck with a Morse taper in the tailstock. Secure the 1¼" multi-spur or Foerstner bit into the chuck and drill the storage area in the box. After the drilling is complete, band-saw the base of the box from the glue block. Sand the base until it is ready for finishing.

5. With very few exceptions, I finish all my turned boxes off the lathe. Finish the base and lid as desired. You may want to write your initials or place your logo on the bottom of the base before you begin the finishing process.

Design B 16-1: Turned Box with Lid (Illus. 72)

1. This design is somewhat larger than the previous one and uses different procedures both in its preparation and turning. The box in Illus. 72 has a base made from spalted sycamore and a lid and knob made from spalted hackberry. This design is a good size for storing jewelry or other items. It can also be made into a music box. For the necessary procedures and dimensions for making a music box, refer to Design A 1-2. The base is 2¼" (9/4's) thick and has a diameter of 3⅜". The lid fits inside the base and rests on a turned shoulder. The knob on this design extends 3½" from the top surface of the lid. The knob piece is glued to the lid block prior to

72

turning. As you consider designs for turning, you may want to examine the collection of turned boxes in Illus. 73. As the picture indicates, there is no end to the design possibilities for the turned box with lid. Most of these designs have a turned shoulder inside the box upon which the lid rests.

2. Because of the size of this design, you will no doubt have to use good stock rather than scraps. The major issue regarding the dimensions of the design have to do with the thickness of the stock for the base. You may want to use 2″ (8/4's) or, if not available, thinner stock. You can, of course, laminate two 1″ (4/4's) boards together for use as the base. The base should be rough-cut on the band saw to a diameter of at least 3½″. This diameter becomes critical if you plan to turn the box to house a musical movement. If you use the design for other functions,

such as storing grimple, you may want to reduce the diameter of the block.

I turn this design using a glue block and a 3″ faceplate for the base. Most of the boxes in Illus. 73 were turned using a glue block and faceplate. You may, however, prefer using one of the many commercial chucks on the market. Because of the cost of these chucks, I've decided to continue using either a glue block or a block with double-face tape. The additional procedures for preparing a block to be held in a chuck have also discouraged me from their use. You may find the opposite to be true. In any event, use what works best for you.

After the base block has been cut to diameter, glue it to the glue block and clamp. For glue blocks, I use ¾″-thick pine, cut to a diameter of 3¼″. I do not use paper between the turning block and the glue block. Using a thin coating of white glue and then separating the turned piece from the glue block works better for me. I separate the pieces with the band saw. This eliminates all the mess that usually accompanies the use of paper and glue. I frequently use commercial double-face tape instead of glue for securing the turning block to the scrap block. It's very effective and simple to use. You may find the cost a bit high for the amount of turning you do. On the other hand, a full roll of the tape will last a long time and it seems to have a good shelf life.

3. The base of the lid should be cut from 1″ (4/4's) stock to a diameter of at least 3½″. The lid-knob extension is also cut from 1″ (4/4's) stock, with the grain. As indicated, this design has a lid extension that is 3½″ long. You may want to reduce its length. Sometimes turning these longer lid knobs from spalted wood can be a problem. When you turn them, you need to use a light touch or they will break. Glue the lid knob to the middle of the lid block and clamp. Be certain the two surfaces are in good contact after the clamp is in place. Sometimes, with the glue, the assembly will slide during the clamping process. Allow the glue to dry. Incidentally, you will want to use wood glue with the lid and its knob. It will hold better in the long run.

4. With a 3″ faceplate mounted on the box-base assembly, begin turning the walls of the base. Depending on your preference, use either scrapers or gouges for shaping the outer surface. When the outer portion of the base is turned to your satisfaction, align the tool rest in

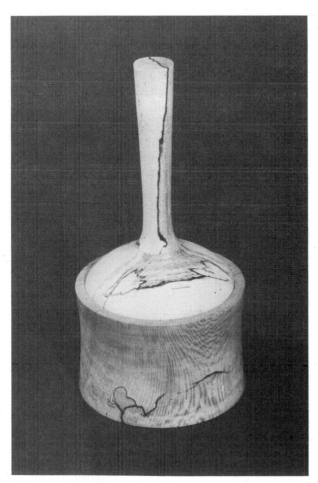

Illus. 72. Turned box with lid

Illus. 73. Collection of turned boxes with lids

front of the block. For removing the wood from inside the base, I use a ½″ square-nose scraper. This tool also works well for cutting the lid shoulder. The initial turning task involves squaring the top edge of the block. Next, cut the lid shoulder to a depth of at least ⅛″. The base wall that surrounds the insert area should be ⅛″ thick. The actual shoulder that the lid rests on should be a little more than ⅛″ wide. This extra dimension allows for the possibility of a lid being turned too small. Even though the diameter of the lid base is turned a bit small, the lid will still rest on the lid shoulder (Illus. 74).

After the lid-insert shoulder has been prepared, remove the wood from the storage area. You can turn to within ¼″ of the bottom. You will want to leave some thickness for cutting the base off the glue block and also for sanding the base for finishing. If the surface needs it, sand it to finishing readiness. Do not sand the top edge of the base round. Having a sharp edge around the top of the base looks better.

5. For turning the lid and its knob, I use a small screw chuck mounted on a 3″ faceplate (Illus. 75). The chuck can be made from any 1″(4/4's)-thick stock. A ¼″-diameter lag screw penetrates the center of the chuck about 1″. An undersized hole is drilled in the bottom center of the lid. To make the turning of the lid base easier, I thread a small block onto the lag screw and tight

against the face of the chuck. The lid and knob are then threaded tight against the small block. To prevent the long lid knob from breaking, I bring the tailstock with a revolving center up

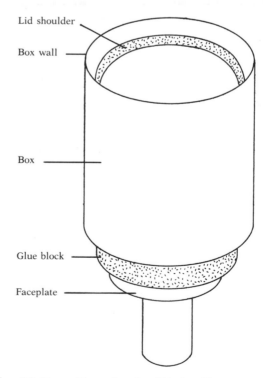

Illus. 74. Turned box showing lid shoulder

74

against the top of the knob. Don't put too much pressure on the knob with the tailstock or it will break. After the lid and knob have been turned, I cut the top of the lid knob at an angle on the band saw. This gives it a nice appearance, but it also removes the hole made by the revolving center. These procedures are especially important when turning lids and knobs from spalted woods.

Before you begin turning the base and knob of the lid, measure, with a vernier caliper, the diameter of the base opening. The lid base needs to be turned a touch smaller than the diameter of the base-lid insert. You don't want the lid to fit too tightly in the base-insert area. It's better a bit too loose than too tight. Turn the base of the lid and the knob using tools of your choice. Be sure to frequently check the lid-base diameter with the preset vernier caliper. When the turning has been completed, you may want to use some abrasive paper to bring the surface to finishing readiness. Remove the lid from the chuck and check for fit in the base. If it's too tight, remount it on the chuck and remove a bit

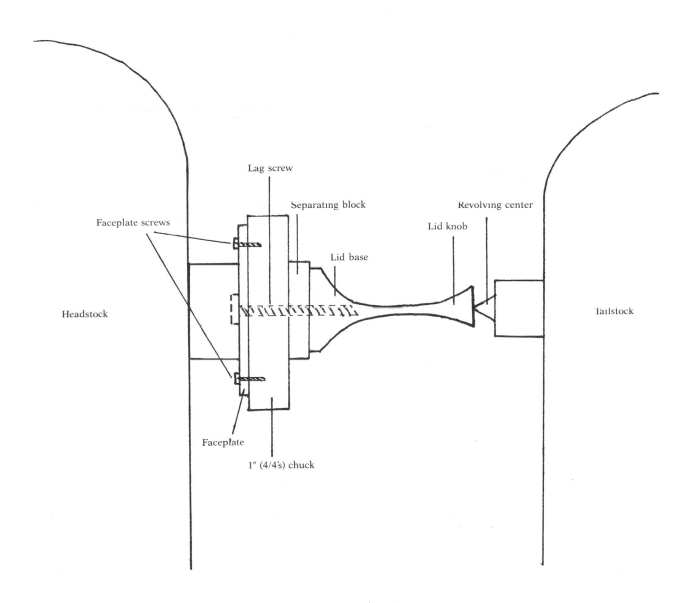

Illus. 75. Self-made chuck: turning lid

more wood. Be careful not to remove too much. Frequently I use only abrasive paper for this procedure. With turning tools, it's too easy to remove too much wood. Remove the lid and, again, test for fit. Using the band saw, carefully cut the top section of the knob off at an angle. It's best to rest the knob on a small block when cutting it on the band saw. If the blade catches, it could break the knob. I place a dab of wood filler in the bottom of the lid where the screw-chuck hole was drilled. When dry, sand the entire surface to finishing readiness.

6. Finish the box as desired.

Design B 17-1: Log Box with Lid (Illus. 76)

1. The name of this design not only describes the box, but also the material I used for turning it. While not actually made from a log, the box in Illus. 76 was turned from a chunk of hedge firewood. Hedge is one of the more difficult woods to turn, especially when turning into the grain for the storage area. I use hedge because it's a beautiful wood for boxes, bowls, and inlay work. It's impossible to match the lovely golden color it develops with time. When it's turned into the grain, the annual rings remain a yellow color while the wood surrounding them turns a golden tan. You can see how the annual rings stand out on the top of the lid in Illus. 76. It's tough turning but well worth it. Depending on the length and diameter of the log you use, you can turn a rather sizeable storage container with this design. The box in Illus. 76 is 4½″ tall and has a diameter of approximately 4″. I turn the lid with a tenon that extends into the base. Because of its size, the storage area of the base must be turned out on the lathe.

2. The size of the storage area and the type of turning that's required make it necessary to use a faceplate for this design. Illus. 77 shows a block on the lathe that is partially turned. You should note the tenon being cut. Also, a small block is placed between the revolving center in the tailstock and the top surface of the lid. The block is held firmly in place while being turned to shape, but the small block prevents the revolving center from marking the lid surface.

Select a log of reasonable length and diameter for your box. I generally pull one from the woodpile in the backyard. You will want to find a log that's good and dry. Almost any of the woods that you would normally have for firewood can be used for making this design. Cherry or oak make for an excellent log box.

Square the base of the log on the band saw. You need a square surface on the end where the faceplate is secured. For an initial box, I wouldn't use a block much longer than 6″. The diameter is less fixed. Use a log of a diameter that will meet the anticipated storage function of the box. Attach a 3″ faceplate to the base and

Illus. 76. Log box with lid

secure the assembly on the lathe. Bring the tailstock with a revolving center forward to the top surface of the block. Insert a small circle of wood between the revolving center and the surface of the block. Tighten and secure the tailstock against the block.

3. The log is being turned with the grain so you can use any method of turning desired. If the log still has bark on it, you would be wise to wear a face mask to protect yourself from flying bark. Shape the base and lid area of the log as desired. Before cutting the lid tenon, remove

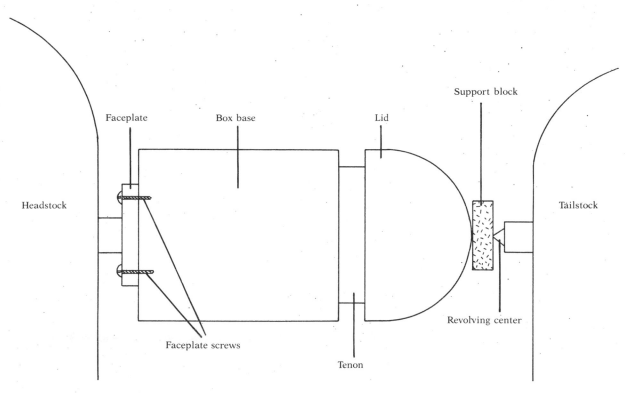

Illus. 77. Log box on lathe

the tailstock and the small block. Finish turning the top of the lid, and then replace the block and tailstock.

It's best to cut the lid tenon with a parting tool. Although it depends on the size of the box, I generally make the tenon at least ¼" long. You may want to cut the tenon a bit longer than ¼" because a portion of its length is removed when the lid and tenon are separated from the base. I separate the lid and base with a band saw, as opposed to using a parting tool. The band saw tends to be easier to use and more accurate. As you cut the tenon to length, you also need to determine how thick the base wall should be. I usually make the base walls at least ¼" thick. Thus, in cutting the tenon, you should only cut into the block surface ¼". Refer to Illus. 77 to get an idea of how this procedure appears when completed. Using abrasive paper, sand the entire surface to finishing readiness. Be certain not to round the top edge of the base and the bottom edge of the lid with the abrasive paper. You will want a nice sharp line where the lid and base fit together.

4. Leaving the faceplate attached to the base, remove the entire box from the lathe. Using the band saw, cut through the box where the tenon attaches to the base. You may want to support the curved areas of the box when cutting. If the box is not supported under any curved areas, the band-saw blade can grab the box out of your hand. When cut, sand the bottom of the tenon on a belt sander. You only need to clean up the band-saw marks that are on the surface. Those saw marks that are on the base will be turned away on the lathe.

5. Remount the base on the lathe and align the tool rest in front of the block. Before you begin turning out the storage area, place a vernier caliper on the lid tenon and set the caliper to its exact diameter. Using the preset caliper as a guide, mark the tenon diameter on the base surface. Using a ½" square-nose scraper, turn out only a small portion of the storage area until the tenon diameter has been reached. Place the lid with its tenon into the turned out area and check for fit. Continue these procedures until the lid tenon fits snugly into the box. After these fitting procedures are complete, turn out the remainder of the base for storage. Be careful not to widen the diameter of the base at the top where the lid tenon fits. The depth of the storage area will, in part, be determined by the length of the faceplate screws you use. Monitor the depth so that you do not hit the end of the faceplace screws with the tool. I always turn the bottom inside of the box flat. You may need to use some abrasive paper to clean up the inside of the base.

6. Remove the faceplate from the base. I usu-ally cut ⅜"-diameter plugs from the same wood as the base for use in covering the faceplate screw holes. Drill a ⅜"-diameter hole into each faceplate screw hole and glue one of the plugs in place. When dry, sand the surface of the base flush.

7. Finish the box as desired. You may want to refer to the next chapter for a few ideas on finishing methods and products.

Design B 18-1: Turned Box with Floral Inlay (Illus. 78)

1. This box is clearly one of my favorites. No doubt it's partly because it is a totally turned box. Also, the lid of this design presents an endless series of inlay options of a size that I enjoy making. I've inlaid the lid for this design with cats shaped from ebony, zebrawood, and hedge. I've also shaped and inlaid pears, apples, birds, flowers, and many other objects in the lids of this design. Another reason for my fondness probably has something to do with the fact that the design does not consume great quantities of wood. With this design, you can make an attractive box that can serve a range of functions, while using only a minimum of wood. The box can also easily house a Model 1.18 musical movement. As a matter of fact, the box was originally designed as a music box. If you want to make it into a music box, refer to Design A 1-2 for specific procedures and dimensions. These are the approximate dimensions of this design: The base is 2" (8/4's) thick; the lid is 1" (4/4's) thick; the box diameter is 3½". You can, of course, vary these dimensions as you see fit. You may want to change them in relation to some special storage need.

2. A circle template is an effective way to pattern out the base and lid for a turned box. I use the kind of template that has a series of circles with graduated diameters. Then I cut the traced base and lid with a band saw.

3. Depending on your own preference, you can either glue the base block to a scrap of wood attached to the faceplate or attach the faceplate directly to the base. If you prefer the glue-block method, refer to Design B 16-1. You will find all other necessary procedures for turning the base of this box also in Design B 16-1. Turn the base and the lid area using these procedures.

4. I turn the lid for this design using the same screw chuck that is presented in Design B 16-1. However, the lid for this design must have a recess turned into its top surface for a back-

Illus. 78. Turned box with floral inlay

ground insert and the inlay. The lid on the screw chuck with the turned inlay recess is shown in Illus. 79.

Drill an undersized hole through the middle of the lid and mount the lid on the chuck. You may want to have a small block between the base of the lid and the face of the chuck. Using procedures presented in Design B 16-1, turn the lid to the appropriate diameter for a good fit in the shoulder of the base. After turning the lower portion of the base to the correct diameter, I

Illus. 79. Lid on screw chuck

roll the upper portion of the lid. I also make a slight rolling indentation in the upper side portion of the lid. Refer to Illus. 78 for an idea of how this upper lid portion is shaped. Realign the tool to rest in front of the lid. The next procedure involves turning out the lid recess that will hold the background insert and the inlay. A ½" square-nose scraper works well in preparing the recess area. First, square the outer portion of the lid surface. Cut into the top of the lid approximately ¼" from the outer edge. Make the cut into the lid at least ⅛" deep. Systematically remove the wood from the surface of the lid to a uniform depth. The lag screw will no doubt be penetrating through the surface of the lid. Allow a small pillar of wood to develop around it. You can chisel away this excess wood when the lid is removed from the chuck. You may want to sand the surface of the wall on the top of the lid that surrounds the recess. Don't round the inside edge of the wall. You will want it sharp so it blends in with the background-insert piece (Illus. 80).

While you may want to turn the lid recess to an exact diameter, it's not necessary. It does simplify the preparation of the recess insert and, when I'm doing production turning with this design, I generally make the insert area a uniform 2¼". However, for one box, you can easily measure the recess diameter and prepare the insert. For specific procedures involved in preparing the insert and the flower inlay, refer to Design A 5-2. You should design and cut the flower inlay in relation to the diameter of the

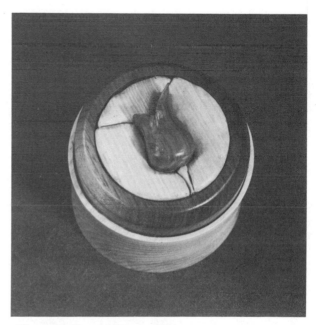

Illus. 80. Floral inlay on lid

lid recess. If desired, the stem for the flower can extend onto the shoulder of the recess. Trace the width of the stem onto the surface of the shoulder, and cut out the area to the same depth as the recess.

5. Finish the box as desired. Refer to the next chapter if you need some assistance with the finishing process. If you made the design into a music box, you may want to refer to the Appendix for some specifics on cutting a glass insert.

Design B 18-2: Turned Box with Apple Inlay (Illus. 81)

1. This design is exactly the same as the previous one, except for the lid embellishment. Refer to Design B 18-1 for the various procedures in making the base and lid. The apple inlay is made from padouk. For assistance in preparing the apple and other components of the inlay, refer to Design A 6-2. You need to take into account the reduced size of the apple for this design.

2. You may prefer using another inlay design. Better yet, design and prepare one of your own for use on this turned box. The procedures are basically the same no matter what design you use. Do some pencil-and-paper design work and develop an inlay that may better reflect your interests or taste.

Illus. 81. Apple inlay on lid

Design B 19-1: Apple Music Box (Illus. 82)

1. This is one of those box designs that compromises the sound and volume of the musical movement for the sake of the apearance of the box. When using the smaller Model 1.18 movements, this is a reasonable trade-off. However, you can use a larger movement in this design, as well as a pull-string stopper (Illus. 83). I've used both a Model 1.28 and a Model 1.36 musical movement in this design with the pull-string stopper system.

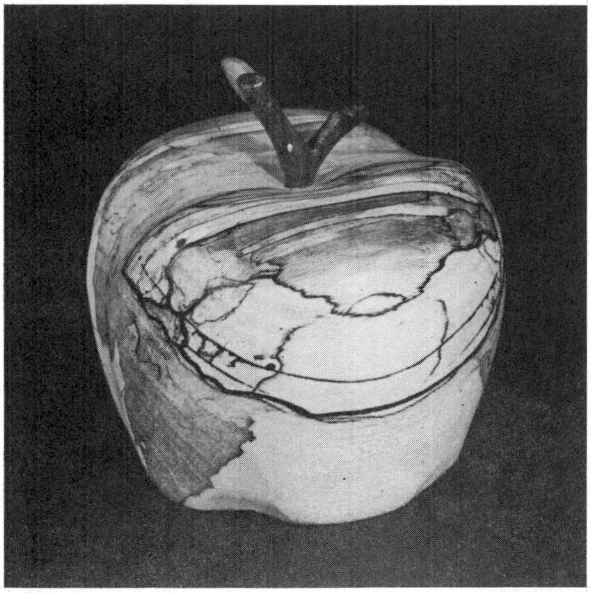

The design, as you might guess, is a consumer of wood. I have made the apple from padouk, walnut, or spalted wood. Any wood looks good for this design, but the red padouk is an obvious choice. To achieve the necessary thickness for the design, I usually laminate two 2″ (8/4's) pieces of padouk. These are the approximate dimensions of the apple: The height (thickness of block) without the stem is 3½″; the diameter is 4¾″. These dimensions give you some idea of the sizeable wood requirements of this design. On occasion I've crafted the apple design as a solid piece. When this is done, the dimensions can easily be reduced.

While it's often difficult to find wood thick enough for this design, it is available. If you live in an area where there is a small sawmill, this is a likely spot for finding the thicker stock. The wood is usually air dried (AD), but for turnings

Illus. 82. Spalted apple music box

that's no problem. You can also hunt for a size-able block of spalted wood. The apple in Illus. 82 is made from a spalted sycamore log end.

To meet the dimensional requirements of the apple design, you can also laminate standard-thickness boards (4/4's) together. To achieve a different effect, you may want to mix woods in the laminating procedure. Another way of laminating involves placing the boards in opposite grain alignment. This gives the turned apple a very interesting visual effect.

2. Mount a 3″ faceplate on the bottom of the block. I usually use the least desirable surface for the bottom because most of it will be turned away for the musical movement area. Turn the block to resemble the shape of an apple. I taper the bottom of the block to a diameter of about 4″. If you're using spalted wood, use the tail-stock and revolving center for support while turning. Faceplate screws can easily pull out of the spalted blocks. You may want to use the support system while turning any large block regardless of the type of wood that's used. It's a good, safe turning procedure and it also provides excellent stability to the block being turned.

Roll the upper edge of the block to resemble the upper area of an apple. While rolling, begin tapering the top surface of the block downwards. The stem area should be quite a bit lower than the upper edge of the apple. You should be able to turn this area even with the revolving center in place. You may want to examine Illus. 82 again to see how the top area of the apple should look. You should leave or make a mark at the center of the top surface. This will be the exact center of the apple and also the point where the stem will eventually be placed. If you used a revolving center, a mark should already be on the surface. You will need to drill a small pilot hole at this center point for mounting the apple on a screw chuck. This same hole will eventually hold the stem and leaf.

3. After removing the turned apple from the faceplate, drill the pilot hole in the top center of

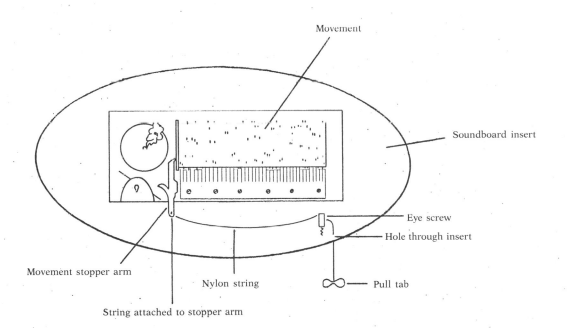

Illus. 83. On/off stopper system

the apple. The hole should be substantially smaller than the diameter of the chuck-lag screw. This is especially important when turning an apple from one of the spalted woods. Design B 16-1 includes a description of the screw chuck that I use for turning the apple design. Unless you have one of your own design or a commercial one, you may want to make the chuck described in that design.

Secure the apple to the screw chuck on the lathe and bring the tailstock and revolving center into it. Regardless of the type of wood used for the apple, you should definitely support the block while turning out the movement and insert area. Illus. 84 shows the bottom musical movement area and the insert shoulder that must be made to hold the soundboard in place. Using a ½" square-nose scraper, turn out the movement area to a diameter of at least 2¾". If there is sufficient space, make the diameter larger. You also need to turn a shoulder in the movement area that will hold the soundboard insert (Illus. 83).

Turn the movement area to a depth of at least 1½". You can get by with less depth, but the sound reproduction of the movement is better if there's more space around it. Leaving the apple wall at least ¼" thick, cut the insert shoulder.

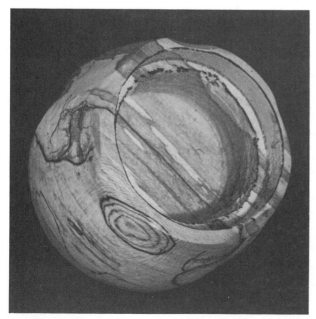

Illus. 84. Movement area and insert shoulder

The shoulder should be at least ½" down from the bottom edge of the apple. The shoulder should be at least ¼" wide so that the insert can easily be screwed into it. The winding key needs the depth from the bottom edge of the apple to the insert. You may want to check the length of your movement key while turning this area.

4. Remove the piece from the chuck and begin shaping it to resemble an apple. I do the initial shaping on the end of a 6"×48" belt sander using a 60- or 80-grit belt. The belt grit is partially determined by the wood used for the apple. The round end of the belt sander is ideal for rough shaping. Be certain you don't sand through the thin wall at the bottom of the apple. For the shaping process, you may want to examine Illus. 82 again or use an actual apple as a model. When shaping on a large belt sander, hold onto the apple or the tool will pull it from your hands. A smaller belt sander will accomplish the shaping equally well. Using an electric finishing sander and a series of finer abrasive grits, bring the surface of the apple to finishing readiness.

5. It's now time to prepare the ⅛" plywood insert. You should use a vernier caliper for transferring the diameter of the base to a plywood disc. I rough-cut a circle of ⅛"-thick plywood that's larger than the actual base diameter. I usually use a cabinet-grade plywood for the inserts. To turn the insert to the proper diameter, I must drill a hole in the middle so the insert will fit on a screw chuck. If you can cut a perfect insert to the correct diameter, you can eliminate the chuck-lathe procedures. For those who need the lathe, mount the insert on the chuck screw. To hold the insert in place and tight against the chuck surface, I thread a ¾" piece of dowel onto the lag screw. Drill a pilot in the middle of the dowel and twist it on the lag screw until it's tight against the insert surface. Using the preset vernier caliper, a ½"square-nose scraper, and a light touch, turn the insert to the required diameter. Touch up the insert edge using abrasive paper. Remove the insert from the chuck. To check for fit, place it in the apple base, on the shoulder. If the insert is too tight, remount it on the chuck and remove a bit more edge, using abrasive paper. If the insert is too small, start the procedure over.

6. With the musical movement close at hand,

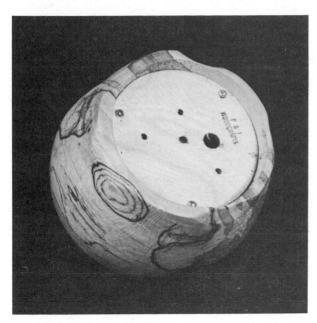

Illus. 85. Insert soundboard

7. Place the insert on the shoulder and, using an electric drill and small bit, drill three properly placed holes around the outer edge of the insert and into the shoulder. These three holes will receive screws that will secure the insert assembly to the shoulder. You may want to use small, round head screws for reasons of appearance. Before removing the insert from the shoulder, place alignment marks on the insert surface and the inside wall of the apple. This helps when you assemble the finished insert, with the movement in place, back into the apple.

8. Prepare a stem and leaf that are proportional in size to the total apple. Referring back to Illus. 82 should help you visualize the size and shape of the stem and leaf. I cut the stem about ¼" square. You can shape the stem round using a finishing sander or a Moto-Tool with sanding sleeves. Be careful not to break the stem while shaping it. So that the base of the stem will fit in the pilot hole used for chuck mounting, you need to reduce its diameter. If necessary, you can also widen the hole to accommodate the base of the stem.

Before shaping the leaf, I drill a small hole in one end that will hold a piece of wire. By the way, I usually cut the leaf to a thickness of ¼". You need to drill a hole of a similar size in the stem at the point where you want the leaf to protrude. After cutting a small amount of wire, glue the wire into the leaf. When the glue is dry, shape the leaf as desired. After placing a bit of glue on the wire that extends from the leaf, insert the wire into the hole in the stem. Cut off any excess wire. Allow this assembly to dry Spread glue in the pilot chuckhole and on the bottom of the stem. Insert the stem-leaf assembly into the hole and allow it to dry. Remove any excess glue that may squeeze out from the hole.

9. After finishing the apple, secure the movement and insert the soundboard into the base area.

mark the insert surface for drilling the key-shaft hole and mark the screw holes for attaching the movement. Remember, the insert is your movement's soundboard in this design. Center the movement on the insert and press down on the spring housing. This procedure will mark the insert surface with the key-shaft end. Drill a ⅜" hole at this mark. Support the insert with a block when drilling or else the plywood may tear out. Place the winding key shaft through the ⅜" hole, center it in the hole, and allow the movement to lie flat on the insert. To do this, you will have to elevate the insert. Also, be sure that the movement is centered on the insert surface. Using a sharp pencil, mark through the screw holes of the movement onto the insert surface. Drill these three holes using a bit with a diameter that is a little larger than the diameter of the screws. Mark the surface of the insert indicating which side faces into the apple.

Design B 20-1: Apple Jewelry Box (Illus. 86)

1. The apple jewelry box is very similar to the apple music box described in the previous design. Although the dimensions are the same, you can reduce them or enlarge them for the jewelry box. As Illus. 86 indicates, the jewelry box is cut in two sections. The top section is the lid and the bottom section is the storage area for jewelry or other items. The suggested dimensions provide you with a box that has enough space to house a musical movement. Because you are not using a movement, you have more dimensional options with this design. If you prefer to avoid having to find and pay for the thicker stock that is recommended for the design, use the laminating process discussed in Design B19-1. By using this process, you can create a unique and extremely attractive jewelry box. If you do laminate the wood, be sure to spread glue on all surfaces, clamp, and allow ample time for the glue to dry.

2. Mount the block on a faceplate after it has been rough-cut round. Secure the assembly on the lathe and bring the tailstock with revolving center forward for support. Follow the turning procedures discussed in Design B19-1. Do not, however, taper the base of the apple too much. You should leave as much wood as possible for the storage area. When the apple has been turned to your satisfaction, you can start the procedures for separating it into a base and lid.

To separate the apple, I use a parting tool and a hack saw. Before proceeding, examine Illus. 87. Determine where you want the apple to be divided. I usually remove the upper third for the lid, which leaves the bulk of the apple for storage area. Using the parting tool, make a cut ¼″ deep and ¼″ wide. The width will eventually

be the length of the lid tenon that fits into the base. With the lathe shut off, using the hack saw, make a cut into the apple along the edge of the base portion. Remember, you need to leave the tenon on the lid section so don't cut it off with the saw. After you've made a starting cut into the apple, remove the saw and turn the lathe on. While the apple is rotating, carefully place the blade in the cut and apply light pressure on it. Periodically remove the blade from the cut so the blade doesn't overheat and bend and then burn the wood. When approximately ¼″ of wood holds the two sections together, stop the lathe and finish the cut. The tenon surface will be rough, but it can easily be sanded.

3. Realign the tool rest, remove the tailstock, and find a ½″ square-nose scraper or similar tool. Remove some of the wood from the middle of the base, being careful not to remove any from near the edge. Using a large caliper or ruler, measure the diameter of the lid tenon. Transfer the diameter to the base surface, and make a mark that is visible when the block is rotating. This mark will be the outer edge of the storage area and the surface against which the

Illus. 86. Apple jewelry box

Illus. 87. Separating apple jewelry box

Illus. 88. Turned storage area

lid tenon will fit. Cut this area with the scraper, and check the fit of the lid tenon. Remove wood in small amounts so you don't take out too much and have a loose-fitting lid. Once the lid tenon fits perfectly, cut the inside wall and remove all the wood from the storage area. Remember that you have faceplate screws penetrating into the base. You will need to plan the depth of the storage area accordingly. Square the bottom surface of the storage area. Illus. 88 shows how the lid and base look after turning.

4. Shape the apple, following the procedures in Design B19-1. Be sure to hold the two sections firmly together and properly aligned. Match up the grain so the piece will resemble a solid apple. When shaping the sides, don't remove so much wood that you expose the tenon or the storage area. You should focus the shaping more on the top and bottom of the design or where there are substantial amounts of wood. Bring the surface to finishing condition.

5. Cut a stem and leaf, shape, and use an attachment wire, as described in Design B19-1. Drill a hole in the middle of the lid for receiving the stem and leaf assembly. Glue the assembly in place.

6. Finish as desired or refer to the next chapter.

Design B 21-1: Mushroom Music Box (Model 1.18 Movement) (Illus. 89)

1. While this design can be crafted from any wood, I tend to make it from spalted wood. Because mushrooms are a type of fungus, it seems only appropriate to craft the box from wood that has been enhanced by fungi. With this design, the musical movement is activated by a slight tip of the box.

The height of the box is approximately 10″; its diameter is approximately 6″. These dimensions reflect the overall size, regardless of the wood used. For turning the top section of the mushroom, I use stock that is roughly 3″ (12/4's) thick. For the stem, I also use stock that is 3″ (12/4's) thick. You don't need to use wood this thick, however. The stem block is cut lengthwise, with the grain, because it needs to be at least 5″ long. The musical movement area is then turned into the end grain. Except for tearout, end-grain turning is not a major problem with the spalts.

To limit your wood costs, you may want to search for spalted woods of the proper thickness. If your trek through the woods is not productive, find a small sawmill. As discussed in Chapter 1, often mills have cut-off sections of logs and other interesting chunks of wood lying around in their yards. You may find some excellent spalted wood that can be purchased very reasonably. If you do not have access to spalted woods, you may want to laminate stock to the proper thickness. A mushroom crafted from laminates can be a very interesting-looking piece. It's certainly worth a try.

2. Mount a faceplate on the block selected for the stem. Secure the plate to the end grain of the block. While holding the block with the faceplate bolt, you can trim the corners off the block on the band saw. It's a great help if the block is at least partially rounded. Many band saws are incapable of cutting a piece this long, standing on end.

With the block mounted on the lathe, bring

Illus. 89. Mushroom music box

the tailstock and revolving center tightly against the block's surface. Screws do not generally hold well in spalted wood. When the screws are placed in the end grain of spalted wood, they will definitely pull out unless the block is supported.

After aligning the tool rest, turn the mushroom stem to shape. The stem should be tapered towards the faceplate. You need all the wood you can spare on the base end, so leave it as wide as possible. The more diameter you have on the base end, the easier it will be to turn the movement area. When you have completed the turning on the stem wall, use abrasive paper to bring the surface to finishing readiness.

Realign the tool rest for turning out the movement area. Leave the tailstock in place. As you will discover, there's not a great deal of room for moving the tool around but it should be sufficient. You need to turn out an area that is approximately 1½" deep. The lower 1" of this area should have a diameter of at least 2½" because this is where the musical movement will be installed. Additionally, you need to cut a shoulder for the soundboard insert that is at least ½" from the bottom edge of the stem. The shoulder should be approximately ¼" wide. This information is presented in greater detail in Design B 19-1. The important thing, however,

is understanding that the musical movement is attached to a ⅛"-thick plywood insert. You need to screw this insert to the shoulder. The area below the shoulder is where the winding key extends.

When the movement and shoulder areas have been completed, remove the assembly and chisel out the wooden support post that developed while turning the movement area. This post should extend from the revolving center to the top of the movement area. Be sure you don't remove it until all turning has been completed. The post is your primary support in holding the stem in place on the lathe.

3. Mount the faceplate on the block that will be used for the mushroom top. Examine the wood so you have the most attractive part of the block on top. If the wood is spalted, examine the end-grain area to see how far the black zone lines penetrate. Select the side that clearly has the most zone lines for the top surface. Secure the faceplate and block on the lathe. Use the tailstock and revolving center for support, but place a small piece of wood between the center point and the block surface. This piece of wood will prevent the point from boring into the surface, while also allowing for sufficient support.

Turn the block to shape, and then round the top area so it will resemble a mushroom. I also roll and turn out a portion of the base area. I cut a rolling trench between the outer edge and the faceplate. I do this to make the bottom area resemble the underside of a mushroom.

Using several grits of abrasive paper, prepare the surface for finishing. If you have a lot of tear-out from turning tools, use 60-grit abrasive paper for shaping. You may want to wear a dust mask while using the abrasives. You will also probably have some "mouse" on the cross-grain areas of the piece. Although some of this can be cleaned up with abrasives, a certain amount will remain. It's difficult to deal with end grain in spalted woods because it tends to tear out. It's the nature of decayed wood and little can be done about it. Remove the mushroom top from the faceplate, and mix sawdust and white glue for plugging up the faceplate screw holes. If the holes are not filled, they will show.

4. Prepare a ⅛″ plywood insert for securing in the base of the stem. Refer to Design B 19-1 for specifics on this procedure. Also, follow the procedures for making the various drilled holes in the insert.

5. The top of the mushroom should be set at an angle on the stem. This will make it look more realistic. To achieve this angle, cut the top end of the stem at a slight angle using the band saw. Do not make the angle too radical or the mushroom, already top-heavy, will tip over when assembled. Set the mushroom top on the stem, after the angle has been cut, to see how it will look (Illus. 90).

6. To secure the stem and mushroom top together, I use a piece of ½″-diameter dowel. You need to drill a ½″-diameter hole in the middle of the stem, at an angle. The hole that you need to drill in the base of the top should not be angled. Place glue on the dowel ends and in the holes and assemble. Allow the glue to dry and, if you can manage it, clamp the pieces together.

7. You may want to refer to the next chapter for some suggestions on finishing spalted wood.

C: Joined Boxes

The box designs presented in this section rely almost entirely on joinery techniques. You will be able to do most of these techniques even if you are a beginning woodworker. As a matter of fact, you will probably find the procedures for the various designs relatively simple to do. You may even prefer using more complex joints or techniques for some of your boxes instead of using the ones I've suggested.

The size of the box designs presented in this section range from the very large to the small. As in the previous designs, the dimensions for any of the boxes can be significantly increased or reduced. Remember, the size of a box should relate to the anticipated usage of the box. Thus, you can take a small design and easily enlarge it to meet your needs.

Any number of designs in this section can be used for storing large pieces or quantities of jewelry or other personal items. Some designs can be used as cigar boxes, storage containers for desk tops and, of course, grimple boxes for around the house. Some designs include a tray for additional storage. As a rule, the trays are used for storing and separating pieces of jewelry. Other designs can be made for storing recipes. These recipe boxes can be redesigned to house something else. The pencil box that's presented can be readily made into a jewelry box. You will find that these projects have a diversity of designs and possible functions.

In addition to the functional designs, this section also presents designs that can be made for holding the larger cylinder and disc musical movements. As you review the music box projects, you will see that each one could be readily used for a jewelry box or other kind of functional container. This interchangeability in box designs can be an exciting challenge for the box maker. You may prefer to use one of the jewelry box designs for housing a large cylinder musical movement. On the other hand, you may find that one of the music boxes with extended legs may be more appropriate as an elaborate jewelry chest.

The music box designs are presented in a way that will help you develop a working knowledge of the larger movements and their requirements. The designs present all the necessary information for crafting boxes that maximize the sound potential of the larger movements. Once you understand the various needs of the movement, you can readily design your own music boxes or modify some of the other designs to house a large unit. To eliminate repetition, the procedures for preparing a box to hold a large cylinder or disc movement are stated only once. While a number of the box designs in this section can be modified to house a large musical unit, you will need to refer to the music box projects for specific procedures.

You can use embellished lids with many of the box designs presented in this section. The lids that are either solid or framed lend themselves to a range of decorative inlays. While some of the box lids in this section employ designs and methods from previous projects, many present new and different options for your consideration. In some instances, the entire lid can be inlaid with a picture. This type of embellishment confronts you with some interesting and challenging design and inlay work. You may want to look over the various box designs and their inlays that are presented in this section. It's rather simple to interchange the inlays and the box designs. You may prefer using a different inlay for a box design than the one presented. I also encourage you to develop your own designs that can be inlaid on the boxes you make. Once you understand the various procedures, you can design and make any inlay you want.

Design C 22-1: Fulcrum Box (Illus. 91)

1. The name of this design is based on the way you open the lid. The lid is tapered on both ends so that when you push down one end, the lid opens at the other end. The principle is ancient and its use in boxes is historic. The design has a substantial storage area for jewelry, desk-top items, or anything else that can be placed in a long box. You can make the box with a Model 1.18 musical movement in one end and a storage area in the other. You can also make the box in various sizes. Illus. 91 shows two different-sized boxes. These are the approximate dimensions of the large fulcrum design: The length is 10"; the width is 3½"; the height is 2¼". For making the box, I use ½"-thick stock for the larger design and ⅜"-thick stock for the smaller one. The lid on the larger box needs to be ripped to a thickness of ³⁄₁₆". It's rather simple to rip the stock on the band saw. I use the thinner stock for the lid so that it will open more easily. Also, a thinner lid makes for a more attractive box.

You can use almost any wood for this kind of box. For an initial box, you may want to consider using pine. Pine is rather easy to saw to the required thickness. The bottom of the box is

Illus. 91. Fulcrum boxes

a piece of ⅛" plywood. This thickness is adequate for supporting any items that will be stored in the box. If you plan on installing a musical movement, it's an ideal thickness for a soundboard.

Because of the fulcrum lid, the design lends itself to mitred joints. This is a good design for refining or developing your mitring skills. As you will note in later procedures, the mitred joints on this box have decorative splines placed through them. Illus. 91 shows how the joints will look when the box has been completed.

2. You can make the walls of this design from a single length of stock. This one-piece approach greatly simplifies the various routing procedures that are necessary in the design. A board that is 30" long is more than adequate for cutting all four walls to length. Rip the board to a width of a little more than 2¼". I usually rip the stock at least ⅛" wider than needed in anticipation of the rough edges that will need to be sanded. If you do not have a jointer, you can clean up and square the edges on a shaper using a fence and a ¾" or 1" straight cutter. For those lacking both these tools, a 6" × 48" belt sander can do the job. Don't rule out the use of a hand plane. If you use a belt sander, be careful not to significantly change the width of the stock. You can also clean up the edges on a belt sander after the box has been assembled.

3. Before cutting the board to the lengths required for the walls, you may want to do the necessary routing. You need to rout a groove ⅜" to ½" from the bottom edge of the walls. This groove should be ⅛" or ¼" wide, depending upon the thickness of the plywood to be used for the bottom piece. The routed groove should be at least ⅛" deep to provide adequate support for the bottom section when in place.

In addition to the routed groove, you need to rout a rabbet along the top inside edge of the walls. The lid will fit in this rabbet and also fulcrum against it when opened. The rabbet should be approximately ³⁄₁₆" deep and at least ³⁄₁₆" wide. The depth of the rabbet is, of course, determined by the thickness of the lid. Depending on the depth of the rabbet, you may have to do some sanding on the lid and the top edges of the box to make them flush when the unit is assembled (Illus. 92). One of the joys of working with wood, especially when you lack the appro-

priate tools, is that you can always use abrasive paper to make things fit or work right. For routing boxes, I use a table-mounted router. A piece of pine with a clean straight edge and two bar clamps serves as a moveable fence guide.

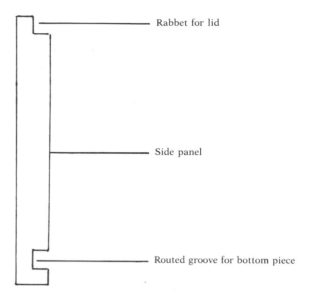

Illus. 92. Edge of fulcrum box

After adjusting the fence on the router table, using a ⅛" or ¼" straight bit (the bit size is based on the plywood thickness), rout the groove the entire length of the board. The groove, as you may recall, needs to be ⅜" to ½" from the bottom edge of the walls and at least ⅛" deep. Remember, this is the area where the bottom section will fit. Realign your router fence and, using a rabbeting bit, rout the rabbet on the top edge. The rabbeted area will hold the lid. As indicated, the rabbet should be at least ³⁄₁₆" wide and deep. Set your bit accordingly.

4. The end and side walls need to be cut to length according to how you plan on mitring the box corners. Cut two side walls to a length of 10¼". The additional ¼" in length allows for dimensional loss from the mitre saw. Also, cut the two end walls to a length of 3¾".

If you're fortunate enough to have a power mitre saw, set it at 45°. When cutting mitres, I always cut one end of each piece first. Align the board so that the mitre cut removes only the thickness of the blade. Cut mitres on one end of each of the four sides. To make the second cut, I clamp a stop block on the mitre-saw table. I adjust the block so that the second mitre cut also removes only the thickness of the blade. If the blade removes a bit more wood, it's not a problem because the stop block assures accuracy in length. You need the stop block at different points, obviously, for the side and end walls. Cut the mitres using these procedures. If you do not have a power mitre saw, use the procedures for cutting mitres with a table or radial arm saw. A mitre box with a backsaw is another option to consider.

5. Before proceeding, you need to assemble the box in order to check the fit of the mitred joints. To hold the box together for this procedure, slip large rubber bands over the entire assembly. I always use large wide rubber bands of varying lengths for clamping mitre-joint boxes together. They assure uniformity of pressure on the joints and force the joints to fit tightly together while the glue is drying.

After checking your mitred joints, remove the rubber bands and disassemble the box. Now you need to prepare the plywood according to the width of the groove cut for the bottom piece. To prepare the bottom insert, you need to measure the inside walls. Measure the length of the side and end walls between the inside edges of the mitre cuts. Also measure the exact depth of the routed groove, and add this measurement to the lengths of the side and end walls. This procedure should give you the exact length and width of the plywood bottom insert. Cut the bottom piece to these dimensions.

To assure the fit of the bottom piece, reassemble the box with the bottom piece placed in the grooves. Secure the assembly with rubber bands. Check the mitred joints, especially the bottom part of the joints, to see that they're not open. If the plywood insert is too large, it will force the joints open. If the bottom section is too large, determine whether it's the length or width and then remove the extra wood accordingly. You may want to assemble the box again to check the fit. It's much easier to solve these kinds of problems before you have glue spread in the grooves and on the joint surfaces.

6. Using abrasive paper or a belt sander, bring the inside surface of the walls to finishing readiness. Be careful that you don't round off the inside edges of the mitre. Do not sand the outside walls.

7. To glue the box, first squirt some wood glue on a piece of paper. Using a small nail or wood splinter, randomly place glue in the grooves that will hold the bottom piece. Be certain you get glue on the bottom shoulder of the groove because this is where the insert will rest. Spread glue lightly and with care so you don't end up having glue marks on the inside of the box. Wipe off any glue spillage and lightly sand the area. Now spread glue on the mitres with your fingertips. Be sure you glue both sides of the joint. Spread a thin coat of glue over the entire surface. If you use too much glue, it will squeeze out and mark the inside corners of the box.

The easiest way of assembling the box after gluing is to lay one of the side walls on a flat surface. Now slip the plywood bottom into the glued groove. Put both end walls in place. Before placing the final side wall, make sure you have some large rubber bands, or some other means of clamping, close at hand. Place the side wall in position, turn the entire box right side up, and slide it against something that will hold it in place. It helps if you have a board or something clamped on your assembly table so you can force the box against it when placing the rubber bands. Place a rubber band over the end nearest you and stretch it so it slips over the other end of the box. This is a rather awkward procedure, but one you will pick up rather quickly. Watch what you're doing with the rubber band, however. If it breaks or slips off, you may get smacked in the chest. If this happens, you may be surprised to the point where you let go of the box, and then the box will fall apart. You will need to use two or three rubber bands for clamping. Place one near the bottom of the box, one in the middle, and the last near the top. Allow the glue to dry.

8. There are any number of options for decorating the mitred joints. Of course, you may prefer not to enhance the joints at all, letting them stand as crafted.

One way of decorating the joints is placing ¼"- or ⅜"-diameter plugs in the surface of the walls around the corners. Plan the dimensional locations, sizes, and number of plugs you want by the joints. Prepare the appropriate-sized plugs, drill the holes, and then glue and tap in place. I frequently use padouk or hedge for decorative plugs on the corners. You can sand the

plugs flush with the walls when all the plugs are in place. As an alternative, you can use plugs with varying diameters, alternating the sizes up and down the surface near the corners. Something else that works is using square plugs cut to a dimension at which they can be tapped into the round holes. The square plugs provide a very interesting effect. When tapped in place, they force the wood in the hole to become square. It's best to taper the end that will be placed in the hole. This simplifies the entry process.

I frequently embellish the mitred joints with decorative splines. While you can cut the splines using a table-saw jig, I have developed my own jig for use on a router table (Illus. 93). The piece to be routed is set in the jig, with the corner pointed downwards, and the entire assembly is moved into and through a straight router bit. I use a clamped board as a fence or guide on the router table. The fence is adjusted according to where on the corners you want the spline located. Once it is set, you can cut the spline recess in the exact location in all four corners. When you use the router and jig setup, you can vary the width of the splines. Depending on the size of the box or desired spline width, you can use ⅛″, ¼″, or ½″ straight bits for making the cut. By raising or lowering the router bit, you can also vary the length of the cut and thus the length of the spline itself.

I make the jig from 1″ or ¾″ pine, with ⅛″ strips on each side of the cutout area. The strips support the walls of the box and allow for different-sized boxes to fit into the cutout for routing. I make a pencil mark in the middle of the inside support board. To use the jig, you simply place the corner of the box in the cutout area, align the joint cut with the pencil mark, firmly hold the box and jig together, and slide over the router bit. This, of course, assumes that you have set the appropriate depth of cut of the router bit.

If you have sharp bits and the spline recess is not cut too deep, you should not have any tear-out. You may, however, place small strips on both sides of the corner to be cut, hold them in place, and then slide the assembly over the bit. This should prevent any tear-out. If you review Illus. 91, you can see the end result of this method.

After the spline recesses have been cut on the router, rip strips of the wood to be used for the actual splines. Use either a contrasting wood or one of the colorful ones mentioned earlier. You need to cut these strips to the exact thickness that will allow them to fit tightly into the spline recess. For example, if you used a ¼″ router bit, cut strips that are ¼″ thick. You may want to check the thickness of the cut spline recess for accuracy. Often, especially when they are old or dull, bits are not dimensionally accurate. After ripping the spline strips, cut them to an over-sized length and width for slipping into the recess. They're much easier to handle and to insert in the recess if they're cut oversized. Spread glue in the recess and tap the spline in place. Check to make sure that the inserts are tight against the bottom of the recess. If they aren't, there will be small holes between the wall and the spline. Allow the glue to dry, bandsaw off the excess spline wood, and sand the entire wall surface to finishing readiness.

9. To prepare the lid, measure the internal length and width of the top rabbeted area. Also, measure the depth of the rabbet. Transfer these dimensions to your lid wood and cut the lid. Check for fit. If necessary, reduce the size of the lid. If the lid is too tight, it will not fulcrum out of the rabbet. So that the lid will fulcrum off the bottom edge of the rabbet, sand the bottom end areas of the lid to a gradual taper (Illus. 94). Place the lid in the box and press down on one end. The lid should raise up on the other end. To increase the opening of the lid, remove more

wood from the taper. I sometimes put a ⅜" decorative plug in the surface at both ends of the lid. These plugs serve as touch points for the opening process and also look rather nice.

10. If desired, you can install a musical movement in one end of the design. However, you need ample space under the bottom piece for the winding key to fit. Place the movement in the box and mark the various hole requirements. These dimensions are the same as those shown in Illus. 26.

To protect the movement from objects in the box and to serve as a support if you use a glass insert, cut a wall and place it in the box next to the movement edge. If you will be using a glass insert, you should glue a support shoulder on the inside end wall, directly opposite the divider wall. Then attach the glass to the shoulder and wall. I usually rabbet a groove in the divider wall for supporting the glass (Illus. 95).

Whether you use a glass insert or not, you can make an on/off system with a small piece of dowel. Place a ⅛" piece of dowel in the bottom

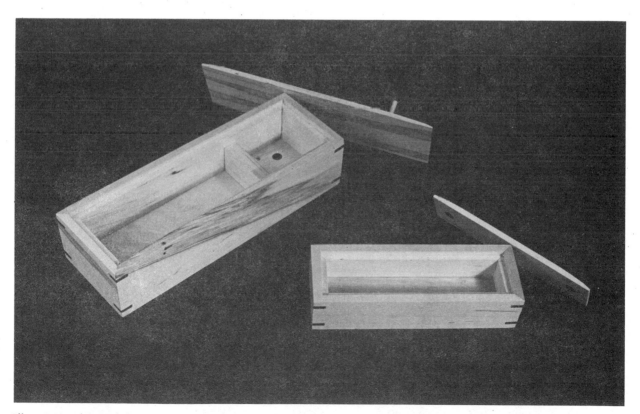

Illus. 94. Fulcrum lids and inside of boxes

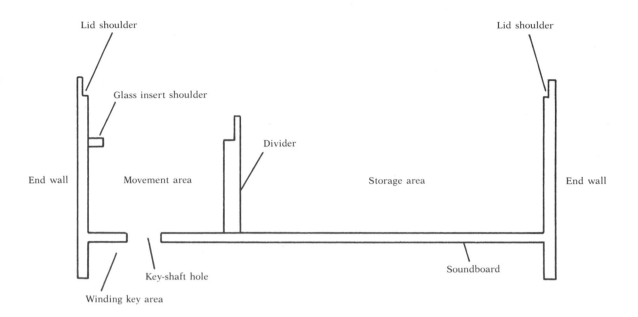

Illus. 95. Musical movement area—side view

of the lid, aligned directly between the flywheel and spring housing of the movement. When the lid opens, the dowel raises and releases the flywheel, and then the movement begins to play. If you use a glass insert, you need to drill a small hole through the glass for the dowel to move in and out of. There are any number of suppliers that stock glass-cutting bits in various diameters. To simplify the entire procedure, you can use Plexiglas acrylic plastic for covering the movement and a standard bit for drilling the hole. I prefer glass over movements, but this is a matter of personal taste.

If you use the dowel on/off system in the lid, be certain you measure carefully after you've placed the movement in the box. You must place the dowel in the lid so that it will intercept the flywheel. Usually, it's best to do this when the dowel drops between the flywheel and the spring housing.

11. Finish the box as desired or refer to the next chapter for some assistance.

Design C 23-1: Pencil Box (Illus. 96)

1. Although this design has been around a long time, it's still one of the most popular. It seems that any small box with a sliding lid is considered a pencil box by most people. You can make this pencil box design as large or as tiny as desired. I've made the box with 2″ walls and 1″ side panels. It can also be made much smaller.

You may want to revise the dimensions of the box shown in Illus. 96. The box has mitred walls and its sides and ends are decorated with ¼″ strips that are also mitred at the corners. The strips are placed in routed grooves in the walls. The sliding lid has a ½″-diameter knob extending from its surface. You may want to cut

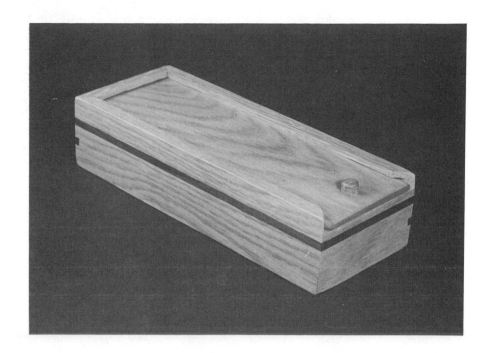

Illus. 96. Pencil box

a finger recess into the surface instead of using the knob. If desired, you can embellish the lid with a surface or sculptured inlay.

2. The box is 10⅝" long, 4¼" wide, and 2½" high. It's made from ½"-thick red oak. The lid needs to be ripped to a ¼" thickness so that it will slide in a ¼" routed groove. The bottom of the box is a piece of ¼" plywood, also set into a ¼" routed groove.

3. Cut the sides and end pieces to the appropriate length and width. Mitre the ends of all pieces. Assemble the panels to check for fit.

4. You need to rout grooves on the inside walls of both the top and bottom of all four panels. You should rout the grooves ¼" from the top and bottom edges and to a depth of ¼". It is especially important to make the lid groove at least ¼" deep.

Illus. 97. Pencil box with lid removed

5. Cut both the ¼″ plywood bottom piece and the ¼″ lid piece to dimension. Remember to add the depth of the routed grooves onto their length and width. Assemble the box and check for fit. If the joints are forced open, you need to remove some wood, especially from the bottom section. You can reduce the lid to fit later.

6. Before assembling the box, you should cut out the top portion of one end wall. You should make the cut at the bottom of the routed groove. You need to remove this section so the lid, with its knob, can slide in and out over the remaining piece. Another design for this box leaves the piece in place and allows the lid to slide through it.

7. To assemble the box, first spread glue on the joints and then in the grooves of the bottom section. When the box has been assembled, clamp it together with large rubber bands until the glue is dry.

8. So that the lid will slide freely in the routed grooves, you need to taper its edges. For reasons of appearance, do not taper the front edge.

Test the lid for fit. It it's too tight, remove more wood from the edges. Continue the process until the lid slides in and out freely. Drill a ½″-diameter hole and glue a small plug in place for the lid opener (Illus. 97).

9. To rout the inlay grooves in the wall surfaces, use a ¼″ straight bit on a table-mounted router with a fence/guide. Set the fence/guide to a position that will rout the groove on the surface where you want it. You should rout two different sets of grooves at two different locations on the walls. Rout the grooves to a depth of ³⁄₁₆″. After the grooves have been routed, prepare strips of walnut that you will insert into the grooves. The pieces need to be mitred at the corners so they will fit properly in place. Spread glue in the grooves and insert the inlays. Allow the glue to dry.

10. Using a belt sander, remove the excess wood from the inlays. Sand the box walls and lid surfaces to finishing readiness. Finish the box as desired or refer to the next chapter.

Design C 24-1: Rectangular Box (Illus. 98)

1. This small but functional box can be used for storing jewelry or other items, or for housing a musical movement. The lid, as shown in Illus. 98, has a strip of laminated veneer through its entire length. This makes for a very clean-looking lid design, but one that also exposes the wood. Should you want to design a more elaborate embellishment, there is sufficient surface

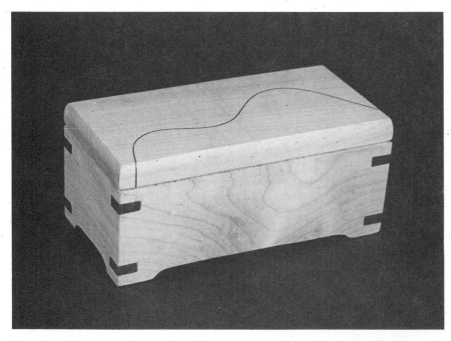

Illus. 98. Rectangular box

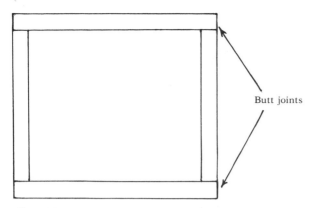

Illus. 99. Butt joints—top view

on the lid to do so. The joints on this box are mitred and enhanced with splines. You may want to use a simple butt joint with screws and decorative plugs (Illus. 99). These are the overall dimensions of the design: It's 7″ long, 3½″ wide, and 3″ high (including the thickness of the lid). As with other designs, the box can easily be increased or reduced in size depending on your needs and interests. The wood thickness, at least for the dimensions of this design, can be reduced but not increased. Thicker walls on a box with these dimensions would look heavy and overbuilt. They would also significantly reduce the internal storage area.

If you don't have a planer, you can use a band saw with a ½″ blade to re-saw any stock you want to use. When I make boxes from stock that has been ripped on the band saw, I put the cut surface on the outside of the box walls. After

I've assembled the box, I bring the box surface to finishing readiness with a belt sander. This is a quick and easy way of obtaining ½″ or thinner stock that can be used for making many different box designs.

While you may prefer to make the box from one of the hardwoods, pine is a good choice for an initial box. Easily ripped to thickness on the band saw, pine provides an excellent surface for a range of decorative designs on both the walls and lid. After you've perfected some of your procedures on boxes made from pine, turn to the hardwoods for crafting similar boxes.

2. Cut the end and side walls to the width and length desired or to the dimensions of the box shown in Illus. 98. This procedure assumes that you are using wood that's ½″ thick or wood that's even thinner.

3. To make the box more attractive, I frequently cut out a decorative area from the bottom edge of the box. I generally make this cutout on all four sides to give the box a more balanced appearance (Illus. 100). Even though making the cutouts may appear to be a simple task, it's wise to make a pattern for the front and back walls as well as the side walls. It's easy to make a pattern for design in Illus. 100 by using a piece of construction paper that's the exact length of the long walls and the side walls. Fold the pattern paper exactly in two and work out the design. You need to measure from the end and draw the design to the fold. You can have legs on the box that are 1″ long and a curve on the inside wall of the leg to an opening that extends

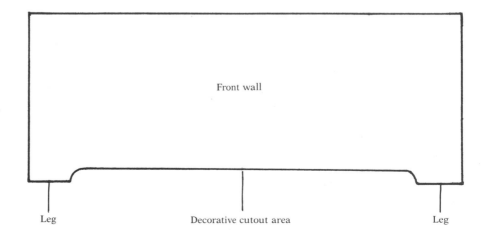

Front wall

Leg   Decorative cutout area   Leg

Illus. 100. Panel cutout design—front view

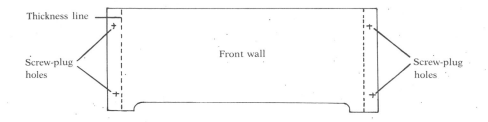

Illus. 101. Wall thickness lines—front view

to the leg on the opposite end. You can draw this kind of design on the pattern to the fold. Cut out the area with a scissors while the pattern is folded, open the pattern, and then trace on the wall surface. The design should be dimensionally perfect and look balanced. Follow the same procedure for the end walls. Using paper for patterning bottom edge designs not only makes complicated designs possible, but also assures dimensional accuracy. I frequently use this procedure on music box designs so that the sounds will emerge from the soundboard. This is another way of enhancing the volume produced by the movement. Cut out the decorative design that you traced on the bottom wall edges.

4. Before you can decide on the bottom piece for the box, you need to make a decision about the kind of joint you plan to use. If the bottom piece is to be placed in grooves routed in the inside walls of the box, the way these grooves are cut is partially determined by the type of joint that's used. With a mitred joint, you can rout the groove through a portion of the joint and it will not show when the box is assembled. If you use a butt joint, you should not cut the groove along the entire length of the butted walls. The ends of these walls are exposed on the sides of the boxes so that the grooves will show. More about this procedure shortly. If you plan on mitring the box joints, refer to Design C 22-1 for procedures on cutting and embellishing the joints. You may also want to refer to some of the designs that appear later in the book for the procedures used with the larger boxes. If you want to use butt joints, refer to Illus. 99 before proceeding. This is a rather easy way of assembling a box and, with decorative

plugs, the box looks very attractive. I always use screws for assembling the butt joint, but more from habit than necessity.

5. The end and side walls should already be cut to the appropriate lengths. To prepare the front and back walls for drilling screw and plug holes for the butt joint, trace the thickness of the boards on the edge surface of the walls. I usually set one of the side or end pieces on edge and trace a line from it. You need this wall thickness so that the drilled holes through which the screws will pass will be centered. It also gives you a guide for measuring where the holes should be placed on the surface (Illus. 101). You should put at least two screws—one high, one low—through the front and back walls into the butted side walls. You may, however, drill blind holes for holding plugs. The number of blind holes you drill depends on how embellished you want the joint area to look. You can drill as many blind holes for plugs as desired. I usually use a ¼"-diameter bit and plugs for the smaller boxes. You may, however, prefer ⅜"-diameter plugs.

Drill the screw holes to the plug diameter to a depth of at least halfway through the board. You need to leave support in the hole for the screwhead. When all the holes have been drilled on the front and back walls, drill a smaller hole through the remaining part of the plug-screw hole. This last hole should be a bit larger than the diameter of the screws to be used. It makes putting screws into the butted wall much easier. You don't have to screw them halfway through the walls before you hit the butt edge surface. This method makes assembling a little easier. The walls are now prepared for assembly, but before it can be done, you need to rout the inside of the walls to hold the bottom section of the box. Refer to Design C 22-1 for routing and preparing the bottom section to dimension. With the butt joint, as mentioned earlier, you do not rout the groove over the entire length of the front and back walls. A good procedure is using the wall thickness already traced on the front and back wall surfaces as a guide for routing. When you are routing the groove for holding the bottom section, cut beyond the traced line a little more than the depth of the router. While this cut will permit the bottom section to fit in the groove, it will not show on the wall edges. You can rout the side panels their entire length.

6. Assemble the box using the gluing procedures for the bottom section, as discussed in Design C 22-1. With the butt joints, spread a light coat of glue on the surfaces to be joined. Drill a small pilot hole through the plug-screw hole. Assemble using small wood screws. If your screwdriver tip is too wide to slip into the ¼" screw-plug hole, grind it narrower so it doesn't rip out the hole, especially the top edge. I always clamp the butt joints although they've been assembled with screws. When the glue is dry, glue and tap the decorative plugs in place. With a belt sander, bring the plugs flush with the wall's surface. Prepare the surface for finishing.

7. With the base of the box completed, you can now make plans for the lid. If you want a strip of veneer running through the lid, you need to cut the width of the lid oversized. This is to allow for wood loss when the lid is cut into

pieces for receiving the veneer laminate. Incidentally, the lid thickness should be the same as the wall thickness. Before making the cut through the lid, draw a line—either straight, curved, or at an angle—to represent the inlay and serve as a cutting guide. Remember that the lid and veneer will have to be clamped while the glue is drying, so make the cut clampable. Cut the lid into the desired parts. Prepare an oversized strip of veneer to be placed between the parts. Glue all surfaces and clamp together. Be certain the ends of the pieces don't slide out of alignment with one another when you tighten the clamps. Allow the glue to dry. When the glue is dry, cut the lid to final dimension and bring the surfaces and edges to finishing readiness. If you prefer to use one of the inlay designs presented earlier for the lid, refer back to the appropriate procedures before continuing.

8. A brass hinge system is needed on this design. Refer to Design A 6-1 for the procedures involved in preparing and installing metal hinges. I often use a small brass chain with small escutcheon pins as a lid stopper. The chain can be pinned to an inside side wall and to the underside of the lid directly over the side pin. Cut the chain to a length that will allow the lid to fall back far enough so it will not close when left open.

9. Finish the box as desired. If you want to make a music box, refer to some of the designs that present both dimensions and procedures related to the bottom section that holds the musical movement.

Design C 25-1: Jewelry Box with Tray (Illus. 102)

1. This is a sizeable design that provides the user with considerable storage area plus a removable, divided tray. It is especially popular with people who have quite a collection of jewelry and want a box where it can be organized and stored. You can, of course, omit the tray and use the box as a general storage container. It is deep enough to hold all kinds of items. You can also increase or reduce the size of the design. You may want to alter the dimensions so that the box will accommodate a particular item. You have any number of dimensional options with this design.

The design in Illus. 102 is made from low-grade white ash. I used a large alternating lapped joint along with plugs and screws for assembly. You will note the lid stopper on this design. The lid stopper, as indicated in an earlier project, prevents the lid from falling back over the back edge of the box when opened. This is an excellent alternative to using chains or metal lid supports. The lid stopper also keeps the lid open, allowing easy access to the items in storage. You may want to integrate a stopper in your design. The box also employs a 12"-long brass jewelry box hinge that is recessed in the edge of the ball wall. In the under-side of the lid, I cut finger slots for opening the lid. Including the 1″ (4/4's) solid lid, these are the overall dimensions of the design: It's 8″ wide (not including the length of the lid stopper), 6″ high, and 16″ long. The tray is 14⅜″ long, 6½″ wide, and 2″ deep. The tray rests inside the top portion of the box on support pieces attached with glue and screws to the side walls. The stock used for the box and lid is 1″ (4/4's) thick. For the tray, I use ½″-thick stock.

2. Cut the front and back walls from your stock to a length of 16″ and a width of 5¼″. Cut the two side walls to a length of 8″ and a width of 4¼″. I rip these pieces on a band or table saw, and then cut them to length on a radial arm saw. You may want to cut the width a bit over-sized so that you can square the edges on a jointer or a shaper with a 1″ straightedge cutter. As mentioned previously, a shaper with a straightedge cutter works very well on edges if you don't have a jointer. Be certain to keep the

width of the boards dimensionally the same. I usually don't cut the solid lid until the box has been assembled. This assures more accurate dimensions.

3. To make the alternating lapped joints, you should begin with the front and back walls. The cuts for the laps are made from these walls, and then traced on the side walls for cutting. To begin the process, you need to trace the thickness of the walls on the ends of the outside surface of the front and back panels. You can do this by placing one of the side walls on edge and tracing its thickness onto the walls. With a ruler, find the center of the width (2⅝″) of the walls, and mark it on the traced thickness line. Draw a horizontal line from this point on the traced thickness line to the edge of the wall. This procedure marks out the exact size of the lap joints for this design. Illus. 103 shows this layout and the portions of the walls that are to be cut out for the lapped joints.

The back panel should have its cutout sec-

Illus. 102. Jewelry box with tray

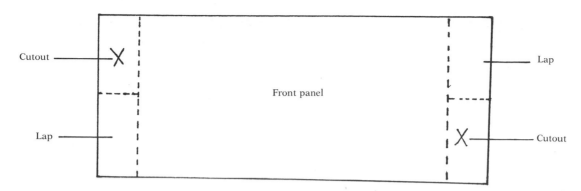

Illus. 103. Lapped joints—front view

tions on opposite edges to the front panel. They should alternate from top edge to bottom edge. This procedure will result in your side walls also having alternating cutouts and laps. You should always mark the portion of the wall that is to be cut out. It also helps in cutting and assembling if you number the various laps on the front, back, and side walls. This simplifies the cutting procedure and eliminates the possibility of error. For example, I will number the cutout area on one end of the front panel with the number *1*. The lap from the side wall that is to fit into it is also numbered *1*. You can assign numbers like this to all the joint components on the box.

4. A band saw with a set rip fence works best for cutting out the marked areas for the joints. I set the rip fence with a stop block for cutting on the traced lines. Proceed to cut out the marked areas on the front and back walls. Do not cut out the side walls at this point. It may seem that, with the rip fence set, it would be a good time to also cut the side walls. It isn't. For a good tight fit, you need to trace each cutout area from the front and back panels onto the side panels. When these are eventually cut out on the band saw, you need to cut on the inside of the line towards the end of the board. Trace the cutout areas from the laps of the front and back walls onto the side walls. Use a sharp pencil and get close to the edges when tracing. Remember to use a numbering system. The traced cutout should be the same number as the lap it

was traced from. Set the band saw fence and, if desired, use a stop block to cut the side-wall traced areas inside the line. When the side walls are done, assemble the box to check for appearance and fit. You may want to clamp it together with rubber bands to get a better look at the joints and how they fit. If there is some overlap of the laps, they can be sanded off after the box has been assembled.

5. The next procedures are preparing a bottom piece for the box and routing grooves in the inside walls that will hold the bottom section. Before you begin these procedures and while the box is still loosely assembled with rubber bands, label the outside surfaces of each wall. For example, write *top* at the top edge and *front wall* on the front wall. You need to make some notes on the surface along with the numerical marking of joints you should have already done. While this may seem a bit simplistic, it's well worth the effort before you begin routing. You can easily remove the pencil marks when you sand the outside walls in preparation for the finishing process.

On boxes of this size, I use ¼″ plywood for the bottom piece. I have found that ⅛″ plywood is too thin and tends to sag in the middle if heavy items are stored in the box. You definitely want to use cabinet-grade plywood for these larger boxes. If you have a planer, you can also plane a bottom piece from the same wood the box is made from. For those who can afford it, numerous hardwood dealers stock surfaced ¼″ stock.

A contrasting wood also looks good for the bottom piece.

Measuring the inside dimensions of the box for cutting the bottom piece requires a little time and thought. You need the length of the front or back wall and the length of a side wall. Then you must add the routed groove depth in all four walls to these dimensions. Combined, these dimensions will give you the exact length and width of the bottom section. To obtain the measurements from the walls, you need to measure from the edge of the cutout up to the point where the lap extends from the edge of the wall. Illus. 104 shows these points on a box wall. As mentioned, you need this measurement from one long wall and one short wall. You need to remember that the bottom is set into the grooved recess that is routed in all four walls. Thus the depth of the groove must be added from all four walls to the length and width of the bottom piece. Cut the bottom section to dimensions.

To rout the grooves for holding the bottom piece, determine where you want them placed in relation to the bottom edges of the box. On large boxes, I usually rout the grooves approximately ¼″ to ½″ from the bottom edges of the walls. There is no need to waste storage space, so place them as near to the bottom as possible. If you get too close to the edge, the router bit could break the edge support off.

It's easiest to rout the grooves with a table-mounted router (refer to Design C 22-1) and a fence/guide. For a ¼″ bottom piece, you obviously need a ¼″ straight router bit. Mark the edge of the wall where the bit will enter for cutting the groove. Set your router fence accordingly. Set the depth of cut a hair deeper than the depth used for measuring your bottom piece. This small overcut will assure that the bottom section will fit comfortably in the walls' grooves. Before routing, check to make sure you will be cutting the groove on the inside walls. Look at the notes on your outside wall surfaces. Also, you do not want to rout through the entire length of the lap. If you do, the groove will show when you assemble the box. Rout the grooves in the laps just far enough so that the bottom piece can comfortably fit in them. Think about the procedure before you do the actual routing. When the rout must be started on a lap, place the wall against the router fence/guide. Holding

tightly onto the piece, force it down into the router bit and rout the groove in the wall. Rout the bottom support grooves in all walls according to these procedures.

Assemble the box, with the bottom section in place, using rubber bands. If the bottom piece is too large, cutting a little wood from it is easier than rerouting the wall grooves. Reassemble and check for fit.

6. To prepare for the final assembly of the box, you need to mark and drill plug-screw holes in all the laps. Your box has eight laps so you need to find the center of each lap and mark for drilling. Because of the size of this box, I use a ⅜″ wood bit and plugs. You can cut plugs from a ⅜″ dowel, but I prefer to cut them using a plug cutter. While you can cut plugs from any wood, I prefer to make the plugs from the same wood that the box is crafted from. This is not one of my more decorative designs. It's a plain, straightforward box that relies totally on the wood for aesthetic effect. I use a wood screw for assembly that has a rather narrow-thread diameter and is at least ⅝″ long.

With the screw-plug holes marked in the center of the laps, drill the holes. The depth of the screw-plug holes is arbitrary, but I tend to drill at least halfway through the wall. I want to leave ample wood in the hole for supporting the screwhead as I tighten the screws in place. You should probably do this according to your own shop procedures. You may prefer a deeper hole.

After you have drilled the screw-plug holes, using a bit that is a little larger than the diameter of the screw thread, drill through the wood remaining in the screw hole. This simply makes the screws easier to turn into the side walls when assembling. You won't have to thread the screws through all the extra wood. You should have within reach an electric drill with a very small bit for drilling pilot holes for the screws. Also, you will want to have some large wide rubber bands on hand for use when assembling.

7. Before spreading the glue on the laps and cutouts, spread it in the bottom section grooves. Using a small nail or wood splinter, spread the glue in the grooves, concentrating on the bottom. Don't use too much glue or it will simply squeeze out when the bottom section is put in place. Wipe any glue off the walls. When the glue is dry, sand over the areas with

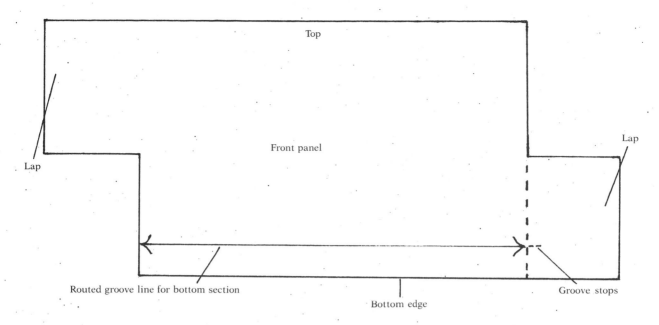

Illus. 104. Routed areas—front view

fine-grit abrasive paper or the glue will stain the wood. While you can use warm water on a cloth to wipe off glue, often the water will also stain the wood.

Spread glue on the laps and cutout joint edges. Again, don't use too much glue. More glue is not better. Assemble the box by laying the back wall, outside face down, on a flat surface. Place the bottom piece in the grooves and align. Next set the side walls in place being certain that the bottom section slips into the grooves. Place the front wall on the assembly, again being certain that the bottom section slides in the groove. Turn the box, carefully, upright. Slide it against something that will hold it in place, and stretch rubber bands around the assembly. Remember, those rubber bands can hurt if they break or slip.

After drilling small pilot holes, insert the screws in the screw-plug holes. After all the screws are tightened, check for any gaps in the joints or along the wall edges. If you find any, use a small bar clamp or similar clamping device and try to clamp them out. Allow the glue to dry while clamped. Spread glue in the screw-plug holes and then tap the plugs in place. When the glue is dry, you can sand the plugs flush when you sand the entire box surface with the belt sander.

8. Use a belt sander to rough-finish the box walls. Bring the walls and joints flush. Using finer grits and a pad sander, prepare the box surfaces for finishing.

9. The next procedure is preparing the lid. Place the lid stock, top surface down, on a flat surface and then set the box upside down on it. If the lid board has a good straight edge, use it for the front edge of the lid. Mark the side edges of the lid from the box onto the board surface. If you plan on using a lid stopper, this must also be drawn on the lid surface. I tend to make the lid stopper at least one-third the length of the lid. It usually extends away from the back wall of the box at least 1¾". Although these dimensions are a matter of personal taste, they are also, in part, determined by the width of the lid board you are using. If you plan on using a lid stopper, make it look consistent with your design. You will need to mark the back edge of the box on the lid board surface and then draw the stopper freehand. Cut the lid to the marked dimensions. A combination of a radial arm saw for cutting the lid to length and a band saw for cutting the back edge with its lid stopper is a good way to proceed. Check the lid fit on the box.

Bring the lid edges to finishing readiness. The end grain on the sides of the lid usually needs some extra work. Also, clean up the curve on the lid stopper. I usually rout the top edges of the lid with a rounding-over bit. All other edges on the box and lid need to be lightly rolled with abrasive paper. I simply take the sharp edge off. Using a belt sander or finishing pad sander, bring both lid surfaces to finishing readiness. Using the pad sander, roll the top of the lid stopper to a slow taper towards the back. With the roller end of a belt sander, make finger slots at the side edges on the bottom of the lid. I make the slots about 1½" back from the front edge of the lid. You may prefer to cut some other configuration in the lid that will make it easier to open. Another option is omitting finger slots altogether.

10. Before placing a long brass jewelry hinge or a pair of butt hinges on the box and lid, you may want to make the tray. The first procedure in the design gives you some approximate dimensions for a tray that you may want to consider. In measuring the internal dimensions of the box for the tray, you will want to reduce them by at least ⅛" both in length and width. The tray needs to be made so that it can be easily removed. In planning your tray design, you may want to consider using small lapped joints. You can follow the same procedures for them as used for the box. Another option is making mitred joints with decorative splines or plugs. For these procedures, refer back to Design C 22-1. You may also want to consider the butt joint presented in Design C 24-1.

I tend to make the trays rather sturdy because they're subjected to considerable use. I usually make the frame of the tray from ½"-thick stock. You can obviously reduce this thickness to ⅜" or ¼", depending on your own design ideas. You can easily rip the stock to the desired thickness using a ½" blade on the band saw. For the bottom of the tray, I use ¼" plywood or whatever wood I used for the bottom of the box. I rout a groove in the walls to support the bottom piece. Again, the procedures are the same as those used for the box proper. The bottom piece is placed in routed grooves approximately ¼" from the bottom edges. If you do not have a router, the bottom piece can still be inside the walls. Cut the length and width of the bottom section to the exact internal dimensions of the box or tray. Glue strips on the inside walls approximately ¼" from the bottom edges to support the bottom section. The bottom piece can then be glued to these support strips.

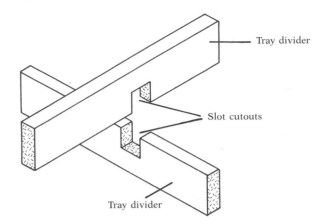

Illus. 105. Tray divider slots

For added security, you can place small screws through the bottom section and into the support pieces.

Usually, I cut, rout, and assemble the frame walls and the bottom section of the tray before adding any dividers. When the dividers have been cut and put in place, I glue the edges against the walls and secure them with screws through the bottom piece. These divider procedures would be different if you wanted to rout grooves vertically in the frame walls for holding the dividers. The divider grooves would be routed down the side walls and into the bottom section grooves. The width of the divider grooves would be dependent on the thickness of the divider stock. These routing procedures for divider grooves need to be done prior to assembling the frame and bottom section of the tray. You can do all the routing on a table-mounted router using a fence/guide. It's important, however, to have a dimensional plan for the tray dividers and to lay it out on the tray-frame edges and walls before routing.

Where the dividers intersect in the tray, you can use slot cutouts instead of cutting the dividers into pieces. You should make the slot cutouts in each divider at the point they intersect in the tray. They need to be cut to the exact thickness of the divider wood and halfway into each divider section. Illus. 105 shows how the dividers look with the slot cutouts. After the slots have been made, you need to place the slot of one divider into the slot of the other. The top edges of both pieces should be flush. If the edges are not flush, remove a bit more wood from the length of the slots. Make the tray with as many dividers as desired or according to your design based on user needs. Assemble the tray and dividers and then bring the surfaces to finishing readiness.

11. To support the tray inside the box, I cut two small strips approximately ¼″ square and 4″ long. You need to place the tray in the box to make sure that a ¼″ square support piece is ample for the tray to rest on. It may be necessary for you to increase the width of the support piece. Measure the height of the tray and then mark this dimension on the inside of the two side walls where the tray supports will be secured. I usually make two small marks on the walls separated from each other by about 3″. These two marks make it easier to align the support piece on the wall and secure it at the right point. Remember that you should place the top edge of the support piece on the bottom edge of the two marks on the side walls.

To keep the tray supports in place, I screw and glue them in place. I drill two small holes, placed towards the end of the support piece, for the screw threads to pass through. Use round-head screws or countersink flathead screws when assembling the supports. Drill a small pi-

lot hole, with the support in place, into the wall. Be careful not to drill through the wall. Spread glue on the supports and then screw them into place. When the glue is dry, test the supports with the tray. The tray and the wall edges should be flush when the tray is resting on the supports.

12. For placement of the hinges, refer to the procedures in Design A 6-1. If the lid has a lid stopper, you will need to mark the hinge location on the underside of the lid more carefully. Approach the task slowly, both measuring and marking before drilling holes and securing the hinge on the lid. As indicated earlier, I use a 12″ jewelry box hinge on this design. If you decide to use butt hinges, you may want to consider a more costly pair than the usual discount shop variety. Because of the weight of the lid and its continual use, rather substantial hinges are required.

13. Finish the box as desired. You may want to review the chapter on finishing for a few ideas on products and methods that I find helpful in this process.

Design C 26-1: Large Box with Inlaid Face (Illus. 106)

1. This is a rather nutty design, but one that's fun to make. It demonstrates how you can make a decoration with a touch of humor on a box lid. Furthermore, the design shows how inlays can be both affixed to and inserted in an inlay surface.

The mitred lid with walls is quite different from the solid lid. You rout a plywood insert into the walls of the lid. This type of lid design significantly changes the overall appearance of the box and also provides new and different options for inlay work. An inlay background can be set into the lid, which affords large and picturesque designs.

This box design is 8¾″ wide, 10½″ long, and 3½″ high. Except for its height (1¼″), the lid has the same dimensions as the box. The wall thickness of this design is ½″. This box design has short front and back walls and long side walls. The design employs a standard metal lid support that holds the lid open when in use. It does not include a jewelry tray although one could certainly be included. This design is large enough to have a tray as well as a large storage

area. Because of its size, it's ideal for general storage. In your planning and design work, you

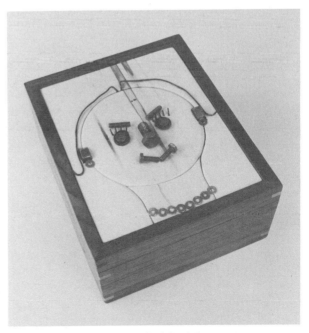

Illus. 106. Large box with inlaid face

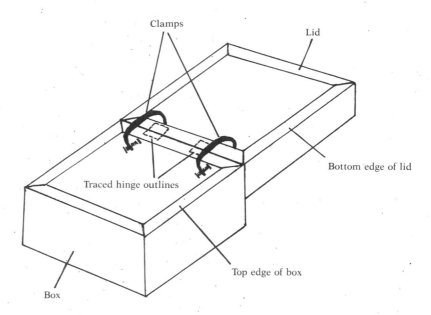

Clamps

Lid

Bottom edge of lid

Traced hinge outlines

Top edge of box

Box

Illus. 107. Preparations for hinge placement

may discover a wide range of possible functions for this box.

2. Cut the box and lid walls to the lengths desired or to those presented in the first procedure. As mentioned, I use ½"-thick stock for the design, but you can reduce or increase it. However, don't use stock that's thicker than ⅝" unless you significantly increase the overall dimensions of the box.

When you cut the mitred joints, refer to the procedures in Design C 22-1. You may want to follow these procedures for cutting mitres or other things that you normally do in your shop. As indicated in Design C 22-1, I use a power mitre saw. You may prefer or have to use a table or radial arm saw for cutting the mitres. In any event, when you cut the mitres, be sure to maintain the exact length of the pieces.

3. I use ¼"-thick plywood for the lid insert as well as the bottom section of the box. I glue both of them into routed ¼" grooves in the walls. I cut the grooves on a table-mounted router with a fence/guide and a ¼" straight bit. You may want to refer to Design C 22-1 for more detailed procedures. For this design, the plywood bottom section should be placed at least ¼" up from the bottom edges of the box. The plywood lid insert should be placed ac-

cording to your planned inlay design. For example, with this inlay design, I use a piece of soft maple that is ⅜" thick for the inlay background. The inlay background needs to be recessed at least ⅛" from the top edges of the lid. Thus, I rout the ¼" insert grooves ½" from the top edges. You can, of course, lay out the insert position measuring either from the top or bottom edges of the lid.

When a box has this type of lid design, the planning and design process becomes critical. You may want parts of your inlay to protrude from the background inlay. If so, the plywood insert should be placed farther away from the top edge of the lid. A number of later projects employ this same lid design, but use veneer glued to the insert surface. The veneer is slightly recessed in the lid to prevent wear and also to provide a more attractive appearance. With these designs, the lid inserts have been placed near the top edges of the lid. Thus, before cutting the insert grooves in the lid walls, you should have a good idea of how you plan to embellish the lid. Incidentally, you rout the lid insert into place the same way the bottom section of the box is done. Both the lid and box groove routing should be done at the same time using the same depth of cut.

4. Before gluing the assembly, test-assemble the box and the lid using large rubber bands. Be certain the bottom section and the lid insert fit comfortably into their respective grooves without forcing the joints open. Using wood glue and the rubber bands as clamps, assemble the box with its bottom section and lid insert in place. You may want to refer to Design C 22-1 for a discussion on gluing methods and using rubber bands as clamps. Remember to allow the glue to dry.

5. I use ¼" splines for decorating the mitred joints on this design. To maintain the comic theme, I use different-colored woods for each of the splines or in alternating splines. You may also want to vary the length and width of the splines. Plugs, of course, can be used to decorate the edges of the joints. To make a jig for cutting splines on a table-mounted router, refer to Design C 22-1. You may prefer designing and using a similar type of jig on your table saw. In addition to demonstrating how to cut the spline areas in the joint, the discussion in Design C 22-1 also shows you how to cut the spline inserts and secure them in the recesses. After the joints have been embellished with the splines, bring the wall surfaces to finishing readiness.

6. Before beginning work on the lid inlay, I mount the hinge system on the box and lid. Usually, for this design, I use a 6"-long jewelry box hinge. As mentioned, I also use a metal lid support for holding this rather long lid in place. You may want to consider using a lid support because all the metal makes the lid rather heavy. While you can attach the hinges following the procedures presented in Design A 6-1, you may want to consider another option for this type of lid. The procedures in Design A 6-1 are effective when a solid lid is used on a box, and they certainly will work on this design. However, you may want to consider other procedures when placing hinges on a box-type lid, as used with this design.

Using bar or C clamps, clamp the lid to the back of the box, being certain that the edges and walls are flush (Illus. 107). The clamps should be placed near the walls so they don't interfere with the placement of the hinges for measuring. Depending on whether you're using jewelry or butt hinges, center the respective hinge leaf on one of the edges. Using a pencil, mark the end edges of the hinge leaf on the edge

surface. These marks should clearly indicate the exact length of the hinge leaf and the recess that needs to be cut. Using a square, trace these two lines onto the other edge. Next, place the hinge leaf back between the two marks but have the hinge knuckle extending beyond the back wall edge. The knuckle should extend only its thickness beyond the wall edge. The inside surface of the knuckle (where the leaf becomes the knuckle) should just touch the back wall surface. The knuckle needs to extend beyond the walls in order for the hinge to function smoothly and prevent binding. In any event, with the leaf and knuckle properly placed, mark the front edge of the leaf on the edge surface. You only need to mark one front edge because the recess is cut with a Moto-Tool that has a router attachment and guide. Once the router guide is set for cutting the width of one recess, it can be used for cutting the unmarked recess. When the hinge dimensions have been marked for cutting the recesses, remove the clamps.

Using a Moto-Tool with a router attachment, guide, and small bit, cut out the recess to a depth that is the exact thickness of the hinge leaf. The guide, of course, must be properly set. Refer to Design A 6-1 for specifics on routing hinge recesses with a Moto-Tool. This discussion will also be helpful when you place the hinge leaves in their respective recesses.

7. For the inlay work on this design, I cut the background inlay to the exact dimensions of the lid recess. Measure and cut carefully so you have a good snug fit. The face section is 6" in diameter and made with a school compass. Before cutting the circle for the face, draw the neck area extending from the chin to the bottom of the inlay. Cut out the face circle and the neck. The two should also be separated by cutting. Before replacing the various pieces, sand all the edges including the outer edges of the inlay piece. It's a good idea to mark the top surface of each part so they will be assembled properly. By the way, the edge sanding helps to make the profiles stand out better and gives the insert edge a more finished look. Place the various pieces back into the lid recess. Be certain the grain is lined up on the face circle and the insert.

Now get ready for some fun. Find some old bolts, screws, nuts, washers, or whatever else you want to use for making the facial features.

Every woodworker seems to have a catchall can in the shop where these kinds of things are stored for future use. When you lay out the face, you only need to do additional cutting if you use large nuts for the ears. I mark the length and width of these nuts on the inlay surface, next to the face wall, and then cut a recess for them. While you can use a male counterpart to the female design in Illus. 106, this design offers more possibilities for detail. You may note the earrings and necklace. They're both made from small brass washers. The eyes are lock washers with heads of bolts cut off with a hack saw to fit inside. The eyelashes and hair are made from old wire that I inserted into small drilled holes and bent. Let your can of junk and your imagination generate the design. First I lay out the total design. When I'm satisfied with it, I glue the parts in place on the surface.

Other glues will work but I use cyanoacrylate or what is generally referred to as "superglue." It's a good idea to purchase this glue from a mail-order craft supplier rather than from a local store. You can often get it in larger quantities and it's also less expensive. In the event of an accident, it's wise to have the solvent for the glue on hand. *This is very powerful glue, so be sure to keep it away from your eyes, and be certain to read the directions on the label.* Incidentally, the glue will stain the wood, so place it only where needed. To remove any spillage on the surface, allow the glue to dry and then lightly sand it off using fine-grit abrasive paper.
8. When the design has been completed, finish the entire box, including the inlay and lid. By way of information, lacquer holds well on the metal inlay parts.

Design C 27-1: Equilateral Triangle Box with Lid Inlay (Illus. 108)

1. Although this design has a rather complicated-sounding name, equilateral simply means equal sides. With its triangular shape, this design is an interesting configuration for a storage or music box. The lid on the design is hinged with a 6″ jewelry box hinge and uses a brass chain with escutcheon pins as a lid stopper. The joints have splines cut with a ½″ dovetail router bit. By the way, don't drop carbide-tipped router bits on concrete shop floors. They tend to chip, as I recently discovered again after dropping the ½″ dovetail. The dovetail cuts can be made through the joints using the jig described in Design C 22-1 and a table-mounted router. The walls of the box are 12″ long and 2¼″ high. The lid, of course, has the same wall length but is 1¼″ high. I use ½″-thick stock for the box and the lid. For the box bottom and lid insert, I prefer to use ¼″ plywood.
2. The first step in this challenging box design is cutting the walls to length for both the box and the lid. The length needs to be exact for all pieces, so you may want to use a stop-block setup on your radial arm or table saw. To cut the mitred joints at a 60° angle, I devised a jig for use on a radial arm saw. Using one of the mitre grooves on a table saw, the jig can be modified for use on this tool as well. Illus. 109 shows the jig placed on the table of a radial arm saw. While you may have a similar system or an easier way of cutting 60° angle joints, the jig has worked well for me. There is a detailed sketch of the jig in Illus. 110 should you want to make one.

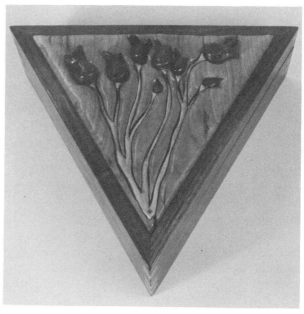

Illus. 108. Equilateral triangle box with floral inlay

Illus. 109. Jig for cutting equilateral triangles

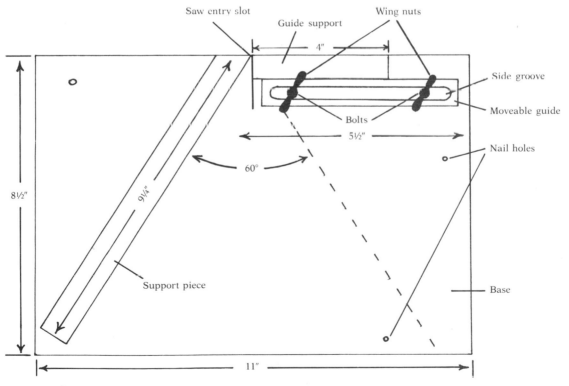

Illus. 110. Triangle jig

My jig is a rather poorly crafted assemblage of board pieces glued together. While it does the job, it certainly isn't much to look at. To align the jig on a radial arm saw, I place a block that is approximately 3″ wide between the front edge of the jig and the support piece at the front of the radial arm saw table. I draw a straight line on the top surface of the block. I use this line to align the saw blade and the entry point in the front end of the jig. Although it's an eye-ball-alignment process, it does work. When the saw blade and the jig are in perfect alignment, I carefully nail the jig to the table surface. I have predrilled holes through the jig surface to make the nailing procedure easier and to prevent the jig from moving out of alignment. When the jig has been securely nailed so it won't move from alignment, I remove the guide block. By the way, you should have a rather fine tooth blade or at least one that will give you good smooth cuts.

Before using your jig for cutting sample or final joints, you should practise with the jig and the saw with the power *off*. When you use the jig, hold a board against the support piece with your left hand and pull the saw blade towards you with your right hand. *Be certain your left hand, holding the board in place, is out of the path of the saw blade. Do a number of practice cuts, with the power off, to determine the safest place to put your left hand when you are holding the board.* The board needs to be held firmly against the support piece, so find the safest location for accomplishing this procedure. Always remember that a radial arm saw blade is an unforgiving tool. When I cut the mitred joint, I pull the saw blade through just far enough to make the cut and then, holding the board firmly in place, back the saw away. *There is no need to pull the saw blade far into the jig base. It only increases the chance of injury and cuts up the jig.*

Align the wall piece against the jig stop, holding it firmly in place, and then cut the mitre. Repeat the process on the other end of the board and on all the wall pieces for both the box and the lid. *When making repetitive cuts like these, you can be lulled into carelessness. Stay alert and watch your hand by the saw blade.* After the mitres have been cut on the box and lid pieces, assemble the pieces using rubber bands so you can check the various joints and their fit.

3. You need to route grooves in the walls of both the box and the lid for holding the bottom section and the lid insert. As mentioned earlier, I use ¼″ plywood for both the bottom piece and the insert. For procedures on routing the grooves, refer to Design C 22-1. Additional information on routing procedures, especially pertaining to the lid insert, are presented in Design C 26-1. These procedures for the lid are critical to the inlay work that will be done on the lid of this design.

4. To pattern and cut the bottom section and the lid insert, first assemble the box with rubber bands. Be certain the joints are snug. Lay the assembled box on the surface of the ¼″ plywood you plan to use. Align the box on the plywood so the grain runs up and down, vertical to the wall that will be the back of the box. With a sharp pencil, trace the inside of the box onto the plywood surface. Next, measure the depth of the routed grooves. Mark at several points the groove depth along the three sides of the triangle. Using a ruler, draw the larger triangle using the groove depth lines as guides. When cut, the piece should fit perfectly into the grooves of the box walls. When you cut the triangle from the plywood piece, cut on the traced lines. You do not want the triangle too large or it will force the joints open. It's better for the plywood bottom piece to be a little loose in the grooves than too tight. Using the bottom section triangle as a pattern, trace the lid insert triangle from it. They should both be the same size. Cut the lid insert on the traced lines. Assemble both the lid and box with their plywood pieces so that you can check for fit. Use rubber bands to hold them together. If they're too tight, remove a little wood from the plywood. Don't rout the grooves deeper.

5. Using the gluing procedures in Design C 22-1, assemble the box and lid with the bottom and insert pieces in place. Use rubber bands for clamps. If you prefer to use another method of clamping, by all means use it. Allow the glue to dry before proceeding with the next step.

6. If you have a small dovetail router bit and table-mounted router, you may want to cut dovetail recesses for decorative splines through the joints. I use the router jig described in Design C 22-1 and shown in Illus. 93 for cutting the spline recesses. To avoid tear-out when the bit exits the wall, place a small strip of board along the wall of the box when it's placed in the jig. Place and cut the dovetail recesses wherever you want them on the joints. I tend to cut one near the top edge of the joint and the other an equal distance from the bottom edge. On the lid, I cut one recess on each corner, centered.

7. After the dovetail recesses have been cut into the box and lid corners, you will need to prepare dovetail splines to fit tightly into the recesses. This can be a bit of a problem, but the end result is worth the effort. Use a wood for the tails that will make them conspicuous. For example, with a walnut box, I use either hard maple or white ash. However, you may prefer a less conspicuous wood. If you used a ½″ dovetail bit, the widest part of the cut recess should then be ½″. Rip strips from the wood you plan to use for tails that are exactly ½″ wide and at least ¾″ thick. Strips this thick not only make the tails easier to insert into the recesses, but also assure that the tails will be long enough. Measure the depth of the dovetail cut in one of the corners. This dimension should be the same for all the cuts because the router bit was set and used at the same depth for every rout. On the butt end of the ½″ × ¾″ strip(s), mark the cut depth from one surface that is designated the top on the butt face. Use this designated top surface as the point of origin for the next measurement. Using a ruler, measure the opening of the recess at the corner of a joint. Before placing this measurement on the butt end of the strip(s), find and mark the center of the ½″-wide strip. Draw a line on the butt-end surface at the center point. You need to place the opening measurement at the point where the strip center line and the depth-of-cut line intersect on the butt surface. However, because this is the narrow end of the taper, the measurement must be placed half on one side of the center point and half on the other. When these two points have been placed on the depth-of-cut line, draw lines from them to the upper corners of the butt face. Illus. 111 shows how the butt end will look after all the lines are in place. This procedure should lay out tails that will fit snugly into the dovetail recesses on the joint corners.

I use the band saw for cutting the strips to the marked angles. Tilt the band-saw table and set it at an angle so that, with the fence in place, it will cut one tapered wall of the strip. An easy way of aligning the table angle and the fence setting is by using the tapered line on the butt surface, placed against the blade, as a guide. Cut the tapered edge on one side of the strip. You will need to realign or use an alternate fence arrangement to cut the taper on the other

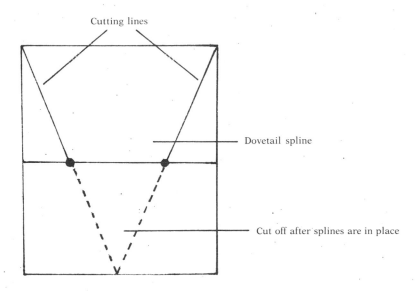

Cutting lines

Dovetail spline

Cut off after splines are in place

Illus. 111. End of dovetail spline—top

111

side. A level table and a guide support piece with the strip placed at the correct angle will also allow you to make the cut.

After the tapers have been ripped on the strips, you need to cut them into pieces that are long enough to fill the recess and extend out a bit on both sides. The strips cut into 1″ pieces are an adequate length. Do not cut off the excess taper. This can be cut off when the box walls have been sanded to finishing readiness.

Spread wood glue in the recesses. Tap a spline tail, from the side, into the recess. Be certain it goes through the recess and there is no gap between the spline and the box wall. After all the tail splines are in place, allow the glue to dry. When the glue is dry, trim off the excess from the splines using the band saw. Using a belt and finishing sander, prepare the surface for finishing.

8. The next procedure is putting the type of hinge you desire in place. Follow the instructions for placing hinges on this type of lid that are presented in Design C 26-1. After the hinges are in place, prepare all surfaces for finishing.

9. The final task in this design involves preparing the lid inlay and then securing it in place. Before beginning the various procedures, you may want to review Design A 5-2. This design includes information that should be helpful as you approach the inlay process.

If you plan to duplicate the floral inlay design in Illus. 108, some information on the wood that's used should be helpful in your planning. The box and lid were crafted from walnut. Hard maple was used for the dovetail splines. The inlay background is made from wild cherry. The stems are cut from the green areas you often find in a poplar board. The roses and buds are from padouk.

The first step in making the inlay is cutting the background triangle. Before measuring and cutting, be certain of the grain alignment and the way the inlay is placed in the lid. The top edge of the inlay where the flowers are placed is on the hinged part of the lid. The stems of the flowers converge at the point of the triangle opposite the hinged wall. The wood grain in the cherry background inlay should thus run vertical to the hinged wall. The cherry background inlay should be made from stock that is 3/8″ thick, if possible. You can use 1/2″-thick cherry but, if you do, add 1/8″ of thickness to all the insert parts. In other words, the roses should be cut from 5/8″-thick padouk, instead of from 1/2″-thick padouk. Remember this dimensional change if the inlay background is thicker than 3/8″. Cut the inlay background so that it fits neatly in place in the lid recess. It's a good idea to bring the surface where the inlays will be placed to finishing readiness. Although there will be pencil marks you will need to remove later, it's much easier to prepare the surface while it is still in one solid piece and not all cut through to receive the inlays.

The design has six roses of varying sizes and two buds. While you may want to vary the number or make patterns for the flowers, I usually draw the roses and buds freehand on the surface of the padouk. By the way, if you don't have padouk, use Osage orange (hedge) or purpleheart. They look just as attractive with the cherry background. The wood for the flowers should be at least 1/2″ thick. The buds should not protrude from the inlay surface, so they can be cut from 3/8″ stock.

Cut out each of the traced roses and buds using a scroll saw or whatever tool you prefer. You may want to use a band saw with a 1/2″ blade for this procedure. When all the flowers and buds have been cut and when the cherry inlay has been placed in the lid recess, place them as desired on the inlay surface. As you place the flowers and buds on the inlay, try to make them resemble a cluster of roses. For an idea, refer to Illus. 108. After you finalize the flower and bud placement, leave them in place on the inlay surface. Each rose and bud must be traced with a pencil on the surface of the inlay. As you trace each one, mark the top of the flower with a number and place the same number near the inlay outline. You need to number each flower and bud and the insert recess where you will place them. Also, the top of each flower should be clearly marked. This numbering and marking procedure becomes critical when you assemble all the finished pieces in the inlay. If the shaping process removes a number when you shape the flowers, transfer the number to the bottom. Do not cut out the traced flower and bud outlines yet. The stem and flowers are all cut out at the same time. More about this shortly.

The next procedure is preparing the stems for each individual flower and bud. All of the stems emerge from a common base in the front corner of the lid inlay. I make all the stems from one piece of poplar. The only problem with making all the stems interconnecting is that they can be easily broken when you are handling and shaping them. When I shape the stems, I lay the entire stem assembly on a flat surface and shape them while they lie against a hard surface. If you try to shape all the various parts of the stem while holding the assembly in your hand, inevitably some part will break. To determine the width of the piece of poplar needed for the stem assembly, measure the distance between the two outer rose patterns on the inlay surface. On the inlay in Illus. 108, the stem assembly required a piece of poplar that is 4½" wide. Measure the length of the stem assembly from the corner of the lid to the base of the rose that's highest on the design. The stem in Illus. 108 required poplar that's at least 7" long. Thus, for the stem, you need poplar that is at least 4½" wide and 7" long. To account for variations in the designs and to also be on the safe side, add to both dimensions. Too much is better than too little. I rip the poplar on the band saw to a thickness of ⅜".

I draw the stem assembly freehand on the poplar, using a ruler to check for length and distances between flowers and buds. This is probably the easiest way to design the stem and you don't need any drawing skills. I draw the stem so that two roses are connected to two sections of the same main stem; another stem might connect both a flower and a bud. In drawing the stem, use your imagination in terms of how everything should be connected and interconnected. I draw the stems to a width of at least ¼" at the bottom, and then taper them to about ⅛" as they near the top. On the top end of the stem where it touches the base of the flower, I flare out the stem. Look at Illus. 108 again to see how the stem flares out.

10. After you have traced the stem assembly on the surface of the poplar board, cut it out. Plan your cuts carefully so you won't break any of the stems. I cut the flared sections that will touch the flowers a little longer than the pattern calls for. You may need this extra length when you test for fit. If it is not needed, it can easily be removed later. Be careful not to cut any of the stem areas too thin. No part of the stem should be less than ⅛" wide. Poplar is a rather soft wood and can break easily, so handle the assembly with care when cutting. Mark the top surface of the assembly.

11. Place the stem assembly on the background inlay surface and line the various stems up with the traced roses and buds. Hopefully, the stems with their flares will touch the traced bases of the roses and buds. If the stem flares extend beyond the traced line on the bottom of the flowers or buds, mark and cut them to length. Now proceed in making each stem and its flare fit against the base line of the flowers and buds. When each stem is in place in relation to its rose and bud and when the bottom of the assembly fits within the inlay wall, you can begin tracing the stem onto the inlay surface. Carefully hold each stem in place while you are tracing it. Be careful not to move the assembly out of alignment when tracing. Make your tracing lines dark so that you can easily see them for cutting.

12. Using a scroll or band saw with a ⅛" blade, cut out the traced stem assembly, as well as the roses and buds. I cut the parts out of the inlay in a way that leaves it in one piece. It looks better this way. You should begin the cut into the inlay from the bottom of the stem assembly. Plan your cuts carefully. Be especially careful when cutting the stem areas. It's easy to confuse an area to be cut out with a stem. Always stop and think before making cuts in the stem areas. When all the parts have been cut from the inlay, carefully place the inlay on a flat surface. You should roll all the edges in the inlay, including the outer ones, while the piece is lying on a flat surface. As with the stem assembly, the inlay can easily be broken.

13. The next procedure is shaping the roses and buds and the stem assembly. Refer to Design A 5-2 for specific techniques, tools, and accessories required in the shaping process. You may want to interject some of your own procedures into the sculpting process.

When all the pieces have been shaped, place the inlay background into the lid recess. Place the roses and buds, using their numbers as guides, into their proper recesses. You should check the fit of all the pieces in their respective recesses. This, of course, includes the stem assembly. Where the fit is too tight, reduce the piece using the shaping tools. When all the parts fit perfectly, remove them and prepare for gluing. Spread a thin coat of glue on the entire plywood insert surface. Place the background into the recess. Next place the roses and buds in their respective areas and press in place. You want to be certain that the parts make good contact with the glued plywood surface. The final piece to be placed is the stem assembly. Place it in the various recesses and press it down to the plywood. Be careful that you don't break a stem. If you do, put a touch of glue at the break and press the parts in place in the recess. You can clean up the edges of the break after the glue is dry. If portions of the stem will

not lie down properly, stretch a large rubber band around the entire lid. Place small blocks between the rubber band and that part of the assembly that needs to be forced down to the glued surface. Allow the glue to dry.

14. Using fine-grit abrasive paper, remove the pencil and other marks from the surfaces of the inlay or shaped parts. Use this abrasive paper to clean off any glue. Be certain to sand lightly with the wood grain so you don't mark the surfaces.

15. Finish the box and inlay as desired.

Design C 27-2: Equilateral Triangle Box with Veneer Inlay (Illus. 112)

1. This design is similar to the previous triangle box, shown in Illus. 108. Unlike the previous box, however, this design can be made to house a large CH (changing) 3.72 musical movement.

2. Each wall of the triangle is 12½″ long and 3½″ high (panel width). You should use ½″ stock. The lid walls are the same length as the box walls, but are 1″ high (width). The lid and bottom insert pieces are made from ¼″-thick plywood. The dimensions have been planned with a large CH 3.72 musical movement in mind. You may, however, prefer to make a large storage container.

Illus. 113 shows the box with the lid removed. Note the Australian lacewood veneer inlaid

Illus. 112. Equilateral triangle box with veneer inlay

It also makes an excellent jewelry box or other type of storage container. The design is made by referring to procedures in other designs. With this approach, you can design and make a unique box by using methods you've already learned. You will have an opportunity to alter some components of the design and develop your own procedures. I think you will find this

approach to making a rather complex box both unusual and challenging.

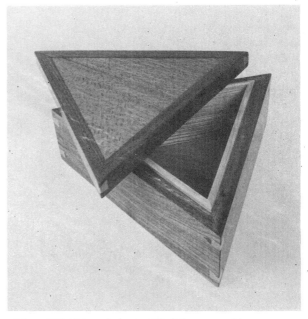

Illus. 113. Triangle box with lid removed

Illus. 114. Triangle box prepared for musical move-ment

gle. It may also be helpful to note that the frame extends beyond the top edge of the box walls in order to hold the lid in place. To embellish the joints, I used a dovetail router bit for cutting the splines.

Here's a final bit of information if you decide to make the design into a large music box. In Illus. 114, there is a similar box showing where the elevated soundboard strips can be placed. The insert frame is also cut out to allow the sliding-on/off assembly to move in its routed groove. Design B 28-1 is a good source of information for the various procedures required by the larger musical movements. Incidentally, when I make a music box with this design, I do not put glass over the movement. You may want to design a divider that will separate the musical movement from the back portion of the triangle. This back area can then be used for storage. If you use this design for a music box, the lid should not be hinged. Have fun.

into the lid. You may prefer designing a sculptured lid inlay instead. You should also note the internal mitred insert frame. As you might suspect, the frame needs to be mitred at a 60° an-

Design C 27-3: Equilateral Triangle Box with Veneer Inlay (Illus. 115)

1. This box presents another alternative lid design for the triangle design. The dimensions and procedures are the same as those presented in Design C 27-2.

2. The lid inlay on this design is burl veneer that has been spot-glued to give it the appearance of leather. To prevent the veneer from being punctured, it has been recessed into the lid. Note the narrow frame around the inside edge of the lid. The frame not only adds a nice touch, it can also cover up any poorly cut veneer edges.

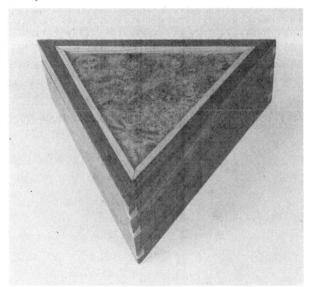

Illus. 115. Equilateral triangle box with veneer inlay

Design C 28-1: Large Music Box (Model CH 3.72 Cylinder Movement) (Illus. 116)

1. This design presents a music box that has all the basic components for quality sound reproduction. It is designed solely for the perfor-

mance of clockwork music. Some of the boxes I make for the larger movements include an area for storing jewelry or other small items. How-

ever, this design does not lend itself to these extra functions. The design integrates a mitred internal frame that holds a piece of glass over the movement. As you will discover in the procedures, the glass slides into grooves in three walls of the frame. The fourth wall holds the glass in place. This wall can also be easily removed if you need to take the glass out in order to work on the movement. The wall permits easy replacement of the glass should it get broken.

The box also includes a spring steel stopper system that is routed into the front panel (Illus. 117). This on/off system is the standard mechanism that is used with the larger movements. Later procedures will assist you with the placement of this mechanism.

As mentioned previously, the soundboard of a

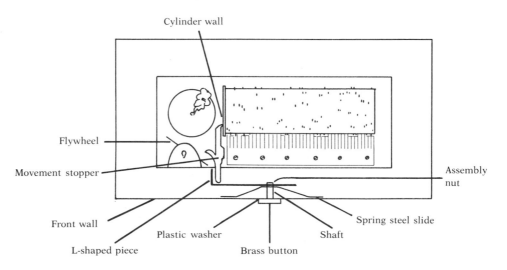

Illus. 117. On/off stopper system

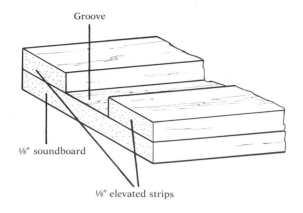

Groove

⅛" soundboard

⅛" elevated strips

Illus. 118. Elevated soundboard

music box is critical to both the quality and the volume of the sound produced. This design employs a three-part, elevated Sitka spruce soundboard that maximizes the sound potential of the movement.

To enhance the appearance of the box, a coved, raised panel from ½"-thick maple fits neatly into grooves in the lid. Also, the mitred joints on both the box and lid are embellished with splines and plugs. The box has a 6" jewelry box hinge recessed into place.

These are the approximate dimensions of the walnut box, not including the lid. It's 10" long, 4¾" wide; and 2¾" high. The lid is 1" high and, as mentioned, the insert panel is ½" thick. The other lid dimensions are the same as those for the box. The soundboard is made from ⅛" Sitka spruce. The walls of both the box and the lid are made from ½"-thick stock.

2. Cut the box and lid panels to the length and width mentioned in the first step. Using a power mitre saw or whatever tools you prefer, cut 45° mitres on the ends of all pieces. Using large rubber bands as clamps, assemble both the box and the lid in order to check the accuracy and fit of the joints. Remedy them, if necessary. Also, place the assembled lid on the box to make sure that all walls are flush on the sides.

3. Before beginning the next procedure, take time to familiarize yourself with the dimensions and parts of your CH 3.72 musical movement. Note its height, length, and width. Become familiar with the stopper that is attached to the movement. Musical movements are mar-

vels of craftsmanship and are well worth studying. If you haven't already done so, wind the movement, place it on a hard surface, and turn it on. The sounds emanating from the instrument, as you will discover, are incredible. The movement will sound even better once it is placed in the box. A word of caution: Do not let the movement lie exposed in the shop or it will get loaded with sawdust.

4. You need to cut grooves in the inside walls of both the box and the lid. To eliminate confusion, the procedures will first be given for routing the grooves on the box. You need to make a ¼"-wide groove in all four box walls. This will hold the soundboard in place. While the soundboard is made from ⅛" stock, when the two strips for elevating the movement are glued to the surface of the soundboard proper, you will have a thickness of ¼". Illus. 118 shows the soundboard proper and the two elevating strips. Procedures for making and assembling the soundboard will be presented shortly. In laying out the dimensions for the grooves on the inside surface of the walls, you first need to measure the length of the winding key. The area under the soundboard must be high enough so that the key will turn freely and not rub on the surface where the box is placed. I generally use keys on this design that are 15 to 20 mm (½" to ⅝") in length. This is measuring from the top of the shaft to the bottom of the key. To simplify these procedures, I will continue to use the dimensions of the box shown in Illus. 116.

Using the inside wall of the front panel as the marking piece, measure ⅝" from the bottom edge of the panel and mark on the wall. At another location on the panel, repeat the procedure so that you will have two marks on the wall's surface. Using a ruler, connect the two marks, extending the line onto the taper of the mitres. The line on the mitre will serve as the guide when lining up the router bit and fence/guide for cutting the groove (Illus. 119).

To route the grooves, I use a table-mounted router with a fence/guide and a ¼" straight bit. To assure a tight-fitting soundboard, the router bit should be set to cut the grooves at least ⅛" deep. A simple way to set the depth of the bit is by making a mark on the edge of a board that is ⅛" from its surface. Slide the board, mark next to the bit, and adjust accordingly.

Place the line on the taper of the mitre against the bit and set the fence/guide. Be sure your fence/guide is set straight and is securely clamped in place. With the depth properly set and the fence/guide in place, rout the soundboard grooves in all four walls. If you want to check the grooves' alignment in the box, assemble with rubber bands.

5. While the ¼″ bit is still in place on the router, it's a good time to cut grooves in the lid walls. These grooves will hold the ½″ maple insert panel in the lid. On other designs, you may want to do an inlay or use veneer. You would then want to use a ¼″ piece of plywood for the lid insert. The inlay or veneer would then be placed on the top surface of the plywood insert.

While it may seem a bit confusing to cut a ¼″-wide groove in the lid walls when the maple insert panel is ½″ thick, the dimensions are correct. The edges of the ½″ lid panel will be routed to a thickness of ¼″ using a cove router bit. Thus, the maple lid panel will fit neatly into the ¼″ wall grooves.

The length of the brass button from its back surface to the two square sides on its shaft are ⁷⁄₁₆″. These two square surfaces are where the spring steel slide fits. The oblong hole in the middle of the steel slide is what fits over these square surfaces. As shown in Illus. 117, the L-shaped piece fits over the spring steel slide on the brass shaft and the small nut secures both in place. The small plastic washer that is included with the assembly fits on the brass shaft between the button and the box wall. Not only does the plastic prevent any damage to the wall's surface, it also permits the button to slide more easily against the wall.

I cut the groove in the front wall using a ½″ straight router bit. You can use a ⅜″ straight bit to eliminate any possible play in the sliding assembly. If the ⅜″ bit is undersized, however, you may get some bind between the edges of the groove and the spring steel slide. You may recall it was ¾″ from the bottom of the base plate of the movement to the stopper arm. When using a ½″ bit, this means the bottom of the groove should be ½″ from the soundboard. For routing purposes, the middle of the groove should be ¾″ from the soundboard or bottom groove. Make two marks ¾″ from the top edge of the bottom groove and draw a straight line that extends onto the joint taper. These procedures are the same as they were for making the soundboard groove. Set the ½″ router bit to a depth of ⁵⁄₁₆″ for routing the groove. This depth allows the ends of the spring steel slide to hold the entire assembly in place but stay loose enough to allow it to slide (Illus. 119).

Rout the assembly groove on the table-mounted router. Set the depth of the bit to ⁵⁄₁₆″ using the procedures mentioned earlier. Align the center of the bit with the line extending onto the joint taper. Set the fence/guide. As the groove for the sliding system is to be only 4″ long, you will be routing blindly. To assist in the placement of the panel on the router bit, mark off 4″ on the top outer surface of the panel. Place a mark on the fence/guide directly opposite the router bit.

When using a solid piece of wood for a decorative lid panel, I usually plan to have the top of the panel flush with the top edges of the lid. However, you may prefer to have it protrude beyond the lid edges or set in from them.

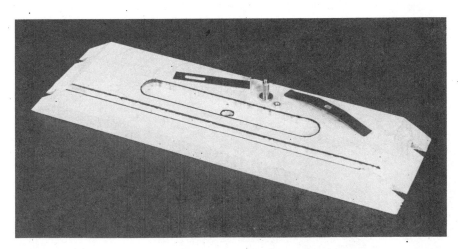

Illus. 119. Front panel: routed for stopper and soundboard

Illus. 120. Routed front panel stopper groove

To simplify the measuring for the lid grooves, I measure from the top edge. On this design using the front lid panel as the pattern piece, measure ½″ down from the top edge and mark. Repeat the procedure at another point on the panel. As with the box wall, using a ruler, connect the two marks with a line that extends onto the joint taper.

The router bit is set to an adequate depth for cutting the grooves. If you want, you can reset it for a deeper cut. Realign and set the fence/guide on the router table so that the bit and marked line are in alignment. Rout the grooves in all lid panels. Incidentally, be certain you make these grooves on the inside walls. Haste can get you in trouble. Always think through the procedures before making the cut.

6. The next procedure involves cutting another groove in the inside wall of the front panel. This groove will eventually hold the sliding stopper system that activates the movement (Illus. 117). The exact placement of this groove and the spring steel slide that moves back and forth in it are critical to turning the movement on and off. You must be careful when measuring for the groove. Although I will provide the dimensions you need for making the stopper system groove for this design, it's worth going through the steps involved in determining the dimensions.

Place the movement on a flat surface. With a ruler, measure from the bottom edge of the movement base plate to the stopper arm on the movement. The distance should be approximately ¾″. Thus, the center of the groove that holds the assembly should be ¾″ from the top edge of the soundboard (groove). Next, measure the spring steel slide from the stopper assembly. You will note that it's approximately 3″ long and not quite ⅜″ wide. As the spring steel must slide back and forth in the groove, you should allow at least ½″ on each side of the slide. Thus, the groove should be approximately 4″ long.

With the router turned on, place the panel edge against the fence/guide. Line up one of the 4″ marks with the bit location mark on the fence/guide. Force the panel down onto the bit and rout to the other 4″ mark. *This procedure must be done very carefully and with a firm grip on the board.* You may want to practise the procedure using a piece of pine before doing the procedure with the walnut panel. When the groove has been cut, the panel can be lifted from one end off the router bit. Again, proceed carefully and slowly (Illus. 120).

7. There's one final step that's needed in order to have a functioning sliding stopper system. You need to make an oblong hole in the middle of the groove you've just routed. The shaft of the brass button will penetrate the hole and, with the small nut, secure the spring steel and L-shaped piece in place. The shaft has a diameter of approximately ³⁄₁₆″. The hole needs to be oblong because the shaft needs to move sideways in the hole when sliding the assembly. I use a ¼″ Foerstner bit for drilling an oblong hole that is ⁵⁄₁₆″ long. You will need to make two holes, one overlapping the other. You should avoid making the hole much wider or longer than the stated dimensions or it will show on the front surface when the button slides to the side.

8. As a reward for the tedium of the previous tasks, assemble the entire sliding assembly into the hole and groove so you can see how it works. Unfortunately, this procedure can also be laced with some frustration. Place the brass button shaft through the hole. While pressing

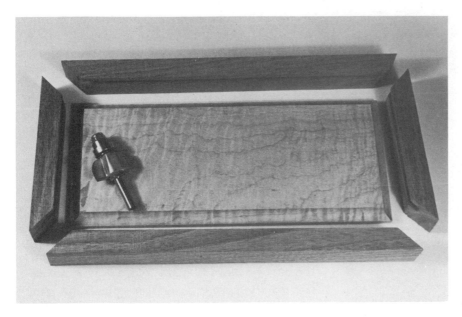

Illus. 121. Lid routed for insert

the spring steel slide into the groove, slip it over the shaft onto the two square sides. Next, place the L-shaped piece over the threaded end of the shaft and secure the nut. This procedure is easier said than done. It's hard to thread the nut on while holding the other pieces in place. If you can get the nut started on the threads, you can realign the spring steel's oblong hole over the square surfaces as you tighten the nut. This is usually the part that can complicate the procedure. Persistence is what this procedure is all about. When the assembly has been secured together, test how it slides in the groove. One of the last tasks is adjusting the L-shaped piece to line up with the stopper arm on the movement.

9. At this point it is worth noting how the slide assembly activates the movement when it's in place in the box. When the sliding assembly has been secured in its routed groove, it is the L-shaped piece, properly adjusted, that pulls the stopper arm to start the movement. The slide mechanism is pushed to the right (when facing the box) and the secured L-shaped piece moves the movement stopper arm to the right. When the stopper arm has been moved to the right, the flywheel is released by the small arm on the stopper. Also, the bent end of the stopper is pulled from a small hole on the side of the cylinder. Now the movement begins to play. If the sliding assembly remains in this position, the movement will continue to play until the spring unwinds. To stop the movement after playing one tune, slide the assembly to the left. The small spring on the movement stopper will simultaneously force the bent end into a hole in the cylinder wall and the small arm into the flywheel.

10. The next procedure is preparing the soundboard. For this design, you should make the soundboard and its two elevating strips from ⅛" Sitka spruce or a cabinet-grade plywood. Determine the internal length and width of the box, then add the depth of the routed grooves in the side walls to these measurements. This should give you the dimensions for the soundboard.

In addition to the soundboard proper, you also need to prepare the two strips that are glued to its surface (Illus. 118). These strips elevate the movement and leave the middle portion of the soundboard as the primary resonator. Not only do the strips provide support, they effectively carry the vibrations from the movement to the middle portion of the soundboard. The width of the strips is determined by where the movement will be placed in the box. You should place the strips so that they are under the screw holes in the bedplate of the movement. On this design, the strips are approximately 1⅜″ wide. Their length, of course, is the same as that of the soundboard proper. Using wood glue, glue the strips, flush with the soundboard edges, in place. Clamp them and allow the glue to dry. You may want to assemble the box, using rubber bands, with the soundboard in place. This is an effective way to check the fit of the soundboard. If the joints are forced open, you need to reduce either the length or the width of the soundboard. A little sanding on the edges usually takes care of this.

11. The lid-insert panel is the next component that must be prepared. If you routed the grooves in the lid panels to the same depth as those in the box walls, the lid insert should have the same dimensions as the soundboard. If the grooves are a bit deeper, simply add this additional depth measurement from all four sides to the length and width of the lid panel. For this design, the lid insert is made from ½″-thick hard maple. To cut the cove on the edges of the insert panel, I use a ⅜″ cove router bit. You may prefer a ½″ cove bit. In routing the cove on the edges of the panel, you are also reducing the edges of the ½″-thick panel to ¼″. The ¼″ thickness is what is required for the panel insert to fit into the lid grooves (Illus. 121). Rout the panel using the appropriate bit. To test for fit, assemble the lid and panel. If the panel is oversized, you have to rout the cove deeper or remove a touch of wood from the edges of the panel. Bring the assembly to a good fit.

12. Using wood glue and clamps or rubber bands, assemble both the box with its soundboard and the lid with its panel. Allow ample time for the glue to dry.

13. This design has decorative splines in the joints on both the box and lid. It also can have ⅜″ decorative plugs with a reverse placement on the joints. For a discussion of the appropriate procedures and those procedures related to the home-made jig for preparing splines, refer to Design C 22-1. Review Illus. 116 to get an idea of the placement of the splines on this design. You may, however, prefer to forego the use of plugs. After the spline inserts and/or plugs are dry, sand the walls of the box and the lid to finishing readiness. After sanding the box, you need to drill a hole in the bottom of each of the four corners. Then you need to glue and insert screw-hole buttons in these holes. These buttons elevate the box off the surface so that the

Illus. 122. Glass-insert frame

musical sounds flow from under the box. It is critical that the box be elevated on small legs (buttons) or the sound will be trapped under the box.

14. You should use a 6″ jewelry box hinge on this box. This hinge has ample length and strength for a box of these dimensions. For a detailed discussion on the placement of hinges, refer to Design A 6-1. If you plan on using a framed insert to hold the glass over the movement, there will be no room for a lid stopper system.

15. If you want to use a glass covering over the movement, you may want to make a framed insert that will hold it in place. You can, of course, place small strips on the side walls of the box as shoulders. The glass is cut and then glued to these shoulders. On boxes that house these larger and more expensive movements, I prefer to make a framed insert that will hold the glass.

The framed insert for the glass is made from ¼″-thick stock. You can use either the same or contrasting wood (Illus. 122). Find the internal dimensions of the box. The frame should sit on the soundboard and extend at least ⁵⁄₁₆″ above the top edge of the box walls. Determine the width of the walls keeping the ⁵⁄₁₆″ extension in mind. Check all dimensions carefully before cutting the mitres. You need nice-fitting joints on the panels because they're exposed, especially the top edges. After the mitres have been cut, check for fit.

You need to cut an area from the front insert panel so that the sliding spring assembly can fit in place and work (Illus. 122). Measure the assembly area and cut out the panel accordingly.

So that the glass will fit neatly in the frame, I rout a ⅛″-wide groove approximately ⅛″ from the top edge of three of the panels. One side panel is not routed. This unrouted panel holds the glass in place. It also is not glued to the box wall. You need to be able to pull this panel wall out when removing or replacing the glass. The mitres hold it in place. I use standard-thickness window glass, which the ⅛″-wide routed groove accommodates very well.

Carefully lay out the wall areas to be grooved using the same measuring procedures as for the soundboard and lid insert. Rout the ⅛″-wide groove to a depth of ³⁄₁₆″ using a table-mounted router and fence/guide. You should leave some

wood in place at the top edge of the frame so that it doesn't break off. This is why I rout the groove to only a depth of ³⁄₁₆″. It's adequate for holding the glass in place.

Place the framed insert inside the box. Measure, including the depth of the routed grooves on the three panels, for the glass. The glass needs to be cut to dimensions that will permit it to fit snugly against the surface of the unrouted side wall.

Cut the glass to its required dimensions. There are some suggestions in the Appendix on ways to reduce the dimensions of the glass using a belt sander. Your glass may be a bit oversized and need reduction.

When the glass has been cut, test for fit with the unrouted panel in place. Remove the glass and sand the inside surfaces of the insert. You should also roll the outside edges on the top of the insert. After sanding, glue the three insert walls in place. Again, do not glue the unrouted panel to its wall. You may want to clamp these walls while the glue is drying.

The hinged lid should fit neatly over the extended glass insert frame. If it does not, sand the inside edges of the lid frame where they fit against the top edges of the insert. You may also want to roll the top outer edges of the insert walls a bit more.

16. At this point, you should finish the box and lid with the products you prefer. It's simpler to finish the box before drilling the winding key shaft and the movement screw holes in the soundboard. By doing it this way, you won't assemble and align the sliding assembly twice. You don't want the sliding assembly in place when finishing.

17. When the box and lid have been finished with whatever products and procedures you prefer, secure the sliding assembly in place in its groove. Do not fully tighten the assembly nut onto the shaft. This will be done later.

Place the musical movement in the box, centering it and being certain it is far enough forward in the box so that the L-shaped piece can grab the stopper arm. At this point, you will want to adjust the L-shaped piece in relation to the stopper arm. Tighten the assembly nut just enough to hold it in place.

With the movement properly placed, press down on the spring housing in order to make a small indentation on the surface of the soundboard. While holding the movement securely in place, using a sharp pencil, mark through the movement screw-hole areas onto the surface of the soundboard. Remove the movement. You should have four precisely placed marks on the soundboard surface.

You should drill the winding key-shaft hole with a ⅜"-diameter wood bit. You can drill the screw holes with a ⅛" bit. Be sure to place a block of wood firmly under the soundboard when drilling the holes. Without this piece under the soundboard, you will get tear-out from the bits. Both Sitka spruce and plywood tear out quite easily when drilled.

18. Secure the movement in the box and align the L-shaped arm so that it will pull the movement stopper to the right. It should also be adjusted so that when the slide assembly is moved to the left, the L-shaped arm will be clear of the stopper as it springs back in place. Tighten the assembly nut. Thread the winding key onto the movement, wind, slide the assembly to the "on" position, and enjoy the marvellous sounds of clockwork music. Slide the glass, cleaned on both sides, into the insert frame and secure with the unrouted panel wall. Finish the box as desired.

19. The tune sheets that come with the movement can be glued in place. You should place the decorative tune sheet on the inside of the lid. The other one is usually glued to the undersurface of the soundboard. Illus. 123 shows the movement in the box.

20. This final procedure is optional. I frequently glue a small designed piece of wood over the brass button. If you like the appearance of the brass button, forego this procedure. I usually make the covering piece from the same wood that's used for the box. On occasion, I will use padouk or some other decorative wood to make it more attractive. Drill a shallow hole, to the diameter of the brass button, in the back of the piece. Apply glue in the hole and place the piece over the press button. Be careful not to smear any glue on the front panel.

Illus. 123. Box with CH 3.72 musical movement

Design C 28-2: Large Music Box (Model CH 3.72 Cylinder Movement) (Illus. 124)

1. This design provides you with another lid embellishment. Instead of using a routed panel insert in the lid walls, as presented in Design C 28-1, this lid employs a ¼" plywood insert routed into the lid frame. Veneer is then cut to the internal dimensions of the lid recess and secured with contact cement. If desired, you can prepare a small frame that's placed over the edges of the veneer (Illus. 115).

2. The dimensions and procedures for this box are the same as those presented in Design C 28-1.

Illus. 124. Large music box

Design C 29-1: Large Music or Jewelry Box (Model CH 3.72 Cylinder Movement) (Illus. 125)

1. This box is designed to function as either a jewelry or music box. It's large enough to be very effective for both. The dimensions of the box are ideal for a large musical movement because they provide a large internal area for sound production. The size of the soundboard and the area surrounding the movement tends to enhance the sound's volume and quality from the movement.

If desired, you can include a small storage tray along with the movement. I have secured a narrow storage tray on the back wall, near the top edge. This placement does not obstruct the view of the movement, and allows easy access to any stored items.

As mentioned earlier, with the larger box designs, I seldom put a glass covering over the musical movement. If this is not your preference, you can design a box with shoulders secured to the side walls. The glass panel is simply secured to the shoulders using a touch of glue and small pieces of trim that cover the glass edges.

This design includes a small piece of wood glued to the brass on/off button. As indicated earlier, I tend to cover up the brass button with a piece of wood glued to its surface. You may want to refer to Illus. 125 to see how this looks.

I've designed a small extension on the lid to serve as a lid stopper. Because the lid is made from a solid piece of wood, the procedures for including the stopper are relatively simple. These procedures are discussed in Design 25-1. In looking over the photograph of this box, you will see that the lid stopper is quite small. I did not want to distract the eye from the unusual piece of curly red oak used for the box. The lid, by the way, is hinged with two high-quality brass butt hinges.

On this box, I've used butt joints that are secured with wood screws and covered with plugs. The plugs are cut from scraps of the same wood I used for the box.

These are the approximate dimensions of the box: It's 9" long, 6½" wide (this includes the front and back panel thicknesses and the butt joint assembly), and 6¼" high (including the ¾" thickness of the lid). The box walls are 7/16" thick.

2. The curved cutout areas on the front, back and side walls greatly enhance the overall appearance of the box. Boxes of this size tend to look very square and boxy without some kind of decorative cutout design. On large music boxes, these cutout areas also allow the sound to emerge from the bottom of the soundboard. It's another way of enhancing the sound produced by the movement. Because the cutout legs also make for a very impressive-looking jewelry box, you may prefer to duplicate the design as a jewelry box instead.

While you may want to duplicate the curved cutout legs on this box, I suggest you try developing a design of your own. The box provides sufficient wood surface for a range of possible cutouts. It would be wise to make a pattern for your design.

3. The soundboard for this box is made from ⅛″ Sitka spruce. It is an elevated soundboard, with two strips supporting the movement over the primary sounding board. For procedures on preparing the soundboard and the box, refer to Design C 28-1. When using a butt joint, remember not to rout the soundboard grooves the entire length of the front and back panels (see Design C 24-1). The routed grooves will be exposed at the ends of both panels.

If you use the design for a jewelry or storage box, use a ¼″ piece of cabinet-grade plywood for the bottom insert. With this kind of box, it is well worth the extra money to buy a better grade of plywood for the bottom.

4. For procedures on preparing the front wall for a sliding on/off stopper system, refer to Design C 28-1. This design will also provide you with the information necessary for making this box into a music box for one of the larger movements.

5. As previously indicated, I use butt hinges on

Illus. 125. Large music or jewelry box

this design. On a box of this size, it's best to buy a quality hinge. It greatly cheapens the appearance of the entire box if you use standard hardware-shop hinges. As mentioned, numerous mail-order suppliers have a wide range of high-quality brass hinges.

6. Finish the box as desired. As a rule, on boxes that are made from choice wood, I usually use an oil finish.

Design C 30-1: Large Music or Jewelry Box (Illus. 126)

1. This design employs some rather unusual leg configurations that showcase the beautiful curly hard maple. The box has a butt-joint design that employs screws and plugs for assembly. The lid insert is made from the same maple that's used for the box and frame. While not visible, the box has a wooden hinge system made from ash. A number of projects that follow include detailed procedures for making wooden hinges.

2. These are the approximate dimensions of the box: The front and back walls are 10″ long. The side walls are 6½″ long (including the front and back wall thicknesses and the butt joint). The box is 5″ high (not including the lid). The lid is 2″ high. The wood for both the box and the lid is ½″ thick.

3. Because of its size, this box can be used for a large cylinder musical movement, a 4½″ disc musical movement, or for jewelry or general

storage. Refer to the designs that have detailed procedures for the function you would like the box to serve.

Illus. 126. Large music or jewelry box

Design C 30-2: Disc Music Box (Model 9131, 4½″ Disc Movement) (Illus. 127)

1. While ideal for jewelry or general storage, this design has been specifically created for housing a 4½″ disc musical movement. It is rather difficult to design boxes for disc movements. In part, the design problems result from the space required by the disc movement. The movement itself is rather large and requires additional space beyond the rotating disc. In some of the disc boxes I make, an air-chamber sound system is designed into them. This, too, places added restrictions on possible designs. With this type of movement, I've chosen not to compromise sound for design. To do so, however, would probably solve some of the problems in designing boxes for these movements.

The basic disc box in Illus. 127 has been designed and crafted to maximize the sound potential of the movement. The lid insert is a beautiful piece of ½″ spalted hickory. As you can see in the photograph, the joints are mitred and enhanced with decorative splines and wall surface inlays.

The box is approximately 8½″ long, 5½″ wide, and 4″ high (not including the lid). The framed lid is 1½″ high. It has the same length and width as the box. The stock used for the box and lid is ½″ thick. The box is made from black walnut and the decorative splines and wall inlays are from white ash.

2. Cut the walls for both the box and the lid to the indicated lengths and widths. Using either a power mitre saw or some other saw you would normally use, cut 45° mitres on all pieces. As always, assemble the panels using a large rubber band so that you can check for fit.

3. I use two pieces of ¼″-thick plywood for the sound chamber in this box. The bottom piece of plywood is inserted into routed grooves in the walls. The other piece of plywood is secured to support pieces that are glued to the inside walls and the bottom piece. The movement is secured to this piece of plywood. The dimensions of this piece are the same as the internal length and width of the box.

Illus. 127. Disc music box

Rout a ¼" groove, using a table-mounted router, ⅜" from the bottom edges of all four box walls. The groove, of course, is on the inside of the walls. For this procedure, as mentioned with other designs, use a ¼" straight router bit and a fence/guide on the router table. You should rout the groove to a depth of at least ⅛".

You also need to rout the lid walls so that they can hold a ¼" plywood lid insert. While you may prefer to do a sculptured inlay or some other embellishment on the lid, I have used ½" spalted hickory for the inlay in this design. So that the spalted inlay will extend above the lid edges, the grooves must be routed ¼" from the top edges of the lid walls. This will permit the inlay to extend beyond the lid edges by at least ¼".

Realign the router fence/guide and rout the lid panels. You may want to leave the depth of the router the same as it was for the box walls. If you do this, you will need to measure only for the bottom plywood piece. The lid plywood insert can be traced directly from it because they're the same dimensions. The plywood piece that holds the movement has different dimensions.

Measure and cut the two plywood pieces. In measuring, remember you have to add the ⅛" depth of cut from all four walls to the plywood dimensions.

Assemble the box and lid with the plywood pieces in their respective grooves and check for fit. If the joints are forced open by the plywood, reduce the wood accordingly.

Now that the box has been assembled with large rubber bands, it's a good time to measure and cut the piece of plywood that fits inside the box and serves as the top of the sound chamber. This is also the piece to which the movement is attached. You should measure and cut the piece to the exact internal dimensions of the box. Do not make the fit too tight because this piece must be removed for assembly and, if necessary, for repairing the movement at some point in the future. Incidentally, a quick way of making the lid inlay fit perfectly into the assembled lid is tracing it from the assembled lid frame. I assemble the lid frame, using rubber bands, without the plywood insert. Then I place the top of the frame on the piece that is to be used for the inlay and trace along the inside top edge of the frame. This is also an excellent procedure

Illus. 128. Sound and support posts

for patterning a piece of veneer to be used as a lid inlay. You're assured of good fit without the hassle of measuring. It's an especially effective method when working with equilateral or other oddly shaped lids.

4. The next procedure is preparing support pieces for the plywood piece that will be placed inside the box. In addition to preparing four support pieces, you must also prepare two sound posts. These sound posts are placed directly under the comb of the movement. They carry sound and vibrations to the bottom piece of plywood. This procedure tends to increase the volume of the movement and, with the sound chamber, generates a very mellow sound from the movement.

In Illus. 128 you can see three box walls loosely standing. The four corner posts set on the plywood surface support the piece of plywood to which the movement is attached. The other two sound posts are put in the marked area that is directly below the place where the movement comb will be located.

When planning for the support pieces and sound posts, you must be familiar with the dimensional needs of the movement. For example, with the winding key in place, the movement is approximately 2¼" from the bottom of the base plate to the top of the key. You need to account for this height when measuring for the sound and support posts. If the posts are made ½" long for this design, there will be ample room for the movement key. This length will also provide more space for the movement to resonate in the box. Incidentally, a framed lid also enhances the sound production of the movement. When closed, it provides more area for the vibrations to resonate in.

In addition to being ½" long, the support pieces should be wide enough to accommodate a small wood screw. The plywood piece that holds the movement will be screwed into the support posts. Cut the support pieces and the sound posts. I usually cut them from the stock used for the box.

Set the disc movement on the surface of the plywood bottom piece, center it, and mark an area for the sound posts that will be directly under the movement comb. You will be approximating the location, but it's close enough.

5. Glue the joint surfaces and assemble the box with its plywood bottom piece glued into the routed grooves. Also, glue and assemble the lid and its plywood insert. Clamp both assemblies with large rubber bands until the glue is dry. Place glue on the edges and bottom of the support pieces, and place them in the four corners of the box and against the surface of the plywood bottom. They should be pressed into the plywood surface and box walls simultaneously for good glue contact. Glue to the two sound posts, within the marked area, to the plywood bottom surface. Press in place and allow to dry.

6. When the support and sound posts are dry, place the plywood insert on top of them. Again, if the fit is too tight, remove some wood from the edges. This piece needs to be removable. The movement is eventually secured to it with its screws or bolts entering the movement from the bottom of the plywood. Also, if the movement ever needs to be repaired, you will want to be able to remove it from the box.

With the plywood in place in the box, mark screw-hole locations at the four corners of the plywood directly over the four posts. Screws are not put into the two sound posts. Next, place the disc movement on the plywood surface and center it. You may want to put a disc on the movement to be certain you allow enough clearance between the front and back walls. With a pencil, trace the base of the move-

ment onto the plywood surface. Remove the movement and the plywood from the box.

7. Drill four holes through the screw locations on the corners of the plywood. I use small round-head screws just long enough to hold the plywood in place. The drilled holes should be of a diameter that permits the screw threads to slip through them. This procedure not only makes screwing them in much easier, it also prevents the screws from cracking the plywood.

Place the movement within the patterned lines on the plywood surface. Screw locations for securing the movement to the plywood must be marked. Using a sharp pencil, you can easily mark through the two movement holes on the comb end of the movement. The two holes on the other end are placed under the movement gears' cover plate. As they are difficult to get at, you can approximate their location by placing alignment marks on the plywood surface. Another procedure involves bending a piece of wire and inserting one end through the movement holes and into the surface of the plywood. If you use this procedure, be sure the wire entering the movement hole is straight. You may be able to devise another way of marking these two movement-hole locations onto the plywood surface.

When the four movement-screw locations have been marked, drill holes through them that will allow the movement screws to pass easily through. Because the movement screws are so long, I usually make small blocks with a hole drilled through them and slide them onto the screws. The blocks are usually about ¼" thick and slip up on the screw under the head. They're a kind of washer-only square. Their use prevents the movement screws from extending too far above the movement.

8. Assemble the movement onto the plywood and secure the assembly, using small round-head screws, into the support posts. Place a disc on the movement, wind, and then turn the unit on. You will be delighted with the sounds you hear. You will also notice how different the sound is from that produced by cylinder movements. When you have finished enjoying the sounds of disc-produced clockwork music, remove the movement so that it doesn't get loaded with sawdust.

9. Before hinging the lid to the box or putting the inlay in place, you need to embellish the box joints and surface. I would suggest you use the home-made jig presented in Design C 22-1. You may also want to refer to Illus. 127 to see how the box looks with the decorative splines and surface inlays. You can do the various splines and inlays on this design with either a ⅛" or ¼" straight router bit. You will want to use the home-made jig for cutting the joint splines. To make the wall inlays, adjust the router guide/fence to the location on the wall surface where you want to place the inlay. Set the router bit's depth of cut to ⅛" or a bit more if desired. Rout the inlay groove the entire length of the wall. I usually rout for the inlay at the same location on both the front and back walls. Reset the guide/fence and repeat the procedures on the side walls but at a different location.

I use a band saw for cutting the inlay strips to length and width. You can sand any excess inlay that extends from the wall surfaces using a belt sander. Glue the strips in place. Also, glue the splines into their respective grooves. When the glue is dry, using a belt sander remove all the excess wood and glue from the wall surfaces. Also, clean up the spline areas on the lid. Bring all walls to finishing readiness.

10. The lid is hinged with a 6" jewelry box hinge. Refer to Design C 26-1 for the procedures involved in placing a hinge system on a framed lid. You may want to use a brass chain or a commercial lid stopper to keep the lid from falling over the back.

11. If you patterned the lid insert from the frame assembly, cut it to the marked dimensions. You will need to measure the lid recess for the inlay if you did not pattern it out. I rout the edges of the inlay using a round-over router bit. Be certain to sand the edges of the inlay before gluing it in place. You also want to be sure that the top edges of the lid have been prepared for finishing. They're tough to sand once the inlay is in place.

Spread glue on the lid insert and place the inlay in the recess. Clamp until dry. You may want to clamp it with rubber bands so that you won't mark the box or inlay surfaces. Spalted wood is very easy to dent, especially with clamps and blocks.

12. Finish the box as desired or refer to the next chapter for some ideas. Secure the disc movement to the plywood insert and the insert to the corner posts.

Design C 31-1: Spalted Walnut Disc Music Box (Model 9131, 4½" Disc Movement) (Illus. 129)

1. This disc music box design is made from a rather unusual piece of spalted black walnut. As the photograph indicates, fungi have created a marvellous piece of wood for the box. If you alter the design, the box can also function as a jewelry box with a tray. The design employs butt joints that are assembled using screws and plugs. The lid is hinged with a 6" jewelry box hinge. And, because it is a solid lid, finger recesses have been sanded into its edges. If desired, a chain or commercial lid support can be attached to the lid and box wall.

Because the box is made from such an unusual piece of wood, a plywood soundboard would simply be out of place. Thus, I've made the soundboard from a planed piece of ⅛" walnut, which I then set in grooves routed in the box walls.

You can see that the bottom edges of the walls have decorative cutouts. Not only does this greatly enhance the flow of sound from the bottom of the box, it also enhances the overall appearance of the piece.

Illus. 129. Spalted walnut disc music box

These are the approximate dimensions of the box: The front and back walls are 8½" long. The side panels are 5½" long (not including the front and back wall thicknesses). The box walls are 5" high or wide. The lid is from a solid piece that is ⅞" thick. The walls of the box are from stock that is ½" thick.

2. Unlike the previous disc box design, this one employs only one ⅛"-thick board, which serves as both the soundboard and support piece for the disc movement. The piece is routed into the walls of the box approximately 3" from the top wall edges. This design is another way of maximizing the sounds of the disc movement. The 2" area below the soundboard functions as a sound chamber. You will find that, with the lid down, the sound is partially held within the box. It's best to play the movement with the lid open so that the sounds emerge from both the top and bottom areas of the movement.

3. As the procedures for making this box are similar to those in Design C 30-2, you may want to refer to it when crafting this design.

Design C 32-1: Large Jewelry Box with Floral Inlay (Illus. 130)

1. This box has a large storage area under the tray. Therefore, it's considerably deeper than most designs and can hold sizeable amounts of jewelry or other items. The design resembles a chest in its dimensional layout. Another feature of this design is its large dovetail joints, which are rather easy to make. The joints make the corners of a box this high really stand out, especially when the corners have been routed or sanded round. The lid on the design is made from a solid board. It employs a lid stopper and finger inserts for opening and it's embellished with a large rose inlay.

These are the approximate dimensions of the box: The front and back walls are 12" long. The side walls are 7" long. Not including the 1" lid, the walls are 6½" wide. The insert tray has 3"-wide walls made from ½" stock. The box walls are crafted from ⅝"-thick stock and the lid, of course, is 1" (4/4's) thick. A 6" jewelry box hinge is recessed in the box edge. The box is large enough to be used as a disc music box (see Design C 30-2 or Design C 31-1).

2. Cut the front and back walls to 12" lengths and make them 6½" wide. Measure and cut the two side walls to a length of 7" and, of course, a width of 6½".

3. The following procedures involve laying out the joints on the outside surface of all the walls. To help you visualize these joints, refer back to Illus. 14. Using the edge of one of the walls as a pattern, trace the thickness of the wall stock on the ends of each panel. Align the thickness pattern with the edge of the boards and then trace. You're making these lines on the outside surfaces of the walls. On the front and back walls only, measuring from the top and bottom edges of the walls, place marks on the thickness line that are 1½" from the top and bottom edges. Again measuring from the top and bottom edges, place marks on the end edge of the walls that are 2" from the top and bottom. Draw a line between the 1½" mark on the thickness line to the 2" mark on the end edge. Repeat this process on all ends of the front and back walls only. Illus. 131 shows how the panel should look and also indicates the areas that are to be cut out. It's a good idea to mark areas that are to be cut out.

Now cut out the traced, angled area at the ends of the front and back panels. For this procedure, I use a band saw with a ½" blade on it. You may prefer to use a backsaw or one of the Japanese handsaws that are available. I make

Illus. 130. Large jewelry box with floral inlay

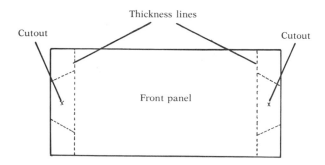

Illus. 131. Front panel joints

the cuts freehand with the band saw. Be sure you cut on or to the inside of the angled line and stop the cut at the thickness line. When you have made the angled cuts, cut the area out on or inside the thickness line. The area is large enough to be cut out with the ½" blade. You will need to make several cuts to clean up the thickness line wall. You want nice straight edges because they do show when the joints are assembled. Repeat these cutting procedures until all four front and back corners are done.

The next procedure is tracing the areas you just cut out onto the end surface of the side walls. Each front and back wall cutout must be traced individually on one of the end surfaces of the side walls. You're literally making four custom joints. Don't try to short-cut the procedure.

When making joints, it's a good idea to label and number the outside wall surfaces. For example, I will write *front wall* and *back wall*, as well as *top edge* and *bottom edge*. I also number the corners of each wall that are to eventually fit together. You should place the numbers where they won't be cut off. Without notes and a numbering system, the process can be confusing.

The tracing procedure that's required is rather awkward but manageable. To simplify tracing the cutout angle lines from the front and back panels onto the end surface of the side walls, clamp the side wall in a vise. If you don't have a vise, use a bar clamp and affix it to something else. Use your imagination. Place the cutout area of a front or back wall directly over the end surface of the side panel. Align the top and bottom edges of both pieces. The wall of the

thickness line in the cutout should be directly over the inside edge of the side panel. When aligned, trace the two angled lines on the end surface. Mark this joint, on the surfaces of both walls, with the number *1* or the letter *A*, or according to whatever marking system you chose to use. Repeat the tracing and marking process on the other three corners. Take your time with this procedure and think about what you're doing. Remember that you're also supposed to be having a good time. The end and outside surfaces on the side walls should resemble those in Illus. 132. An additional line has been added to the drawing so that the areas that are to be cut out are clearly marked.

There are any number of ways to cut out the marked areas on the side walls. You can use a backsaw or the appropriate Japanese saw. I usually cut the ends on the band saw. Use whatever tool works best for you. Be certain, however, that you cut out the right areas on the side walls. When I cut for joints, I tend to cut to the inside of the line. It usually provides a better fit. You can always cut more off if necessary.

Illus. 133 shows the various cutouts on one corner. You may want to look over this drawing before making the cuts on the side panel.

After you have made all the cuts, assemble the walls and check the joints for fit. Remember, you have to slide the side walls into the front and back corner cutouts. If they're too tight, carefully remove a little wood from the appropriate spots.

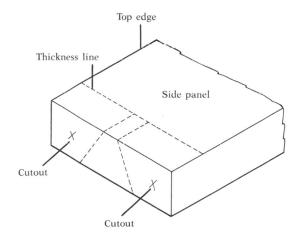

Illus. 132. Side panel joints

4. The next procedure is routing a groove in the box walls that will hold a ¼" plywood bottom piece. With this kind of joint on the box, refer to Design C 25-1 for assistance. The routed grooves, as you will note in the discussion, should not be cut along the entire length of the front and back walls. Follow the procedures on both routing and cutting the plywood bottom section.

5. The procedures for making the tray are also presented in Design C 25-1. You may want to duplicate the box joints on the tray. With this design, you can make a deep tray if desired.

6. When you assemble the box, place glue on all touching surfaces in the joints. Don't use too much glue because it will rub off when the joints are assembled. Remember to place glue in the grooves for holding the bottom section in place. I suggest you clamp the assembly using bar clamps. Rubber bands can't do the job on this type of joint. After the glue is dry, bring the surfaces to finishing readiness. Using a large, round-over router bit, rout the corners. They're more attractive when routed round.

7. Measure and cut the lid. If it's part of your design, include the lid stopper on the back of the lid. For the necessary procedures, refer to Design C 25-1. You will also want to cut the corners of the lid to match the routed corners of the box. If you want to have finger slots on the

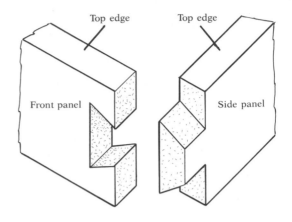

Illus. 133. Corner cutouts for joints

lid, using the roller end of a belt sander is a good way of making them. The finger areas are placed on both sides of the lid on the lower edge of the lid ends and extend onto the bottom surface. For inlay procedures, refer to Design A 5-2.

8. You can review the hinge procedures for a solid lid in Design A 6-1. This lid is not thick enough for wooden hinges, so you should consider a 6" jewelry box hinge or butt hinges.

9. Finish the design using your own favorite products and procedures. Refer to the next chapter for a few finishing ideas.

Design C 33-1: Long Jewelry Box with Ivory Inlay (Illus. 134)

1. This design is rather long and narrow and may contain a tray for jewelry. You may prefer to make the box without the tray and use it for general storage instead. Either way, the design is quite functional. The joints on the design are a lapped-type that are assembled using screws and plugs. The lid inlay employs vegetable ivory for the flower. This ivory is an extremely interesting and challenging substance to work with. It comes from the nut of a tagua palm tree, which is common in South America. The nut ivory is very hard and can be polished to a nice lustre. When soaked in water, the nut becomes quite soft and easy to carve. These nuts are ideal for box lid inlay work because they provide you with a white material that can be tooled easily with microburrs. The use and availability of tagua nuts may also reduce the killing of animals and sea creatures for their

ivory. A number of mail-order craft suppliers stock these nuts (Illus. 135).

These are the overall dimensions of this design, including the 1"-thick lid. It's 13" long, 5" wide, and 5" high. The walls are made from ⅝"-thick stock. The wood I used for the box is emeri, a somewhat tan-colored exotic that is easy to work. The bottom section of the box is made from ¼" cabinet-grade plywood. You can make the tray from ½" material and use mitred joints that are decorated with splines. Although the tray is rather small, it does provide sufficient space for a number of dividers to be integrated into its design. The lid is hinged with two brass butt hinges and employs a chain secured with escutcheon pins as a stopper. I have sanded finger slots into the edge and bottom surface of the lid.

2. Cut the front and back walls to the indicated

Illus. 134. Long jewelry box with ivory inlay

dimensions. You may want to alter the size of the design. If so, cut the walls according to these dimensions.

3. To make the joints, you first need to mark the wall thickness on the ends of all the wall panels. For this design, the thickness is ⅝". A quick way of making these thickness lines is using the edge of one of the panels as a pattern. Align the edge with the end of the panel and trace the line on the outside wall surface.

I do not center the laps in this design, thus the differences in the following dimensions. On the front and back walls only, place a mark on the thickness line that is 1" from the top edge of the wall. Make another mark on the thickness line that is 1¾" from the bottom edge of the wall. You should make these measurements and marks on the thickness lines of all the panels or walls.

Next, on the front and back walls only, draw straight lines from the marks on the thickness lines to the edge of the walls. Draw these lines on the other ends of the front and back walls. These lines, including the thickness line, lay out the area on the walls that will be cut out on the front and back walls. Illus. 136 shows how the front and side ends will look, before assembly, with the joint areas cut out.

Using a band saw or a backsaw and chisel, cut out the marked areas on the front and back panels. You will want to do some labelling on the surfaces of the wall. I generally write such labels as *front* and *back*, *top* and *bottom*, *side 1* and *side 2* on the outside surfaces of the wall. It really helps. It's critical that you use a numbering system when tracing the front and back cutouts onto the side walls. You will have problems down the line if the pieces aren't clearly marked.

The next procedure is tracing the cutouts from the front and back walls onto the surface of the side panels. A good procedure to use for tracing is supporting the pattern piece with the other wall as you trace the cutout onto the side panel. Align the cutout area over the side panel.

Illus. 135. Tagua palm nuts: vegetable ivory

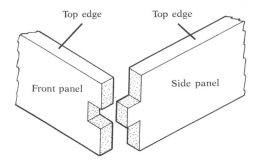

Illus. 136. Joint cutouts on front and side panels

The end of the side panel should be directly below the wall on the thickness line. Be certain to align the top and bottom edges of both walls before tracing. You will be making two lines, traced from the cutout, onto the side wall. The traced lines should stop at the thickness line on the side panel. Refer to Illus. 136 so that you can see the end result of this procedure. You're drawing the tenon or finger on the side wall that will fit into the cutout in the front or back panel.

I recommend that you trace and cut one side panel at a time. This will make numbering the joints easier and will also slow down the process. This is one of those tasks that is easy to rush through. Each joint is custom-made so take your time in tracing, numbering, and cutting.

You can easily cut the traced areas out on the band saw. To assure a tight fit, cut inside the traced and thickness lines. Inside here means towards the piece that is being cut out.

After all the panels have been cut, assemble the box and check for fit. Any pieces that extend beyond the panels' surfaces can be sanded off after assembly.

4. Grooves need to be cut in the walls to hold the ¼″ plywood bottom in place. For this kind of joint, refer to Design C 22-1 and Design C 25-1 for the necessary procedures. Be sure you place glue in the grooves when assembling the box. The bottom section needs to be glued in place.

5. Because the box is assembled with screws, covered by plugs, you need to drill screw-plug holes into the walls. Make the holes, centered on all laps, using a ¼″ wood bit. I cut the plugs with a ¼″ plug cutter. The emeri is so attractive it doesn't need plugs from a contrasting wood. I cut the plugs from scraps of emeri. The screw holes should be drilled at least halfway through the walls. I drill a smaller hole through the rest of the wall that permits the screws to slide through. When the box has been assembled, drill pilot holes for the screws. As the final procedure in assembling the box, glue and tap the plugs into the screw holes.

Before spreading glue on the joint surfaces, place glue in the grooves that will hold the bottom piece in place. Spread a thin coat of glue on all joint surfaces that make contact with one another. I usually clamp the assembly with bar clamps and blocks so the surfaces are not marked. You should clamp the box before the screws are put in place. Don't clamp over the screw-plug holes, if possible. Drill the screw-pilot holes and secure the screws in place.

Sand the box surfaces on a belt sander and reduce any joint extensions. Bring the surfaces to finishing readiness.

6. As previously stated, the design employs brass butt hinges. You may want to use a 6″ jewelry box hinge. For procedures on placing hinges on solid lids, refer to Design A 6-1. Before placing the hinges, remember to sand the bottom of the lid in preparation for finishing.

7. The lid embellishment on this design is placed in a 2½″-diameter recess. The recess is drilled with a multi-spur bit to a depth of ¼″. The background inlay is cut from walnut and is ⅜″ thick. The double stem for the flowers is cut from Osage orange (hedge) and is also ⅜″ thick.

Illus. 137. Ivory inlay

You can see in Illus. 137 that the stem extends onto the lid surface and a small leaf is placed next to it. The leaf can be cut from a green strip of poplar and should be ⅜″ thick.

When I work with the tagua nuts, I first cut them in half on the band saw. Because they are round, they can grab the saw blade. Therefore, you may want to sand a small flat area on the surface that will rest on the table while sawing. The center of the nut usually has a small hollow area and a number of cracks, no doubt from drying. To make the flowers for the inlay, I cut two pieces that are ½″ thick. The nuts are generally about 1½″ in diameter and about 3″ long, so you can get two good-sized pieces for the flowers. As with a wood flower, I draw the flower design on the surface of the ivory and then cut it on a scroll saw. If you have a ⅛″ blade on your band saw, this will do the job. The rest of the procedures for making the inlay are the same as those in Design A 5-2. As you will discover, the ivory shapes quite easily. Although some exotics tend to be toxic, I have no information on whether the dust from the nut is hazardous or not. When I've used it, I have had no adverse effects.

8. Finish the box as desired. Incidentally, I do not put any finishing products on the nut. Paste wax and polishing tend to enhance its appearance enough.

Design C 34-1: Long Jewelry Box with Picture Inlay (Illus. 138)

1. Although this box is a duplicate of the previous design, it's presented as a separate project because it uses different procedures for preparing the lid inlay. For the dimensions and the various instructions, refer to Design C 33-1.

2. To make the inlay picture in Illus. 139 or one of your own design, you need to rout a recess if you're using a solid lid. For a framed lid, you can place the plywood insert into the walls of the lid at the desired depth. Unless you have the router capability to cut a recess in a solid lid, you may want to consider the framed lid as an option. You should rout the lid recess to a depth of at least ¼″ and you should leave a ½″-wide shoulder in place on the lid edges. The corners in the lid recess can be squared with a chisel or a Moto-Tool with a router attachment and microbit.

3. The inlay is a rather uncomplicated picture made from zebrawood, spalted maple, ebony,

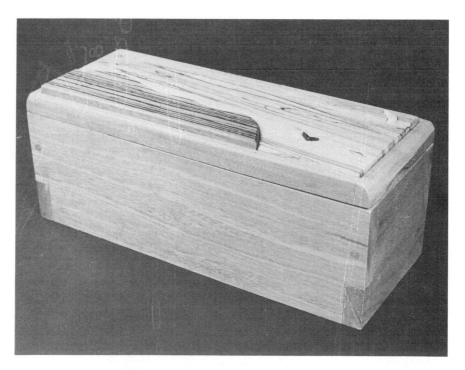

Illus. 138. Long jewelry box with picture inlay

and tagua ivory. The design requires only one basic cut to produce the sky and landscape effect. The ebony bird in flight and the tagua ivory moon are cut with a knife and then microrouted in place.

4. To prepare the inlay, cut a ¼"-thick piece of zebrawood that will fit into the entire lid recess. You should cut it a bit oversized to allow for dimensional reduction from the inlay cuts. The more cutting that is done for the inlay design, the greater the dimensional loss of the inlay piece. You need to plan for this when cutting the inlay for the lid recess. Using the zebrawood piece as a pattern, cut a ¼"-thick piece of spalted maple to the same dimensions. For the purposes of this discussion, I'll assume you are duplicating the design using the same woods.

5. After the two inlay pieces have been cut and checked for fit in the recess, you need to cement or lightly glue the two pieces together. This process is done only to hold the two pieces together while the inlay parts are being cut. As the two pieces must eventually be separated, the kind of cement or glue you use is critical. I usually use rubber cement or one of the many household cements to temporarily secure the two pieces. In a pinch, you can sparingly put drops of white glue on one of the surfaces to hold the pieces together. After you cut the inlay design in the joined boards, you will have an inlay piece cut from one wood and a recess to place it in cut from another. This is an easy way of cutting the various inlays of the design and the perfect recesses for them to fit into. As your inlay designs become more complex and your skills increase, you may want to use three or four boards of varying thicknesses and woods. The procedures are the same for two boards or more. The only limiting factor in this stacking procedure is that you must have the saw capacity to precisely cut out the parts of the inlay design.

6. To make the picture in Illus. 139, draw the design on the surface of the top piece in the cemented assembly. It doesn't matter which wood is on top when you draw the design because when you cut it, you will always have one part from each wood.

Cutting inlay designs following this type of procedure gives you much better-fitting parts, especially when you're doing a detailed design. For example, the multiple roses and stem assembly in Design C 27-1 can also be done fol-

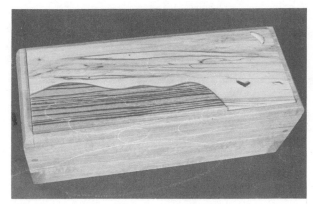

Illus. 139. Picture inlay

lowing this procedure. You would have cemented the cherry, padouk, and poplar inserts together, made the design on the lid, and cut. Assembling the final design is a matter of placing the correct inlay part into the correct recess.

To continue with the inlay for the box lid in this project, first examine Illus. 139 and then draw a line on the assembly surface representing a line of hills. Using a scroll or band saw, cut out the lined piece from the assembly. Separate the two cemented boards. I use the section from the zebrawood for the hills and the spalted section for the sky. When placed in the lid recess, the two parts should fit perfectly. If they're too tight, remove a bit of wood from the outside edges.

7. To complete the inlay picture, design a piece from ebony that resembles wings of a bird in flight. The ebony only needs to be ⅛" thick. You can use this thickness because the bird and the moon are placed into recesses in the inlay that are only ⅛" deep. More about this shortly. Using tagua ivory, you also need to prepare a ⅛"-thick piece that resembles the moon.

Place the bird and moon where you want them to be recessed in the scene. With a sharp pencil, trace their outline on the inlay surface. Cut out the traced area to a depth of ⅛" using a sharp knife or a Moto-Tool with a router attachment and a microbit. Check for fit.

8. Remove the inlay parts and shape the hills if desired. On this type of design, I usually just sand all the edges round. The design does not lend itself to a great deal of shaping. When doing a more detailed inlay that requires shaping, refer to Design A 5-2 for some suggested procedures and tools.

9. After removing the inlay parts from the lid recess, spread wood glue on the surface of the recess. Place the two inlay pieces into the recess and press them into the glue. Put a spot of glue in the two small recesses and set the bird and moon in place. You may want to stretch a rubber band around the entire box and place pieces of wood under the rubber band to clamp the inlay in place. Allow the glue to dry. Finish the inlay and the rest of the box using the same product. I usually don't put any finishing products on the ivory.

10. As mentioned at the outset of this design, this inlay procedure gives you another option for embellishing the lids of your boxes. You may want to try it on your next framed lid, but with a more detailed inlay of your own design.

Design C 35-1: Box with Goose Lid Inlay (Illus. 140)

1. With its side walls a bit longer than its front and back walls, this box design is ideal for inlaying a goose with its long neck. Another feature of this design is that, if you make a few dimensional changes, it can hold a 4½″ disc musical movement. While the design has been created as a large storage box, you can also modify it into a jewelry box with a tray. Should you want to include a tray, refer to Design C 25-1 for the necessary procedures.

As you can see in Illus. 140, the lid and box are made from different woods. The splines in the mitred joints reverse the woods: dark on light, light on dark. The inlay is designed so that a portion of the goose extends out onto the edge of the lid. This extension of the shaped or sculpted design beyond the edges of the inlay background gives the lid a very interesting appearance (Illus. 141). The procedures are similar to those in the designs where the flower stem extends beyond the inlay and onto the lid surface.

The box and the lid frame are made from ½″-thick stock. Both the bottom piece and the lid insert are from ¼″ plywood and held in routed grooves. The front and back walls of the box

Illus. 140. Box with goose inlay

and lid are 7½" long. Their side walls are 8½" long. The box walls are 3" high; the lid walls are 1½" high. These dimensions can be changed as desired. For example, if you want to make the box perfectly square, you can easily do so.

2. After cutting the box and lid walls to length, refer to Design C 22-1 for procedures on mitring and router work. This design also provides you with information on routing the box and lid corners for holding splines. You should review Design C 26-1 for specifics on placing the plywood insert in the lid. For procedures on placing hinges, also refer to Design C 26-1. The hinges should be placed before the inlay work begins. If you would like to use wooden hinges for this box design, follow the next procedure.

3. Wooden hinges can be used for this design and most other boxes, if desired. Not only do I enjoy making these hinges, they're also quite functional as you will discover. In many ways, wooden hinges will outlast and outperform their metal counterparts. Due to the nature of their design, they also stop the lid and hold it open. Illus. 142 shows wooden hinges in place on the goose inlay box design.

Once you understand how wooden hinges are designed and how they work, you can make them to fit most boxes. While excellent hinges can be made from many woods, I have a bias towards using white ash. A number of boxes I made some time ago have ash hinges and they continue to function efficiently and show no signs of wear. For decorative reasons, you may prefer making your hinges from other woods.

In making wooden hinges for this box design, I cut a block of ash that is 2" (8/4's) thick, 3¼" long, and 3¼" wide. Because of the procedures involved, I generally make several sets of hinges when I make a pair for a given design. If you should break one of the hinges or drill a hole incorrectly, another hinge is always available. I simply keep the extra wooden hinges with my metal hinges for future use. This is why I use such a large block for preparing the hinges.

The first task is making a mortise or groove in one end (end grain) of the block. To make the mortise, I use a ¾" mortise router bit on a table-mounted router. For smaller hinges, you can reduce the size of the mortise and its matching tenon. You need the wider mortise for the hinges on this box design. You will want to lay out the block surface so that you can cut the

Illus. 141. Goose inlay

mortise in the exact center of the block. Remember, you will be cutting the mortise in the end (end grain) of the block, so place your pencil marks accordingly. The mortise needs to be cut to a depth of ½". You may have to make two passes over the mortising bit to get the mortise this deep.

Align the fence/guide on the router table to the block. Be certain the marked center lines on the block's surface line up with the mortise bit. Set the bit to the depth of cut and rout the mortise. As suggested, you may want to make two passes over the bit that are set at different cutting depths to achieve the ½"-deep mortise. You are routing into cross grain and also ash, which can be rather demanding on the bit. Be sure to hold the block tight against the fence/guide when moving it over the bit.

After the ¾" mortise has been in one end of the block, I lay out the other end of the block for cutting the tenon. If you haven't figured out the final procedure yet, after the tenon has been cut you simply slice off the hinges with the grain from the block. First, however, you need to prepare the tenon for cutting.

The tenon should be ½" long, but only about ¹¹⁄₁₆" wide. To allow for smooth movement of the hinge knuckle, the tenon needs to be slightly reduced. However, don't reduce the width any more than 1/16". Lay out the dimensions of the tenon on the block surface. It, too, is cut from the end (end grain) opposite the mortise. The tenon is best cut on the band saw using a 1/2" blade that will produce a reasonably smooth-cut surface. Illus. 143 shows how the block will look after the mortise and tenon have been cut. The photograph also shows two sets of hinges and a mortising router bit.

After the tenon has been cut, set the band saw fence for ripping the hinges from the block to a thickness of 1/2". For this style of a box, you need a hinge system that is at least 1/2" thick. You can, of course, increase or reduce the thickness of the hinges according to the size of the box and lid. Slice several hinge sets, two sets for the box and extra ones for use in the event of breakage. Do not cut them into their two-leaf sections yet. You need a little more information before cutting the hinge slices in two.

The hinge leaf that is placed on the back of the box is the one with the mortise. The lid leaf is the piece with the tenon. Review Illus. 142 to get a sense of this and to see their size relationship. I usually cut the leaf for the box twice as long as the lid leaf. With the dimensions of the block used, cut the bottom leaf (mortise) 2" long and the top leaf (tenon) 1 1/4" long. Later you can reduce both in length and also give them some decorative corner cuts.

To hold the two pieces together at the knuckle, I use 1/8"-diameter piano wire. Do not do any shaping or rounding of the tenon until you've drilled a 1/8" hole through the two pieces that will hold the wire. To simplify drilling the 1/8" wire hole, I assemble the hinge, tenon in mortise, and place the assembly in a vise. Be sure the tenon is all the way into the mortise before tightening them in the vise. This vise procedure greatly simplifies drilling the hole through the walls of the mortise and the tenon. Center the drilled hole on the mortise wall surface and make sure it will pass through the middle of the tenon. If a wooden hinge is going to be ruined, it generally happens while doing this procedure. Take your time with the layout and the locking in the vise. When drilling, be certain the hole is drilled straight. Illus. 142 shows how the hinges will look when assembled with the wire. The cut pieces of piano wire are also shown in the photograph. Drill the hole where you will place the 1/8" hinge wire.

Illus. 142. Wooden hinges

You will want to cut the hinge wire that penetrates the knuckle hole longer than required. It helps to be able to slide it in place and pull it out when shaping the tenon and knuckle edges so they move smoothly. With the holes drilled

Illus. 143. Hinge blocks and mortise bit

in the pair of hinges to be used on the box, slide the hinge wires into place. You will note how the knuckle binds when you attempt to move the two parts of the hinge. Examine the tenon and its shoulders to find where the bind originates. With a pencil, darken the wood areas that need to be reduced and rounded over. You will definitely need to round over the end of the tenon. Remove the hinge wire and reduce the marked areas and the tenon end. Assemble again and check the movement of the assembly. You need to repeat this process until the hinge opens smoothly. This needs to be done, of course, on both hinges. When the hinges work properly, leave the hinge wire in place. If the wire is tight, leave it alone. If the wire is a bit loose, after you have sanded the side walls of the hinges, place a small spot of glue on the end of it. You will need to cut off the extra length from the wire. The ends of the wire should be flush with the outer walls of the mortise.

Place the assembled hinges on the back walls of the box and lid. If they look too long for the box, cut some length off both sets. I usually cut or round the corners of the hinges so that they don't look quite so boxy. Using abrasive paper, round the outer edges of the hinges.

While the hinges can be glued to the back surfaces of the box and lid, I always screw them in place in addition to using glue. I drill a screw-plug hole that is 3/8" in diameter in the middle of both hinge leaves. The hole should be drilled at least halfway through the hinge thickness. Drill another hole, through which the screw threads can easily pass. You will also need to drill small pilot holes for the screws in the lid and box surfaces. Prepare 3/8" plugs that you will place in the holes over the screwheads. As Illus. 142 indicates, I used decorative plugs in the screw holes.

Before securing the hinges in place on the box and the lid, place a piece of construction paper between the back edges of the lid and box. This paper will elevate the two edges enough to prevent the hinges from binding. Stretch a large rubber band over the box and the lid that will hold the paper in place and make attaching the hinges easier.

The hinges should be centered on the back surfaces. To properly place the hinges, the top edges of the mortise walls need to be aligned with the top edge of the box. Spread glue on the

surfaces of the hinges, being careful not to get any on the moving knuckle. Put the hinges in place and secure them to the box and lid with screws. Glue the plugs in the screw holes and sand flush when dry.

If the box and lid edges are not flush after the hinges are in place (front and sides), you can use a belt sander that will make them flush. However, don't remove too much wood.

4. With the entire box and lid assembled and hinged, you can begin the inlay process. The box in Illus. 140 is made from walnut and the lid is made from oak. The background inlay in the lid is also from walnut; the goose is from wild cherry; the light neck insert is a piece of soft maple. If you want to duplicate this design, knowing which woods were used should be helpful.

Measure and cut the inlay background from 5/8"-thick stock. Plan how you want the grain of the inlay to run. Be certain the inlay fits neatly into the recess with no gaps between it and the lid edges. Take your time in measuring and cutting. To allow for shaping the edges of the goose round, I use 3/4"-thick cherry for the goose. The goose is approximately 6½" long and 5¾" wide. You can, of course, reduce or increase its size. There is sufficient area in the lid for a larger bird if desired (Illus. 141).

Using the suggested dimensions as a guide, make a pattern of a goose from construction paper. Because the goose design is just a profile, you don't need to concern yourself with a lot of details in the pattern. Much of the fun in doing inlay work is designing and drawing your own objects. For example, as Canadian geese have a white feather section under the bill area and on the neck and I've attempted to approximate a Canadian goose, I used an inlay of soft maple. These are my perceptions of a goose. Yours will be somewhat different, so your pattern will also be different. Work on the pattern until you are satisfied with it.

5. Trace your goose pattern on 3/4"-thick cherry. Remember to lay out the pattern according to how you want the wood grain to run in relation to the inlay background. Cut the goose using either a scroll saw or band saw. Before doing any shaping on the goose, you need to trace it on the surface of the inlay background. As you can see in the photograph of the box lid, the goose is placed in the inlay so that its tail feathers extend onto the edge of the lid.

6. It's best to place the background inlay in the lid recess and then trace the goose onto its surface. You can align the goose so that its feathers extend onto the lid surface. As you trace the goose on the inlay, also trace the feather section on the edge portion of the lid. Cut the goose outline from the inlay background. You also need to cut out the lid edge where the feathers will extend. It must be cut down to the top of the plywood insert but no deeper. I use a Moto-Tool with a small bit and router base for this procedure. You may want to use a saw and chisel in order to remove the wood from the lid edge.

7. Assemble the inlay background into the recess and put the goose in place. Check for fit. While the goose is in place, draw the small triangle area on the bill and neck section. You need to cut out this area and make an exact duplicate of the piece from soft maple. Check again that all parts fit.

8. Using abrasive paper or a finishing sander,

roll the edges of the walnut inlay background. You can also shape the goose with a pad sander. If you want to give it more detail, refer to the procedures in Design A 5-2. I taper the edges of the goose to give it the appearance of roundness and depth. You can indent the body area in front of the tail feathers to create the impression of feathers sticking up and out. You can also reduce and shape the bill. Think about the different ways you can enhance the goose by various shaping procedures.

9. Remove the background inlay from the lid recess and bring its surface to finishing readiness. Spread a coat of glue on the plywood lid insert and place the inlay back into the recess. Press it down into the glue. Place the goose and the neck piece in the recess and also force them into the glue. You may want to clamp the entire assembly using rubber bands until the glue is dry. Remove any excess glue with fine-grit abrasive paper.

10. Finish the design as desired or refer to the next chapter for some ideas.

Design C 36-1: Box with Block Inlay (Illus. 144)

1. This box is similar to the one in Design C 33-1, both in design and type of joints. However, it employs a framed lid instead of a solid lid.

I've made the lid using the same lap joints and procedures that I've used for the base. Before you begin to make this box, you may want to

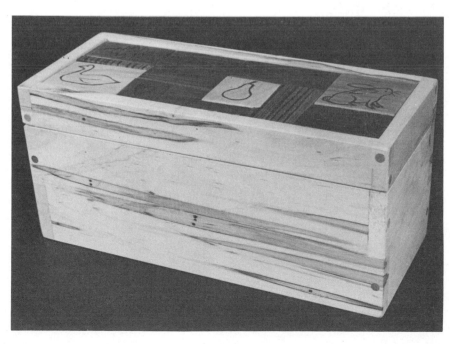

Illus. 144. Box with block inlay

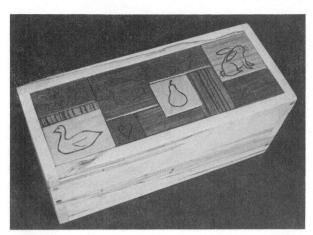

Illus. 145. Block inlay

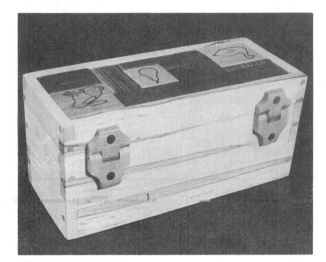

Illus. 146. Wood hinges

review some of the procedures in Design C 25-1 and Design C 26-1 that pertain to this type of joint and the framed lid.

The box base is 12″ long, 5″ wide, and 4½″ high. The dimensions of the lid are the same, except it's 1¼″ high. The box and lid are both made from ½″-thick stock.

The special features of this design are the inlay that is great fun to make and the wooden hinges. Because of its size, the box can be used for a wide range of purposes. You can decorate the inlay according to a theme that relates to the way the box will be used. You can also decorate it in a way that reflects the interests, sex, or age of the user. As you can see in Illus. 145, the

various inlay blocks have a small wood-burned profile on them. More about this shortly.

2. Make the box base and lid using the procedures for lap joints. Depending on the way you plan on using the box, you may want to increase or decrease the dimensions of the design. You should place the plywood lid insert at least ¼″ from the top edge. This depth permits the placement of inlay blocks that range in thickness from ⅛″ to ¼″. You may, however, want the blocks of a uniform ¼″ thickness so that they will be flush with the top edge of the lid.

3. To make the wooden hinges in this design, refer to the procedures in Design C 35-1. I use wooden hinges that are of the same size and design for both of these boxes (Illus. 146).

4. When the box base and lid have been made and the wooden or brass butt hinges have been put in place, you can begin the block inlay process. The inlay procedures on this design are not terribly complicated. I've used a variety of indigenous and exotic woods—purpleheart, Osage orange (hedge), walnut, padouk, Honduras mahogany, zebrawood, and wild cherry—to make the inlay blocks (Illus. 143). There is no decorative rationale for the use of these woods. They simply were pieces of scrap that I had in the shop.

Depending on whether or not you want the inlay flush with the lid edge, you need to rip the blocks to the desired thickness. After the inlay block material has been ripped, begin placing the pieces in the lid. At some point you should sand the top surface of each block to finishing readiness. The placement process is similar to making a puzzle. I usually start in one corner of the lid. Using blocks of differing dimensions, I place them in the lid recess, alternating the types of wood and the direction of the grain. When necessary, I will cut a block to fit in a particular spot. In some instances, I will cut a narrow strip to fit between two blocks that are too small by themselves. Examine Illus. 143 again and you will notice several of these filler strips.

When the lid recess has been filled with blocks, you should number the top surface of each block with a pencil. Then you should remove each block and write its number on the lid insert where it is placed. This numbering system greatly simplifies reassembly. After you've finished this marking procedure, place the blocks back into the lid. You want all the inlay blocks in place so that you can plan your decorative designs on their surface. Do not glue the blocks in place at this point.

5. I use a wood-burning unit to make the various decorative designs on the surface of the blocks. The wood-burning tool that I use is one that was designed for children; it's functional and inexpensive. There are any number of sophisticated wood-burning tools on the market that are probably preferable. You may, however, prefer carving a design in each block rather than burning it in.

The designs I've made on the blocks are rather simplistic. They include a fish, rabbit, goose, tree, apple, heart, pear, and dove. Minimal, if any, detail is burned into each design. A quick examination of my designs and their execution quickly reveals that my skills lie in woodworking and not in art. Do not avoid making this inlay because you feel you can't draw. I can't either, but it doesn't seem to matter.

Before wood-burning the various designs into the blocks, I draw each design with a pencil on the block surface. Again, you can draw anything you want. I avoid any designs that exceed my minimal wood-burning skills. It's wise to keep the designs simple unless you have some expertise with a wood-burning tool.

After the designs have been drawn on the blocks, remove them and begin the wood-burning process. Slowly and carefully, follow the pencil line. Initially, I make a very shallow burn. After the entire design has been lightly burned, I go back over the lines and burn them deeper. It's lots of fun. Continue the process until all the blocks are finished.

6. Because the wood-burning procedures leave a certain amount of residue around the design edges, lightly sand the surface of each block. Also, round the edges of each block using fine-grit abrasive paper. Don't remove the block numbers yet.

7. Spread glue over the entire lid-insert surface. Using the block numbers as a guide, reassemble the blocks into the lid. Allow the glue to dry. After the glue is dry, using fine-grit abrasive paper, sand off the pencilled numbers and any other residue that needs to be removed. Be certain to sand the blocks with the grain.

8. Finish the box as desired. If you use a surface finish, be careful not to use too much on the moving parts of the wood hinges.

Design C 37-1: Bone Music Box (Model 1.36 Musical Movement) (Illus. 147)

1. While this is a rather strange name for a music box design, it does describe the shape of the box. The box in the photograph is made from spalted sycamore. To achieve the bone effect, I cut the walls and lid concave after assembling the box. This procedure not only significantly alters the appearance of the box, it also reduces the wood mass permitting better sound production from the musical movement. The wall thickness at the mitred joints remains at ⅞". The areas that are cut concave with a band saw are reduced to a thickness of ⅜".

The box houses a Model 1.36 musical movement that employs a sliding on/off stopper system routed into the front panel (see Design C 28-1). The movement is secured to a elevated soundboard.

The movement is placed in the middle of the box and a glass insert rests on two dividers. As Illus. 148 indicates, the dividers allow for storage areas on both sides of the movement.

I have hinged the lid with butt hinges placed near the side edges on the back wall. The concave area in the back of the box prevents placing the hinges in a more traditional location.

2. The box is approximately 10" long, 4¾" wide,

Illus. 147. Bone music box

and 3″ high (not including the lid thickness). The lid is made from a solid piece of wood that is ⅞″ thick. The joints are mitred and decorative splines are inserted into the top edge of the joint (Illus. 148). The splines do not run all the way through the joint, but penetrate at both the top and the bottom approximately ¾ of an inch. Their use is strictly decorative and not for strengthening the joint in this design. The spline recess can be routed with a ⅛″-diameter straight bit on a table-mounted router and edge guide. To prepare the box for housing a musical movement, refer to the procedures in Design C 28-1.

Design C 38-1: Spalted Boxes (Illus. 149 and Illus. 150)

1. These two boxes are presented to demonstrate how attractive jewelry or general storage boxes can be when made from spalted woods. Both boxes are approximately 12″ long, 6″ wide, and 5″ high. However, you can make boxes from the spalts in any dimension and they will look superb.

2. Illus. 149 shows a box with a lid made from spalted hickory and a base made from spalted hard maple. The box in Illus. 150 has a lid made from spalted red oak and a base from spalted hard maple. Frequently I will mix spalted woods when I make boxes. The overall effect can be extremely interesting.

3. As both designs employ mitred joints and a solid lid, refer to Design C 24-1 for procedures.

Design 39-1: Spalted Music Box (Model 1.36 Musical Movement) (Illus. 151)

1. This is a somewhat formal-looking design, but one that provides excellent sound reproduction for a Model 1.36 or other large movement. The design also makes for a charming jewelry box. The box in Illus. 151 is made from spalted hard maple that is ½″ thick. This thickness is used for both the walls and the lid. The design has a standard butt joint, assembled with screws and plugs. The lid is hinged with two small butt hinges and employs a brass chain and escutcheon pins for a lid stopper. I do not use a glass covering over the musical movement in this design, but one could easily be included. The soundboard is ⅛″-thick Sitka spruce and the movement is elevated on two strips. If you make the design for storing jewelry or for some similar function, use ¼″ plywood for the bottom section. To prepare the box for housing a musical movement and the appropriate on/off stopper system, you may want to refer to Design C 28-1.

2. The box is approximately 7″ long, and 4¼″ wide (including the wall thickness and butt joint). With the ½″-thick lid piece, the box is 4½″ high. However, this design can be significantly enlarged to hold a CH 3.72 musical movement or to serve as a large jewelry box. It can also be reduced to make a very attractive, chestlike storage box.

3. You should trace the front and back panels from a prepared pattern. This kind of design requires uniformity in its cutout leg panels. Refer to Illus. 151 as you prepare your pattern. You may prefer to make the legs of the design somewhat shorter. Explore with some possible design options before making a final pattern.

4. You may want to refer to the next chapter for a few ideas on finishing spalted woods.

Design C 40-1: Box with Recessed Lid (Illus. 152)

1. This design features a lid that is recessed into the box and hinged on two dowels. It also has a lid extension for opening the lid that rests in a cut insert in the front panel. The box has mitred joints with splines of varying thicknesses. It demonstrates another way of doing decorative work on joints. The lid, as Illus. 152 indicates, also has a decorative strip inlaid into its surface. For an additional decorative touch, a ½″-diameter plug has been inserted into the lid-opening extension.

The box and lid in this design are made from black walnut and red oak. The box is approximately 8″ long, 3½″ wide, and 3½″ high. The

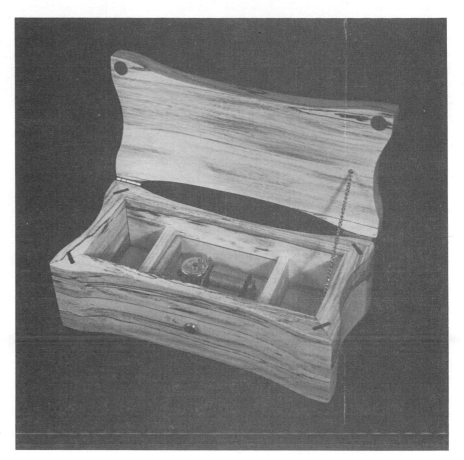

Illus. 148. Movement and storage areas

Illus. 149. Spalted box

Illus. 150. Spalted box

145

Illus. 151. Spalted music box

Illus. 152. Box with recessed lid

walls and lid are made from ½"-thick stock. The bottom section of the box is a piece of ¼" plywood held in routed grooves. I have found a box of this size to be very functional. It has a reasonable amount of storage space but, at the same time, the box is not so large that it overwhelms everything else around it. However, you may want to increase or decrease its size. It's a good idea to reflect on possible uses for the box before finalizing the dimensions.

2. Cut the walls to the desired dimensions. Mitre the wall panels using whatever tools or methods you prefer.

3. A groove needs to be routed into the inside surface of each wall. This groove will hold the plywood bottom section. Refer to Design C 22-1 for some assistance with these procedures. To maximize the storage area, you can place the bottom section about 3¾ inches from the bottom edge of the walls.

4. Using large rubber bands, assemble the box with the plywood bottom section in place. Do not glue. Check the mitres and the fit of the bottom section. Be certain the bottom piece is not too large, forcing the mitres open. Reduce its dimensions if necessary. Disassemble the box for gluing. Spread glue on the joint ends and also in the bottom section grooves. Assemble the box and clamp with larger rubber bands until the glue is dry.

5. To prepare the lid, measure the inside dimensions of the box. Remember, the lid is recessed inside the box in this design. You may want to refer to Illus. 152 to see how the lid will look when in place. Lay out the lid dimensions on the ½"-thick stock you plan to use for the lid. Using a ruler, make a square lid extension on the lid piece. The extension should be at least 1½" long. It must extend over the thickness of the front wall and out far enough to be useful in lifting the lid. You can always reduce its length if it has been cut too long. When cutting the lid, make the cuts on the inside edge of the pencilled dimensional lines. The lid needs to be undersized so that it can move freely in and out of the box. I cut the front part of the lid and the extension using a band saw.

6. After the lid has been cut, place it inside the box with the lid-opening extension resting on the top edge of the front wall. Using a pencil, trace the sides of the extension on the edge surface. You need to remove this area in the front wall so that the lid extension will drop neatly into it. Refer to Illus. 152 to see how the lid extension fits into the cutout area. Using an electric finishing sander, round the back edge of the lid. The front edge should also be rounded, but not as radically as the back edge. Only the sharp edges need to be sanded off the top edges of the lid sides. This rounding procedure on the back and front is critical to the ease of opening and closing the lid. Before proceeding with the lid, you need to decorate the joints and lid.

7. The joints of this design have a number of

splines that vary in thickness and placement. The corners of this design demonstrate some of the different ways that splines can be cut and placed to enhance the appearance of a box. To cut the grooves on the corners, I used the table-mounted router and jig discussed in Design C 22-1. The splines in this design are ⅛″ and ¼″ thick. Thus, if you want to duplicate this spline layout, you need to use both a ⅛″ and a ¼″ straight router bit.

Cut the splines from a contrasting wood and glue into the cut grooves. When the glue is dry, trim the excess spline off with a band saw. Using a belt or finishing sander, sand the box walls to finishing readiness.

The strip of inlay across the lid is ¼″ wide and is routed ⅛″ deep into the lid. You can easily rout the groove on a table-mounted router with a ¼″ straight bit. You should use a fence/guide on your router. It's fine to rout a series of un-usually placed grooves that have varying widths. You may want to do some design work and plan an inlay that is more creative than this one. Use a piece of pine to experiment on. The procedures are relatively simple and there are many design possibilities.

The lid extension has a ½″-diameter plug drilled and glued in place. It adds a nice touch to the lid. As you can see in Illus. 152, I have cut the end of the lid extension at an angle and then tapered the top surface downwards.

8. I have hinged the lid on two ¼″-diameter dowels that are at least 1″ long. The dowels pen-etrate the side walls and into the edges of the lid. The dowels fit loosely in the lid to allow it to open and close (Illus. 153). The accuracy of the dowel placement is critical to a smooth functioning lid. Make a line on the top portion of the side walls that is the exact thickness of the lid. For example, if the lid is ½″ thick, the line would be made ½″ down from the top edge of the wall and it would run parallel to it. Find and mark the exact center between the top edge of the side walls and the thickness lines. Mark this point at several locations so that you can draw a line between the points. Measuring ⅞″ from the outside edge of the back wall, make a mark through the middle line you just made. This is the point where you will drill the dowel hole through the wall and into the edge of the lid. It's worth noting that the ⅞″ measurement was based on a back wall thickness of ½″. The dowel should penetrate the lid approximately ⅜″ from its back edge. These two measure-ments together make the ⅞″ point of entry from the back wall. Make sense? Refer to Illus. 154.

9. Drilling the dowel holes through the marked points on the side walls and into the lid can be a problem. You need to devise a way of securely holding the lid in place while you're drilling the holes. The front part of the lid is adequately supported by the extension resting in the cut-out area on the front wall. The back part of the lid is the problem.

To solve the problem, cut two pieces of pine to a length that, when placed inside the box,

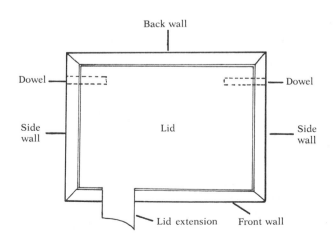

Illus. 153. Dowel-hinge system

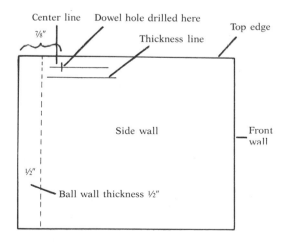

Illus. 154. Side wall layout for hinges

will support the lid so that it's flush with the top edge of the box. The pieces need to be placed against the inside back wall. When in place, the back portion of the lid rests on them, flush with the top edges. To hold the lid and

Illus. 155. Recessed lid open

pine supports in place, use a bar clamp. You can clamp from the back bottom edge of the box to the lid. You may want to put a small block on the surface of the lid so that the clamp doesn't damage it. Don't tighten the clamp too much—just enough to hold the lid in place.

One final procedure before drilling: So that the lid will move freely on the dowels, you need a very slight opening between the back edge of the lid and the inside surface of the back wall. Usually, if the lid has been cut inside the dimensional lines, it will fit loosely inside the box. You need some of this play at the back edge of the lid. Prepare two small tapered shims and tap them between the back wall surface and the back edge of the lid. You should do this procedure with the clamp in place. Tap the shims in only far enough so that you can see a slight

space between the surfaces. If you tap them in too far, you will force the front edge of the lid too tightly against the front wall surface. Take your time with this procedure until you feel it's correct. You can always remove wood from the front edge, if necessary. It's crucial to have the dowels placed properly.

10. If you are using ¼″ dowels, put a ¼″-diameter bit in the drill press. Place the box on its side and drill the dowel hole, at the premarked point, through the side wall and into the lid. Penetrate the lid with the bit to at least a ½″ depth. Repeat the process in the other side wall.

11. Cut two ¼″ dowels at least 1″ long. Using abrasive paper, taper one end on each of the dowels. This rounded end is the one that will penetrate into the lid. With the clamp still in place, tap the dowels through the walls and partially into the lid. Do not drive them all the way in at this point. Leave enough dowel extending beyond the side wall so that it can be pulled out if necessary. Remove the clamp and open the lid. If it binds in the front but opens, lightly sand the front edge until it opens freely. It's best to sand the bottom edge of the front of the lid a bit more round. This usually eliminates the binding, but does not leave a gap between the lid and the wall. You may also have some binding on one or both sides of the lid. Note the area where the bind occurs and mark it with a pencil. If you can't sand out the bind with the lid in place, you can easily pull out the dowels to free the lid. This will permit you to sand the area that binds more easily.

If the back of the lid binds, remove the dowels and sand the surface of the back edge. Remember, the back edge of the lid should be rounded to facilitate opening and closing (Illus. 155). You have to round it more to eliminate the bind. When the lid freely opens and closes, tap the dowels in place and flush with the side wall surfaces. While not mandatory, you may want to place a bit of glue on the dowel just before its final tap into the wall. Do not put glue on the dowel end that enters the lid. The lid needs to move freely on the dowels to open and close. Sand the dowels and wall surfaces to remove pencil marks and any excess glue.

12. Finish the box as desired. I often use an oil finish on this design. For some information on products and methods, refer to the next chapter.

Design C 41-1: Narrow Box with Recessed Lid (Illus. 156)

1. The lid on this design is recessed and operates on dowels. The procedures for placing the lid are the same as those in Design C 40-1. This design, however, has a narrow storage area. It

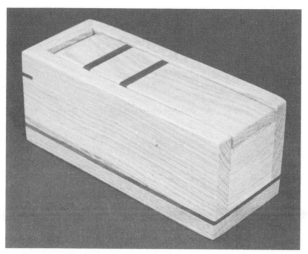

Illus. 156. Narrow box with recessed lid

is very similar to pencil box designs, but has a hinged lid rather than a sliding one. The design lends itself to any dimensions you may want to use. It is especially good for very tiny boxes that hold stamps or grimple or a few pairs of earrings. The box in Illus. 156 is approximately 7¼″ long, 3″ wide, and 3″ high. The walls and lids are made from ½″ stock.

One unusual design feature of this box is that the bottom and the walls have a ⅛″-thick piece of walnut laminated between them. The walnut laminate gives the walls a decorative appearance. Also, it provides a walnut bottom inside the box. Using a laminate can make a rather plain-looking box appear rather attractive.

2. This box employs two types of joints. The back portion of the box where the lid is held has

mitred joints. If you refer to Illus. 156, you will see the splines that cut through the joint. The front portion of the box has a simple butt joint. The front panel is reduced in size so that the lid can rest on its top edge. As you can see in Illus. 156, the lid is flush with all edges. To simplify opening the lid, I have sanded a finger slot into the front underside of the lid. Illus. 157 shows the box with the lid open so you can see the reduced dimensions of the front panel where the lid rests.

The two strips that run across the lid are placed in ¼″-wide routed grooves that are ⅛″ deep. You can easily make the strips on a table-mounted router and cut them to dimension on a band saw. Even though it's a small area, the lid can be embellished in any number of ways. You may want to do some design work that will enhance the lid with something that's more suited to your taste.

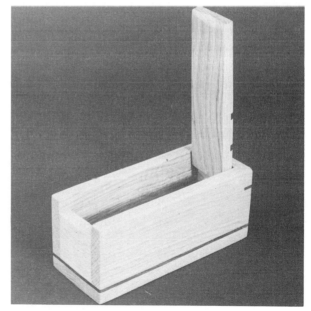

Illus. 157. Narrow box with lid open

Design C 42-1: Recipe Boxes with Inlay Lids (Illus. 158)

1. The two larger boxes are designed to hold 4″ × 6″ recipe cards and the smaller box is designed to hold 3″ × 5″ recipe cards. Of course,

you can also use them for other purposes. Usually I plane down standard-thickness pine to ½″ thickness for these boxes. The smaller box design has mitred joints and ⅛"-wide splines cut from pine. I have glued the top and bottom pieces of this box to its walls. The larger box design employs a butt joint with screws and ¼" plugs. It, too, has the top and bottom pieces glued to the edges. I've cut the lids for both designs from the boxes at a diagonal so that the user can have immediate access to the recipe cards. The lids have an intarsia-type inlay that enhances their appearance.

The larger box design is 7¼" long, 5" wide (including the wall thicknesses in the butt joint), and 5½" high (including the ½" top and bottom thicknesses). The smaller box design is approximately 6½" long, 4" wide, and 4⅜" high (including the ½" top and bottom thicknesses).
2. To make the larger box, cut the front and back walls to a length of 7¼" and the side walls to a length of 4". As mentioned, the stock should be ½" thick. The four panels should be 4⅜" wide. You need to measure and cut the top and bottom pieces after you've assembled the box proper.

To make the smaller box, cut the front walls to a length of 6½" and the side walls to a length of 4". The panels should be 3⅜" wide. As with the larger box, the top and bottom pieces are measured and cut after the box has been assembled.
3. For the larger box, you need to mark the

front and back panels for screw-plug holes. Since the box lid will be cut at a diagonal, the placement of the screw-plug holes is critical. You can see a side view of the box in Illus. 159 that shows the diagonal, its distance from the lid, and marks where the screw-plug holes should be drilled. Incidentally, the lid should not be cut until the entire box has been assembled.

Mark and drill the screw-plug holes on the front and back walls of the box. I use a ¼" wood bit and cut the plugs from pine with a plug cutter.

Using glue and ½"- or ⅝"-long wood screws, assemble the box. Clamp and allow the glue to dry. Glue and tap in the screw-hole plugs.

For the smaller box, mitre all wall pieces to a 45° angle. Do not cut the lid or bottom piece. Spread glue on the joint surfaces, assemble, and then clamp using large rubber bands.
4. Sand all the surfaces on the larger box using a belt sander. Square the top and bottom edges, if necessary. Trace the box frame onto the ½" pine stock for both the top and bottom pieces. Cut the two pieces, glue, and then clamp in place. Don't use too much glue because it will squeeze out on the inside of the box where it cannot be wiped off.

Now clean the wall surfaces and square the top and bottom edges on the smaller box. Re-

Illus. 158. Recipe boxes with inlaid lids

150

peat the procedures that were just used for the larger box.

5. When the boxes are dry, using a belt sander, square the walls, lid, and bottom pieces so that they're flush. To rout the splines in the smaller box, use the home-made jig presented in Design C 22-1. Use a ⅛″ straight router bit for cutting the splines in the joints of the smaller box. Prepare strips to insert in the cuts and then glue in place. Allow the glue to dry before trimming and sanding the walls.

6. The next procedure is cutting the lid, at a diagonal, from the box proper. It's best to do this on the band saw with the table tilted to the correct angle. To lay out the boxes in order to cut their lids, refer to Illus. 159. Draw the angled line on the side wall from the 1″ point on the back to the 2″ point on the front. You can use this line for setting the angle of the bandsaw table. Set the fence and cut. To remove saw marks, sand the edge surfaces lightly.

7. Both boxes are hinged by placing a butt hinge on the back surface of the lid and box. If desired, you can use narrow hinges and recess them into the top edge of the box.

8. You prepare the inlay for all three boxes the same way; you also use the same procedures for routing them into the lid. By the way, for the apple inlay, the apple is made from padouk, the stem is from ebony, and the leaf is from poplar. On the other larger box, the pear is from Osage orange (hedge) and the stem is from ebony. The flowers on the smaller box are padouk and hedge and the stem is poplar.

You should probably make patterns for these designs, although you may prefer drawing them freehand on the inlay wood surfaces. The inlay woods should be cut to a thickness of ⅛″. You should determine the size of the design as you plan the pattern.

Trace or draw the inlay design on the surface of the ⅛″-thick inlay stock. Cut out the inlay designs using a scroll saw or a band saw with a narrow blade.

9. Place the cut designs on the lid of the box and trace the outline of the inlay parts onto its surface. Use a very sharp pencil or scriber for

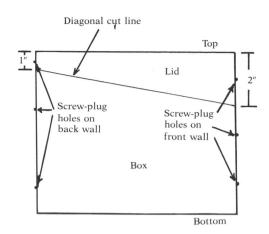

Illus. 159. Side wall layout—side view

tracing the parts. Keep the point tight against the edge of the inlay part when tracing.

10. Using a Moto-Tool with a router-attachment base, remove the wood from the inside surface of the traced inlay. You should use a 3/16″ or larger bit for general wood removal. For detailed routing, use a ⅛″ or 1/16″ bit. Rout the area to a depth of at least 1/16″. Rout very carefully near the traced line. You want to have nice sharp margins. Any cut beyond the traced line needs to be filled. I usually mix pine sawdust with white glue and use it for a filler. Take your time and enjoy the process.

11. When the inlay recesses have been routed, test the inlay piece for fit. You may have to remove a bit of wood from the recess. If it's just slightly tight, you can remove a little wood from the edge of the inlay part to make it fit. Spread a light coating of wood glue in the inlay recesses and put the inlay pieces in place. It's a good idea to place a block over the inlay and clamp it with a large rubber band until the glue is dry.

12. When the inlay is dry, using a belt or pad sander, sand the inlay flush with the surface of the lid. Don't over sand so that you cut through the inlay.

13. Sand all surfaces on the box to finishing readiness and finish as desired.

4

FINISHING

Finishing is that part of woodworking that most of us either love or hate. There seem to be few woodworkers who do not have strong feelings either way about this all-important and necessary process. At the same time, woodworkers probably appreciate a quality finish more than anyone else. We often look with envy at pieces that have been finished with great care. Unfortunately, many of us dislike the finishing process so much that we won't spend the time and effort necessary for achieving high-quality finishes on our pieces. I tend to view finishing as something that has to be done and should be done as quickly as possible. The less time spent on finishing, the more time I can spend working wood. Unfortunately, some of my finishes reflect this attitude.

As a result of my dislike of finishing and need to rush through it, I am endlessly searching for finishing products that are simple to apply, quick to dry, and don't smell. As with many of my fellow woodworkers, I find myself wanting to try almost every new finishing product that comes on the market. I keep looking for that magical product that will make my finishes magnificent and the procedures enjoyable.

Whenever woodworkers gather, the main topic of conversation is, more often than not, finishing procedures. With talk of stirring and mixing and rubbing and boiling, as well as of smells and poisons, these conversations must appear bizarre to the nonwoodworker. However, they are merely attempts to come up with not better, but easier, procedures.

Finishing is hard work and it takes time. There is no easy procedure. Likewise, there is no ideal product, nor will there ever be one. If you prefer surface finishes, find a product that you like and work with it. If oil finishes are your preference, do the same with them. With very few exceptions, the finishing products that are available today are of excellent quality. They won't work miracles, but they'll get the job done. With regard to liking or disliking the finishing process, it has to be done so why not do it well, regardless of how you feel about it.

Preparing the Surfaces

The way the wood surfaces have been prepared is critical to a quality finish. Preparing the surfaces is often an area that we tend to rush through so that we can get to the finishing process. To achieve the kind of finish you want on your boxes, you need to spend some time preparing the wood. The following are some of the ways that I prepare boxes and turned pieces for finishing.

As a rule, I keep an 80-grit belt on a 6″ × 48″ belt sander. This grit, while somewhat coarse, allows me to do any rough sanding that needs to be done on boxes. For example, after cutting the spline edges off the corner of a box, there is always wood and glue on the surface. The 80-grit belt is ideal for removing this kind of material from the walls. It is also good for removing planer and other milling marks from the surfaces of boards. In many instances, I would rather sand these marks off as run them through my planer. You can remove the marks with the belt sander without significantly changing the thickness of the stock. Marks that tend to be on the wood surface, when you purchase wood from a dealer, also can be removed with this grit. I seem to be perpetually removing crayon marks that have been scrawled on the boards by the lumber graders. The belt sander or the same grit on a small electric hand sander removes the marks very quickly.

The 80-grit belt is also effective for cleaning up boards that have been re-sawn on the band saw. It removes the saw marks rather quickly. On boxes that have been cut to pattern on the band saw, I initially sand their side walls using this grit. For example, on the heart or kidney box designs presented in Chapter 3, it's an ideal grit for cleaning up the walls. It removes the saw marks and, when the lid is in place, brings the lid and wall edges flush.

On spalted boards, especially those that are severely decayed, the 80-grit belt is ideal. It removes much of the undesirable wood and, if it's there, exposes a reasonably hard surface.

For general initial preparation of box surfaces, the 80-grit belt is a good choice. However, you pay a price for the convenience of this grit. While the grit does an excellent initial job, it also scratches the surface of the wood. To deal with these scratches, you need a finer grit.

From the 80-grit belt, I usually move up to a 100-grit for going over box surfaces again. While this grit may scratch some of the woods, on most it begins the process of preparing the surfaces for finishing. Some woodworkers prefer starting with a 100-grit belt, as opposed to the 80 grit belt. You might want to experiment with the grits and make a decision based on your own experience.

After going over the surfaces of the box and lid, where possible, with the belt sander and the 100-grit abrasive, I use a small electric palm or pad sander. These small finishing sanders are ideal for working on boxes. I start with sheets of 150-grit and carefully, working with the grain, go over all the surfaces on the box. I use this sander and this grit to cut the sharp edges off the box walls and lids. Although the paper often tears, it's very effective for rolling over sharp edges. I also use the pad finishing sander on the apple and other shaped designs. It's an excellent tool to use on some of the large inlays as well. You can both shape with it and finish the inlay with it. The pad sander is also well suited for removing any scratches that remain on the edges of the lid after an inlay is in place. You can use it in small areas without sanding surfaces that have already been prepared.

If you feel your surface is adequate after going over it with the pad sander and the 150-grit abrasive, begin the finishing process. However, I tend to go up to at least a 220-grit abrasive as a final surface preparation for most boxes. The 220-grit tends to remove scratches on some of the woods that are left by the 150-grit. In general, the 220-grit leaves the box surface in relatively good condition for finishing.

I tend to spend extra time and energy preparing the surfaces of boxes that have particularly involved inlays. With these boxes, I frequently go up to a 320-grit. You may want to try some of the finer grits, especially the silicon carbide ones.

It's difficult to develop a smooth surface on many of the spalted woods. Tear-out is almost inevitable. The cross-grain mouse can be almost impossible to remove. With the spalts, I have found that you give it your best and then let the wood be the way it is. A glass-smooth surface is not necessary nor desirable on many woods, especially the spalts. If you want this kind of surface, you will be hard pressed to get it from many of the spalted woods. On both turned pieces and boxes made from spalted woods, I usually go up to 150-grit before finishing. If I'm removing too much of the soft surface, I'll use a finer grit. You need to experiment with abrasives when working with the spalts. The amount of decay is so unpredictable that each piece almost has to be approached individually.

It helps if you do your sanding work under good light. Most of our shops are so poorly lit that it's often difficult to see what's really happening to the surface as we apply the abrasives. On close examination of the box surface, you will be amazed at the scratches that are left by the various abrasive grits. Actually, the process of sanding amounts to making smaller and smaller and less conspicuous scratches on the wood surface. The finer grits abrade the surface in a way that is not visible to the naked eye.

I encourage you to experiment with different kinds of abrasives and different grits. Above all, remember that finishing products make a poorly prepared surface look worse and a well-prepared surface look better.

Products and Procedures

One of the most frequently used tools in my shop is the air compressor. While I use it with a number of pneumatic tools, I mainly use it to clean myself off and to clean off my crafted pieces prior to finishing. It's an indispensable part of the finishing process. Before I bought the air compressor, I used a shop vacuum to suck or blow the sawdust from the pieces before finishing. It's an effective way to clean off a box if you don't have an air compressor.

I have always needed a special area in my shop for doing finishing. It's next to impossible to finish anything in the shop because of the perpetual dust and clutter. The lack of a proper area for finishing is a major problem for most woodworkers. As a consequence, it's very difficult to obtain the kind of results a piece deserves.

To compound the space problem, many finishing products should not be used in an unvented area because they are toxic and flammable. Before purchasing any finishing product, I always read the cautions on the labels. Among other things, reading product labels can help you determine the best place to work. I suspect that most of us are somewhat careless when it comes to using these chemicals. *You would be well advised, even in a vented area, to wear some kind of mask whenever you work with finishing products.*

One of the reasons I tend to use oil for finishing has to do with the lack of an appropriate environment. In contrast to some of the surface finishes, oil does not attract and hold everything in the air. On oil finishes, you also can do more sanding, using fine grits, than on surface finishes. Sanding the finish tends to remove almost everything that may have fallen on the surface. I use Watco Danish oil on a regular basis. I also use tung oil and a number of products made from it. There is a wide range of commercial oil-finishing products available today. Try a number of them until you find the ones that work best for you within the limitations of your environment.

I use either Deft or a combination of Watco Danish oil and Deft on most of my boxes. Although Deft gives the kind of finish that looks quite nice on most pieces, I especially like the way it enhances boxes crafted from walnut. Deft is a quick-drying lacquer that can be brushed on. I use pure bristle brushes to apply it. If you have an appropriate area for spraying, an air brush can be an excellent alternative. The environment also needs to be considered when you use Deft in pressurized cans.

I generally put five or six coats of Deft on the larger boxes and turnings. This assures that the piece will have a highly resistant finish. After the second or third coat, I rub each subsequent coat with extra-fine (0000) steel wool. The steel wool cuts the gloss, removes any particles that may have gathered on the surface, and prepares the surface for the next application. After the final coat, I go over the piece again with extra-fine steel wool. As a final finish, I apply two coats of clear Trewax or Butcher's wax to the piece and polish it with a flannel rag. I usually maintain the surfaces by adding an additional coat of paste wax.

When finishing pieces from the spalted woods, I also use Deft. Depending on how porous the wood is, I use up to 10 coats of Deft on a piece. I do not use steel wool on the spalts until a good surface has been built up. If you use steel wool too soon, it tends to catch on the wood surface and is difficult to see and remove. Even after many coats of Deft, some of the spalted pieces look as if they're not finished. I've had to resign myself to the semifinished appearance of many of my spalted pieces.

APPENDIX: INSTALLING MUSICAL MOVEMENTS

The musical movement should not be installed in the music box until the entire finishing process is complete. Sawdust is bad enough around a musical movement; but if finishing products got into the working parts of a movement, the results would be disastrous. While the placement of the movement in the box is a relatively simple procedure, the following tips may be helpful.

The movement should come from the supplier with a winding key and three screws for attaching it to the soundboard. In some instances, the screws may be too long. For example, with a ⅛"-thick soundboard, a long screw can penetrate it, the movement bedplate, and the flywheel. You may wind the movement and discover it won't work. The long fixing screw has probably interrupted the movement of the

flywheel. Watch for this, especially when long screws accompany the movement. You will have to use another screw or reduce the length of the screw. You can, in a pinch, get along with only two screws holding the movement in place.

When tightening the movement screws, don't turn them too tight. Too much screw pressure on the movement bedplate can pull the gears out of alignment on the small movements. The movement will play but at a slower speed. Turn the screws up to the soundboard surface, but don't screw them too tightly.

You should place a very small amount of oil on the critical moving parts of the movement (Illus. 160). Use either regular clock/watch oil or sewing machine oil. This procedure should be done at the time of installation and should not have to be repeated for years. Too much oil simply gums up the movement parts and tends to attract and hold dust. The disc movements do not have to be oiled because they are oiled at the factory. The metal plate covering the movement parts also makes oiling an impossible task. Should the movement ever need repairing, it can be oiled again then.

You can have a sliding on/off stopper installed on the smaller movements (Illus. 161). I use this kind of stopper on the Model 1.18 movements. With an on/off stopper, all you need to do is tip the box, and then the stopper will slide away from the flywheel and the movement will play. To shut the movement off, tip the box in the opposite direction and the stopper will slide into the flywheel and shut the movement down. The stopper remains in the placed position until the box is tipped. This type of stopper

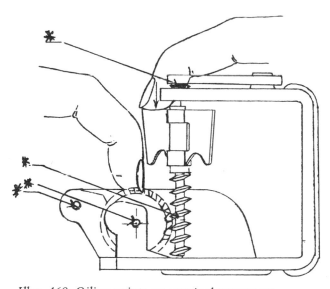

Illus. 160. Oiling points on musical movement

155

Illus. 161. Model 1.18 movement with sliding stopper weight

Illus. 162. Plastic container for Model 1.18 movement

is available from a number of mail-order suppliers that carry Reuge movements. It will, by the way, only fit on Reuge movements. To install the stopper on the movement, remove the comb screw on the treble side of the comb. Place the small washer under the screwhead, and slip the rounded stopper wire on the screw. Replace the screw and assembly in the comb hole, align the stopper with the flywheel, and tighten the screw. You may want to refer to Illus. 161 to see how the stopper is secured and aligned.

A good practice with movements is to wind and test them before securing any glass over them. You will seldom receive a Swiss movement that does not function properly, but it does happen occasionally. You should check for a piece of hair wound around the endless screw on the flywheel or for some packing debris in one of the gear systems. By removing a hair or

some debris, you may be able to make the movement work properly.

If you want to hide the smaller movements in a jewelry box or some other storage box, you may want to use the small plastic container that is available for Model 1.18 movements. This container has a self-contained plastic soundboard and a cover that protects the movement. Usually small screws are provided with the container (Illus. 162).

With the exception of aligning the sliding assembly with the movement stopper arm, the larger cylinder movements are simply secured to the soundboard. When oiling these movements, use clock/watch oil or sewing machine oil, as with the smaller movements. Refer to Illus. 160 for those critical points on the movement that should be oiled.

Cutting Glass Inserts

As many music box designs call for a glass covering over the musical movement, it helps if you know how to cut your own glass. Round glass inserts need to be cut for the smaller music boxes, whereas rectangular pieces of glass need to be cut to specific dimensions for the larger music boxes. Even though you can take the boxes to the local glass cutter, you should at least try cutting the glass yourself. It is not that difficult and is actually rather fun once you get

the hang of it. I use standard-thickness window glass in all my boxes. You can also use Plexiglas of varying thicknesses. I don't like to use Plexiglas in my boxes, but it is much easier to work with than regular glass.

The tools that are necessary for cutting glass are a ruler with a rubber elevated back, a vernier caliper, a regular glass cutter, and one that cuts glass circles (Illus. 163). I use a piece of plywood for a cutting surface. To reduce the diameter of the round glass inserts and to frost the edges, I use a 6″×48″ belt sander with an old 100-grit belt. Coarser belts tend to chip the edges of the glass. You also need a good face mask and gloves. *The mask protects your eyes and face from the small flecks of glass that break off while shaping the edges; the gloves, preferably leather, keep your hands from being burned by the hot glass.* The glass gets extremely hot when held against the sanding belt.

Here are the procedures for cutting the round glass inserts for the smaller music boxes. First measure the diameter of the glass shoulder inside the box with the vernier caliper. Use the internal prongs of the caliper for placement on the shoulders. This, of course, sets the external prongs. You can either read the diameter from the caliper or check the external prongs against the surface of the ruler. While placing the cutter wheel at the end of the ruler, align the center of the suction cup to *one-half* the diameter measured. Remember, the cup is at the center of the circle when cutting; thus, it's necessary to set the diameter of the cutter at only one-half the measured diameter of the insert shoulder. Set the cutter carefully and check it a number of times against the ruler.

Place a small amount of saliva on the rubber cup, force it onto the glass surface, and swing the arm tightly against the glass surface in a full circle. I usually hold the cutter at the cup with one hand and move the cutter wheel and arm with the other. You need to apply some

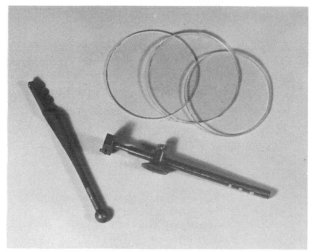

Illus. 163. Glass cutters and inserts

pressure to the wheel or it will not score the glass.

You may want to make a few practice cuts before cutting your final insert. The greatest fear in cutting glass is that you will break the glass. So what! If you break a piece, simply get another piece and start over. Glass is relatively inexpensive.

After the circle has been scored on the glass surface, using the heavy end of a straight glass cutter, tap around the outer edge of the score. Glass cutters, including circle cutters, have small grooves in them for chipping the glass. Find the one that fits the glass and chip away the pieces that surround the scored line. Suddenly, the circle will pop free with relatively clean edges. Test it for fit in the box.

To remove the rough edges on the round glass insert, hold its edge against the 100-grit belt. *Be sure to have your face mask and gloves on.* Rotate the insert on the belt's surface, removing any rough surfaces that might remain from the cutting. If the insert is a bit oversized for the box, you can also reduce its diameter by rolling it on the surface of the belt. You must hang on to the piece or the belt will pull it from your hand. To frost the edges of the glass, hold the piece against the roller part of the belt sander and belt. Frost the edges of the insert on both sides.

Clean the glass insert on both sides before gluing it over the movement. A clear general-purpose glue works fine for holding the insert in place on the box shoulder. Be certain to spread glue on the entire shoulder. You want the glass to be well secured in the shoulder. If the glass is not sealed tightly in place, the vibrations of the movement will make it rattle. To test for a loose-fitting glass insert, turn the movement on and listen just above the glass. Place your finger tightly against the glass and listen again. If the rattle stops, you need to remove the glass insert and glue it in place again.

To cut rectangular pieces of glass for the larger music boxes, measure carefully, and then mark the glass with a soft-tip pen. Align the ruler and score with the regular glass cutter. Move the score to the edge of the plywood cutting surface and press down while holding the other side of the score against the surface. The glass should neatly break off along the scored line. You may want to clean up the edges with the belt sander.

INDEX

METRIC EQUIVALENTS

Inches to Millimetres and Centimetres

MM—millimetres   *CM—centimetres*

Inches	MM	CM	Inches	CM	Inches	CM
⅛	3	0.3	9	22.9	30	76.2
¼	6	0.6	10	25.4	31	78.7
⅜	10	1.0	11	27.9	32	81.3
½	13	1.3	12	30.5	33	83.8
⅝	16	1.6	13	33.0	34	86.4
¾	19	1.9	14	35.6	35	88.9
⅞	22	2.2	15	38.1	36	91.4
1	25	2.5	16	40.6	37	94.0
1¼	32	3.2	17	43.2	38	96.5
1½	38	3.8	18	45.7	39	99.1
1¾	44	4.4	19	48.3	40	101.6
2	51	5.1	20	50.8	41	104.1
2½	64	6.4	21	53.3	42	106.7
3	76	7.6	22	55.9	43	109.2
3½	89	8.9	23	58.4	44	111.8
4	102	10.2	24	61.0	45	114.3
4½	114	11.4	25	63.5	46	116.8
5	127	12.7	26	66.0	47	119.4
6	152	15.2	27	68.6	48	121.9
7	178	17.8	28	71.1	49	124.5
8	203	20.3	29	73.7	50	127.0